Ionic Cookbook
Third Edition

Recipes to create cutting-edge, real-time hybrid mobile apps with Ionic

Indermohan Singh
Hoc Phan

BIRMINGHAM - MUMBAI

Ionic Cookbook
Third Edition

Copyright © 2018 Packt Publishing

Commissioning Editor: Amarabha Banerjee
Acquisition Editor: Isha Raval
Content Development Editor: Mohammed Yusuf Imaratwale
Technical Editor: Diksha Wakode
Copy Editor: Safis Editing
Project Coordinator: Hardik Bhinde
Proofreader: Safis Editing
Indexer: Pratik Shirodkar
Graphics: Jason Monteiro
Production Coordinator: Nilesh Mohite

First published: November 2016
Second edition: October 2015
Third edition: April 2018

Production reference: 1260418

Published by Packt Publishing Ltd.
Livery Place
35 Livery Street
Birmingham
B3 2PB, UK.

ISBN 978-1-78862-323-0

www.packtpub.com

`mapt.io`

Mapt is an online digital library that gives you full access to over 5,000 books and videos, as well as industry leading tools to help you plan your personal development and advance your career. For more information, please visit our website.

Why subscribe?

- Spend less time learning and more time coding with practical eBooks and Videos from over 4,000 industry professionals

- Improve your learning with Skill Plans built especially for you

- Get a free eBook or video every month

- Mapt is fully searchable

- Copy and paste, print, and bookmark content

PacktPub.com

Did you know that Packt offers eBook versions of every book published, with PDF and ePub files available? You can upgrade to the eBook version at `www.PacktPub.com` and as a print book customer, you are entitled to a discount on the eBook copy. Get in touch with us at `service@packtpub.com` for more details.

At `www.PacktPub.com`, you can also read a collection of free technical articles, sign up for a range of free newsletters, and receive exclusive discounts and offers on Packt books and eBooks.

Contributors

About the authors

Indermohan Singh is a Mobile App Developer working in Vienna, Austria, originally from Ludhiana, Punjab. For the past 3 years, he has worked on Angular, Ionic, and TypeScript most of the time. He authored *Ionic 2 Blueprint* for Packt Publishing, and this is his second book on the subject. Before starting the full-time job, he was freelancer with many startups. During his time as a freelancer, he also mentored learners at codementor.io, where he was mostly teaching JavaScript. He is also hobbyist musician and loves to create Indian Compositions and play them on harmonium.

> *I am thankful to the almighty for giving me the strength to write this book. It was challenging, since I moved to a different country. It's tough! I am also thankful to my family; even though they live miles away from me, their encouragement helped a lot. Last but not least, I am really thankful to all the team members from Packt, especially Mohammad Yusuf and Isha Raval, who made this process a breeze for me.*

Hoc Phan is a technologist with experience in frontend development, cloud computing, and big data. He started programming at the age of 12. Hoc has worked on many JavaScript projects by learning from various online sources and was one of the first few developers who tested Ionic for its feasibility as a JavaScript replacement of the native language of a device. He authored the *Ionic Cookbook*.
He frequently speaks at local meetups and cloud computing/big data industry events and conferences. He holds an MBA degree from the University of Washington's Michael G. Foster School of Business.

About the reviewer

Nitish Sinha, a techie from Jharkhand, is a hardcore believer of Steve Jobs's words, "The only way to do great work is to love what you do." Working as a software developer in a reputed firm, he is quite passionate about learning and unlearning things. He has a vast amount of experience in technologies like Angular.js, Node.js, Ionic Framework, and such.

He strongly believes in adapting oneself to an ever-evolving IT sphere, and learning upcoming technologies is his core strength. Not only that, he believes in sharing the learned wisdom with others.

> *I would like to sincerely thank all my mentors who have been a leading light in all my endeavors. Their golden words continue to be an inspiration for me.*

Packt is searching for authors like you

If you're interested in becoming an author for Packt, please visit `authors.packtpub.com` and apply today. We have worked with thousands of developers and tech professionals, just like you, to help them share their insight with the global tech community. You can make a general application, apply for a specific hot topic that we are recruiting an author for, or submit your own idea.

Table of Contents

Preface

Mobile application development has been a hot topic for quite a while now. There are multiple platforms and devices with different screen sizes and form factors out there to accommodate. It makes mobile app development very difficult. Luckily, Ionic is one such tool that helps us mitigate this very problem by allowing us to write code once for all platforms and devices.

In this book, readers will learn how to create mobile applications using Ionic. We will start with very basic things, such as setting up the development environment, using Navigation in apps, working with backend via REST API, Animations, Authenticating Users, Receiving push notifications, localizing an app, generating documentation, and publishing the app, to name a few. Readers will also learn things about Angular and Ionic CLI. I hope that this book will help novice developers as well as advanced developers, because the content is a mixture of easy and advance ionic stuff.

Who this book is for

Ionic Cookbook is for front-end developers who want to create cross-platform mobile apps. This book will help you become a Mobile App developer who is comfortable enough to take on difficult apps by teaching readers about Angular, Cordova, and Sass in depth. The intention of this book is to teach Ionic by solving real-world problems like authentication, push notifications, using the camera to name a few. Nevertheless, if you are new to front-end development, you will still be able to follow the book.

What this book covers

Chapter 1, *Creating Our First App with Ionic*, introduces the Ionic framework with instructions on how to set up the development environment and quickly create and run your first app.

Chapter 2, *Adding Ionic Components*, walks you through some examples of how to manage pages, states, and the overall navigation within the app.

Chapter 3, *Extending Ionic with Angular Building Blocks*, takes a deep dive into the Angular components, directives, and the customization of pipes. You will learn how to leverage the Ionic module architecture to create shared services.

Chapter 4, *Validating Forms and Making HTTP Requests*, explains how to create a complex form with input validation, retrieve data via REST API calls, and integrate with Stripe for online payment.

Chapter 5, *Adding Animation*, provides instructions on how to embed a video as background, create a physics-based CSS animation, and bind gestures to the animation state.

Chapter 6, *User Authentication and Push Notifications*, takes a deep dive into registering and authenticating users using Auth0 and sending and receiving push notifications using OneSignal.

Chapter 7, *Supporting Device Functionalities Using Ionic Native*, explains how to use Ionic Native to access native device functionalities, such as camera, social sharing, InAppBrowser, and map.

Chapter 8, *Theming the App*, focuses on how to customize the app for different platforms using Sass variables.

Chapter 9, *Advanced Topics*, teaches how to use advanced ionic features such as lazy loading, deep linking, and localizing ionic apps.

Chapter 10, *Publishing the App for Different Platforms*, looks into the process of performing the final steps of getting the app published.

To get the most out of this book

1. In the book, I assume that you have some knowledge of Angular. Most of the time the problem that you will face will be regarding Angular instead of Ionic. `https://angular.io` is your best friend in that case.

2. If you want to brush up your information about Angular, I would suggest this book by Victor Savkin and Jeff Cross (former Angular team members) `https://www.packtpub.com/application-development/essential-angular`.

3. Even though you can run most of examples without installing platform SDKs for Android or iOS. I suggest you to do this in the very beginning, in order to test the applications on actual devices. Take a look at these guides:
   - **Android**: `https://cordova.apache.org/docs/en/latest/guide/platforms/android/index.html#requirements-and-support`
   - **iOS**: `https://cordova.apache.org/docs/en/latest/guide/platforms/ios/index.html`

Download the example code files

You can download the example code files for this book from your account at
www.packtpub.com. If you purchased this book elsewhere, you can visit
www.packtpub.com/support and register to have the files emailed directly to you.

You can download the code files by following these steps:

1. Log in or register at www.packtpub.com.
2. Select the **SUPPORT** tab.
3. Click on **Code Downloads & Errata**.
4. Enter the name of the book in the **Search** box and follow the onscreen
   instructions.

Once the file is downloaded, please make sure that you unzip or extract the folder using the
latest version of:

- WinRAR/7-Zip for Windows
- Zipeg/iZip/UnRarX for Mac
- 7-Zip/PeaZip for Linux

The code bundle for the book is also hosted on GitHub at https://github.com/
PacktPublishing/Ionic-Cookbook-Third-Edition. In case there's an update to the code, it
will be updated on the existing GitHub repository.

We also have other code bundles from our rich catalog of books and videos available
at https://github.com/PacktPublishing/. Check them out!

Conventions used

There are a number of text conventions used throughout this book.

`CodeInText`: Indicates code words in text, database table names, folder names, filenames,
file extensions, pathnames, dummy URLs, user input, and Twitter handles. Here is an
example: "Mount the downloaded `WebStorm-10*.dmg` disk image file as another disk in
your system."

A block of code is set as follows:

```
<ion-tabs>
  <ion-tab [root]="tab1Root" tabTitle="One"
    tabIcon="water"></ion-tab>  <ion-tab [root]="tab2Root"
    tabTitle="Two"
    tabIcon="leaf"></ion-tab>  <ion-tab [root]="tab3Root"
    tabTitle="Three"
    tabIcon="flame"></ion-tab>
</ion-tabs>
```

Any command-line input or output is written as follows:

```
$ ionic start LeftRightMenu sidemenu
$ cd LeftRightMenu
```

Bold: Indicates a new term, an important word, or words that you see onscreen. For example, words in menus or dialog boxes appear in the text like this. Here is an example: "Select **System info** from the **Administration** panel."

Warnings or important notes appear like this.

Tips and tricks appear like this.

Sections

In this book, you will find several headings that appear frequently (*Getting ready, How to do it..., How it works..., There's more...,* and *See also*).

To give clear instructions on how to complete a recipe, use these sections as follows:

Getting ready

This section tells you what to expect in the recipe and describes how to set up any software or any preliminary settings required for the recipe.

How to do it...

This section contains the steps required to follow the recipe.

How it works...

This section usually consists of a detailed explanation of what happened in the previous section.

There's more...

This section consists of additional information about the recipe in order to make you more knowledgeable about the recipe.

See also

This section provides helpful links to other useful information for the recipe.

Get in touch

Feedback from our readers is always welcome.

General feedback: Email `feedback@packtpub.com` and mention the book title in the subject of your message. If you have questions about any aspect of this book, please email us at `questions@packtpub.com`.

Errata: Although we have taken every care to ensure the accuracy of our content, mistakes do happen. If you have found a mistake in this book, we would be grateful if you would report this to us. Please visit `www.packtpub.com/submit-errata`, selecting your book, clicking on the Errata Submission Form link, and entering the details.

Piracy: If you come across any illegal copies of our works in any form on the internet, we would be grateful if you would provide us with the location address or website name. Please contact us at `copyright@packtpub.com` with a link to the material.

If you are interested in becoming an author: If there is a topic that you have expertise in and you are interested in either writing or contributing to a book, please visit `authors.packtpub.com`.

Reviews

Please leave a review. Once you have read and used this book, why not leave a review on the site that you purchased it from? Potential readers can then see and use your unbiased opinion to make purchase decisions, we at Packt can understand what you think about our products, and our authors can see your feedback on their book. Thank you!

For more information about Packt, please visit `packtpub.com`.

Creating Our First App with Ionic 1

In this chapter, we will cover the following topics:

- Setting up a development environment
- Creating a HelloWorld app via the CLI
- Creating a HelloWorld app via Ionic Creator
- Viewing the app using your web browser
- Viewing the app using the Ionic CLI
- Viewing the app using Xcode for iOS
- Viewing the app using Genymotion for Android
- Viewing the app using Ionic View

Introduction

There are many options for developing mobile applications today. Native applications require a unique implementation for each platform, such as iOS, Android, and Windows phone. It's required in some cases, such as high-performance CPU and GPU processing with lots of memory consumption. Any application that does not need over-the-top graphics and intensive CPU processing could benefit greatly from a cost-effective, write once and run anywhere HTML5 mobile implementation.

For those who choose the HTML5 route, there are many great choices on the market. Some options may be very easy to start, but they could be very hard to scale or could face performance problems. Commercial options are generally expensive for small developers to find product/market fit. The best practice is to think of the users first. There are instances where a simple, responsive website design is the best choice; for example, when a business mainly has fixed content with minimal updating required or the content is better off on the web for SEO purposes.

The Ionic Framework has several advantages over its competitors, as shown:

- Ionic is based on Angular, which is a robust framework for application development. You have all the components to structure and create an application built into it.
- UI performance is strong because of its usage of the `requestAnimationFrame()` technique.
- It offers a beautiful and comprehensive set of default styles, similar to a mobile-focused twitter Bootstrap.
- **Sass** is available for quick, easy, and effective theme customization.

There have been many significant changes between the launch of AngularJS 1.x and Angular. All of these changes are applicable to Ionic as well. Consider the following examples:

- Angular utilizes **TypeScript**, which is a superset of the **ECMAScript 6 (ES6)** standard, to build your code into JavaScript. This allows developers to leverage TypeScript features such as type checking during the compilation step.
- There are no more controllers and directives in AngularJS. Previously, a controller was assigned to a DOM node, while a directive converted a template into a component-like architecture. However, it is very hard to scale and debug large AngularJS 1.x applications due to the misuse of controllers and/or issues with conflicting directives. In Angular, there is only a single concept—that of a component, which eventually has a selector corresponding to an HTML template and a class containing functions.
- The `$scope` object no longer exists in Angular because all properties are now defined inside a component. This is actually good news because debugging errors in `$scope` (especially with nested scenarios) is very difficult in AngularJS 1.x.
- Finally, Angular offers better performance and supports both ES5 and ES6 standards. You could write Angular in TypeScript, Dart, or just pure JavaScript.

In this chapter, you will work through several HelloWorld examples to Bootstrap your Ionic app. This process will give you a basic skeleton with which you can start building more comprehensive apps. The majority of apps have similar user experiences flow, such as tabs and side menus.

Setting up a development environment

Before you create your first app, your environment must have the required components ready. These components ensure a smooth development, build, and test process. The default Ionic project folder is based on Cordova's. Therefore, you need the Ionic CLI to automatically add the correct platform (that is, iOS, Android, or Windows phone) and build the project. This will ensure all Cordova plugins are included properly. The tool has many options to run your app in the browser or simulator with live reload.

Getting ready

You need to install Ionic and its dependencies to get started. Ionic itself is just a collection of CSS styles, Angular components, and standard Cordova plugins. It's also a command-line tool to help manage all technologies, such as Cordova. The installation process will give you a command line to generate the initial code and build the app.

Ionic uses npm as the installer, which is included when installing Node.js. Please install the latest version of Node.js from https://nodejs.org/en/download/.

You will need to install cordova, ios-sim (an iOS Simulator) and ionic:

```
$ npm install -g cordova ionic ios-sim
```

You can install all three components with this single command line instead of issuing three command lines separately. The -g parameter is to install the package globally (not just in the current directory).

For Linux and Mac, you may need to use the sudo command to allow system access, as shown:

```
$ sudo npm install -g cordova ionic ios-sim
```

The following are a few common options for an **integrated development environment (IDE)**:

- Xcode for iOS
- Android Studio for Android
- Microsoft Visual Studio Code (VS Code)
- JetBrains' WebStorm
- Sublime Text (`http://www.sublimetext.com/`) for web development

All of these have a free license. You could code directly in Xcode or Android Studio, but those are somewhat heavy-duty for web apps, especially when you have a lot of windows open and just need something simple to code. Sublime Text is free for non-commercial developers, but you have to purchase a license if you are a commercial developer. Most frontend developers would prefer to use Sublime Text for coding HTML and JavaScript, because it's very lightweight and comes with a well-supported developer community. Sublime Text has been around for a long time and is very user-friendly. However, there are many features in Ionic that make Visual Studio Code very compelling. For example, it has the look and feel of a full IDE without being bulky. You could debug JavaScript directly inside VS Code, as well as getting autocomplete (for example, IntelliSense). The following instructions cover both Sublime Text and VS Code, although the rest of this book will use VS Code.

How to do it...

VS Code works on Mac, Windows, and Linux. Here are the instructions:

1. Visit `https://code.visualstudio.com`.
2. Download and install for your specific OS
3. Unzip the downloaded file
4. Drag the `.app` file into the `Applications` folder and drag it to Mac's Dock
5. Open Microsoft Visual Studio Code
6. Press *Ctrl* + *Shift* + *p* to open the command palette
7. Type the shell command in the command palette
8. Click on the shell command: Install code command in PATH command to install the script to add Visual Studio Code in your terminal $PATH
9. Restart Visual Studio Code for this to take effect

Later on, you can just write code (including the dot) directly from the Ionic project folder and VS Code will automatically open that folder as a project.

Note that the following screenshots were taken from a Mac:

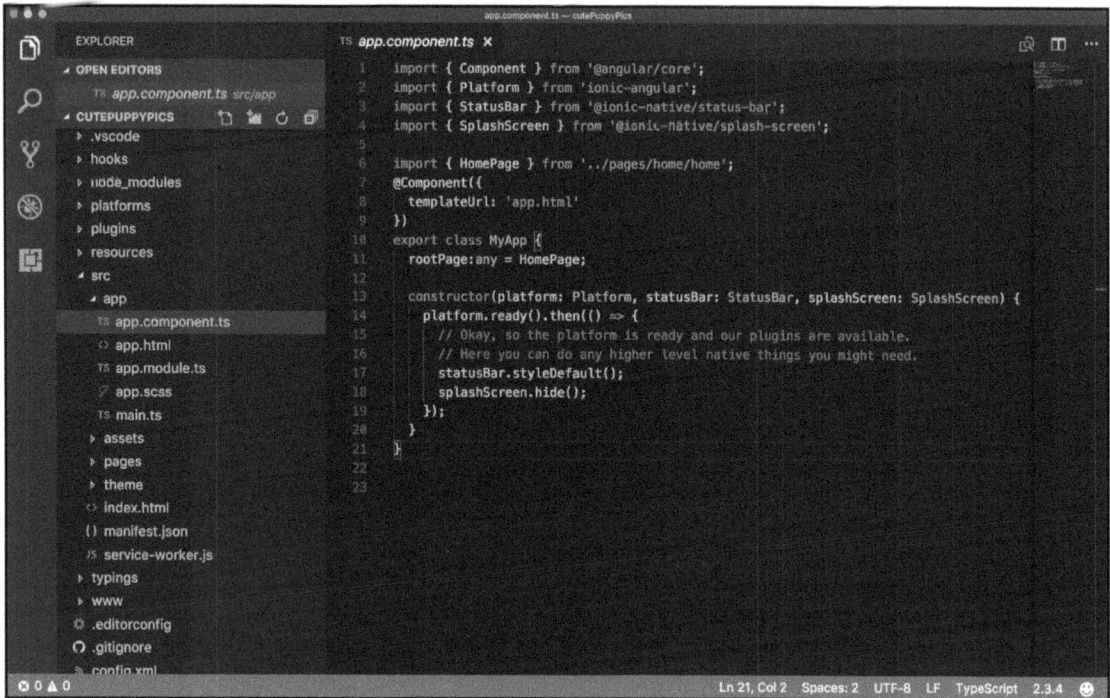

1. If you decide to use Sublime Text, you will need Package Control (https://packagecontrol.io/installation), which is similar to a **Plugin Manager**. Since Ionic uses Sass, it's optional to install the Sass Syntax Highlighting package.
2. Navigate to **Sublime Text** | **Preferences** | **Package Control**.

3. Go to **Package Control**: **Install Package**. You could also just type the partial command (that is, `inst`) and it will automatically select the right option:

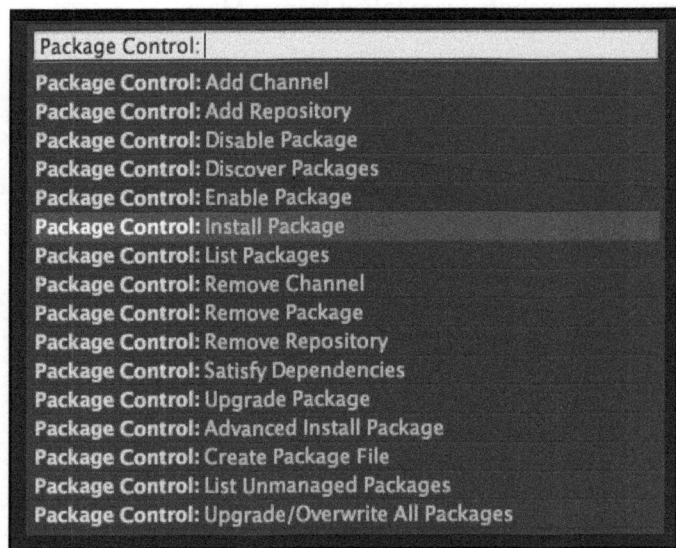

4. Type `Sass` and the search results will show one option for **TextMate & Sublime Text**. Select that item to install:

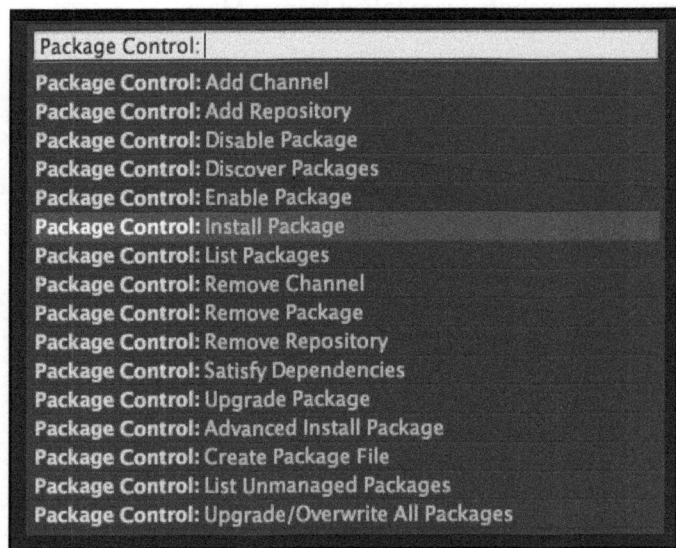

There's more...

There are tons of Sublime Text packages that you may want to use, such as HTML, JSHint, JSLint, Tag, and ColorPicker. You can visit `https://sublime.wbond.net/browse/popular` for additional needs.

Creating a HelloWorld app via the CLI

The quickest way to start your app is using the existing templates. Ionic gives you some standard out-of-the-box templates via the command line:

- **Blank**: This is a simple page with minimal JavaScript code
- **Tabs**: These are multiple pages with routes. A route URL goes to a tab
- **Side menu**: This is a template with a left/right menu with the center content area
- **Super:** This is a template with prebuilt pages and providers, which emphasize the best practices for Ionic app development

How to do it...

1. To set up the app with a `blank` template from `ionic`, use this command:

   ```
   $ ionic start HelloWorld_Blank blank
   ```

2. If you replace `blank` with `tabs`, it will create a `tabs` template, as shown:

   ```
   $ ionic start HelloWorld_Tabs tabs
   ```

3. Similarly, the following command will create an app with a `sidemenu`:

   ```
   $ ionic start HelloWorld_Sidemenu sidemenu
   ```

   4. Likewise, the following command will create an app with the `super` template:

   ```
   $ ionic start HelloWorld_Super super
   ```

Additional guidance for the Ionic CLI is available on the GitHub page: `https://github.com/ionic-team/ionic-cli`.

How it works...

This chapter will show you how to quickly start your code base and visualize the result. More details about Angular and its template syntax will be discussed in various chapters of this book, however, the core concepts are as follows:

- **Component**: Angular is very modular because you could write your code in a file and use an export class to turn it into a component. If you are familiar with AngularJS 1.x, this is similar to a controller and how it binds with a DOM node. A component will have its own private and public properties and methods (that is, functions). To tell whether a class is an Angular component or not, you have to use the `@Component` decorator. This is another new concept in TypeScript since you could enforce characteristics (metadata) on any class so that they behave in a certain way.

- **Template**: A template is an HTML string or a separate `.html` file that tells AngularJS how to render a component. This concept is very similar to any other frontend and backend framework. However, Angular has its own syntax to allow simple logic on the DOM, such as repeat rendering (`*ngFor`), event binding (`click`), or custom tags (`<my-tag>`).

- **Directive**: This allows you to manipulate the DOM, since the directive is bound to a DOM object. So, `*ngFor` and `*ngIf` would be examples of directives because they alter the behavior of that DOM.

- **Service**: This refers to the abstraction to manage models or collections of complex logic besides `get`/`set` required. There is no service decorator, as with a component. So, any class could be a service.

- **Pipe**: This is mainly used to process an expression in the template and return some data (that is, rounding numbers and adding currency) using the `{{ expression | filter }}` format. For example, `{{amount | currency}}` will return $100 if the amount variable is 100.

Ionic automatically creates a project folder structure that looks as follows:

You will spend most of your time in the /src folder because that's where your application components will be placed. This is very different from Ionic 1.x because the /www folder here is actually compiled by TypeScript. If you build the app for iOS, the Ionic build command line will also create another copy at /platforms/ios/www, which is specifically for Cordova to point to. Another interesting change in Angular is that your app has a root component, which is located at /src/app folder, and all other pages or screens are in /src/pages. Since Angular is component based, each component will come with HTML, CSS, and JS. If you add in more JavaScript modules, you can put them in the /src/assets folder, or a better practice is to use npm install so that it's automatically added in the /node_modules folder. Ionic has completely gotten rid of Grunt and Bower. Everything is simplified into just package.json, where your third-party dependencies will be listed.

There is no need to modify the /platforms or /plugins folder manually unless troubleshooting needs to be done. Otherwise, the Ionic or Cordova CLI will automate the content of these folders.

By default, from the Ionic template, the Angular app name is called `MyApp`. You will see something like this in `app/app.component.ts`, which is the root component file for the entire app:

```
@Component({
  templateUrl: 'app.html'
})
export class MyApp {
  @ViewChild(Nav) nav: Nav;

  rootPage: any = HomePage;

  pages: Array<{title: string, component: any}>;

  constructor(public platform: Platform, public statusBar: StatusBar, public splashScreen:
    this.initializeApp();

    // used for an example of ngFor and navigation
    this.pages = [
      { title: 'Home', component: HomePage },
      { title: 'List', component: ListPage }
    ];

  }

  initializeApp() {
    this.platform.ready().then(() => {
      // Okay, so the platform is ready and our plugins are available.
      // Here you can do any higher level native things you might need.
      this.statusBar.styleDefault();
      this.splashScreen.hide();
    });
  }
```

This root component of your app and all content will be injected inside `<ion-app></ion-app>` of `index.html`.

Note that if you double-click on the `index.html` file to open it in the browser, it will show a blank page. This doesn't mean that the app isn't working. The reason for this is that the Angular component of Ionic dynamically loads all the `.js` files and this behavior requires server access via the `http://` protocol. If you open a file locally, the browser automatically treats it as a file protocol (`file://`), and therefore Angular will not have the ability to load additional `.js` modules to run the app properly. There are several methods of running the app, which will be discussed later.

Creating a HelloWorld app via Ionic Creator

Another way to start your app code base is to use **Ionic Creator**. This is a great interface builder to accelerate your app development with the drag and drop style. You can quickly take the existing components and position them to visualize how it should look in the app via a web based interface. Most common components, such as buttons, images, and checkboxes are available.

Ionic Creator allows the user to export everything as a project with all .html, .css, and .js files. You should be able to edit content in the /app folder to build on top of the interface.

Getting ready

Ionic Creator requires registration for a free account at https://creator.ionic.io/ to get started.

How to do it...

1. Create a new project called myApp:

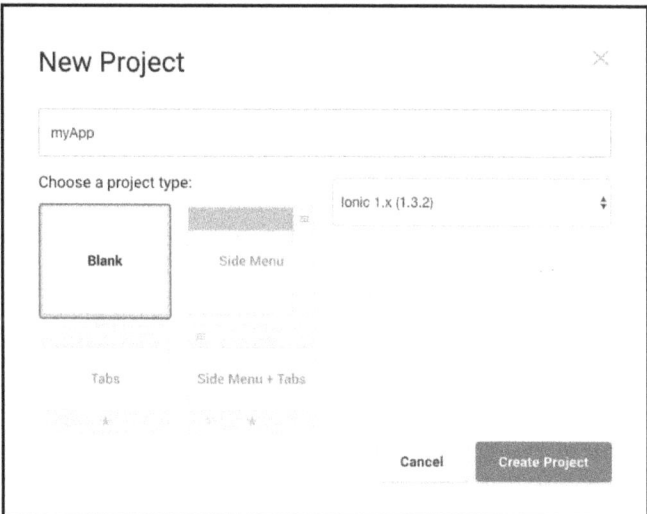

2. Validate, to ensure that you see the following screen:

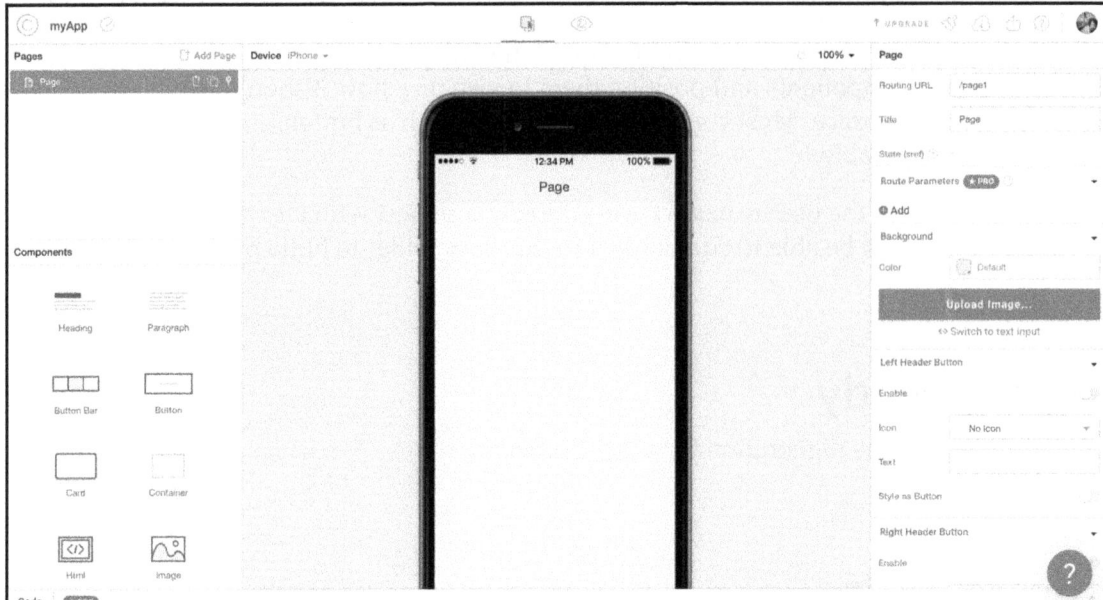

3. The center area is your app interface. The left side gives you a list of pages. Each page is a single route. You also have access to a number of UI components that you would normally have to code by hand in an HTML file. The panel on the right shows the properties of any selected component.

4. You're free to do whatever you need to do here by dropping components to the center screen. If you need to create a new page, you have to click on the **Add Page** in the **Pages** panel. Each page is represented as a link, which is basically a route in Angular UI-Router's definition. To navigate to another page (for example, after clicking a button), you can just change the link property and point to that page.

5. There is an edit button on top, where you can toggle back and forth between the edit mode and preview mode. It's very useful to see how your app will look and behave.

6. Once completed, click the export button at the top of the navigation bar. You have the following four options:
   - Use the Ionic CLI tool to get the code
   - Download the project as a ZIP file
   - Export it to native code (similar to PhoneGap Build), as shown:

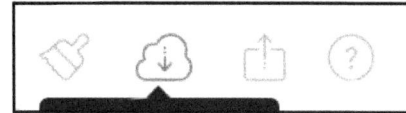

- Export it to the preview mode using the Creator app

The best way to learn Ionic Creator is to play with it.

There's more...

To switch to the preview mode, where you can see the UI in a device simulator, click on the switch button in the top right to enable Test, as illustrated:

In this mode, you should be able to interact with the components in the web browser as if they're actually deployed on the device.

If you break something, it's very simple to start a new project. It's a great tool to use for prototyping and to get the initial template or project scaffolding. You should continue coding in your regular IDE for the rest of the app. Ionic Creator doesn't do everything for you yet. For example, if you want to access specific Cordova plugin features, you have to write that code separately.

Also, if you want to tweak the interface outside of what is allowed within Ionic Creator, it will also require specific modifications to the `.html` and `.css` files.

Viewing the app using your web browser

In order to run the web app, you need to turn your `/www` folder into a web server. Again, there are many methods to do this and people tend to stick with one or two ways to keep things simple. A few other options are unreliable, such as Sublime Text's live watch package or a static page generator (for example, the Jekyll and Middleman apps). They are slow to detect changes and may freeze your IDE, so won't be mentioned here.

Getting ready

The recommended method is to use the Ionic serve command line. It basically launches an HTTP server so that you can open your app in a desktop browser.

How to do it...

1. First, you need to be in the project folder. Let's assume that it is the side menu HelloWorld:

```
$ cd HelloWorld_Sidemenu
```

2. From there, just issue the simple command line, as shown:

```
$ ionic serve
```

That's it! There's no need to go into the /www folder or figure out which port to use. The command line will provide the following options while the web server is running:

```
[ising:~/Learning … HelloWorld_Sidemenu] 4s $ ionic serve
[INFO] Starting app-scripts server: --address 0.0.0.0 --port 8100
       --livereload-port 35729 --dev-logger-port 53703 - Ctrl+C to cancel
[12:20:40]  watch started ...
[12:20:40]  build dev started ...
[12:20:40]  clean started ...
[12:20:40]  clean finished in less than 1 ms
[12:20:40]  copy started ...
[12:20:40]  transpile started ...
[12:20:42]  transpile finished in 1.80 s
[12:20:42]  preprocess started ...
[12:20:42]  deeplinks started ...
[12:20:42]  deeplinks finished in 9 ms
[12:20:42]  preprocess finished in 11 ms
[12:20:42]  webpack started ...
[12:20:42]  copy finished in 2.00 s
[12:20:48]  webpack finished in 6.30 s
[12:20:48]  sass started ...
[12:20:49]  sass finished in 878 ms
[12:20:49]  postprocess started ...
[12:20:49]  postprocess finished in 16 ms
[12:20:49]  lint started ...
[12:20:49]  build dev finished in 9.04 s
[12:20:49]  watch ready in 9.09 s
[12:20:49]  dev server running: http://localhost:8100/

[INFO] Development server running!
       Local: http://localhost:8100
       External: http://10.158.8.23:8100, http://10.158.8.30:8100

[12:20:51]  lint finished in 2.03 s
```

The most common option to use here is *Ctrl + C* to quit when you are done.

There are additional steps to view the app with the correct device resolution:

1. Install Google Chrome if it's not already on your computer.
2. Open the link (for example, `http://localhost:8100/`) from Ionic serve in Google Chrome.
3. Turn on Developer Tools. For example, in Mac's Google Chrome, navigate to **View** | **Developer** | **DeveloperTools**:

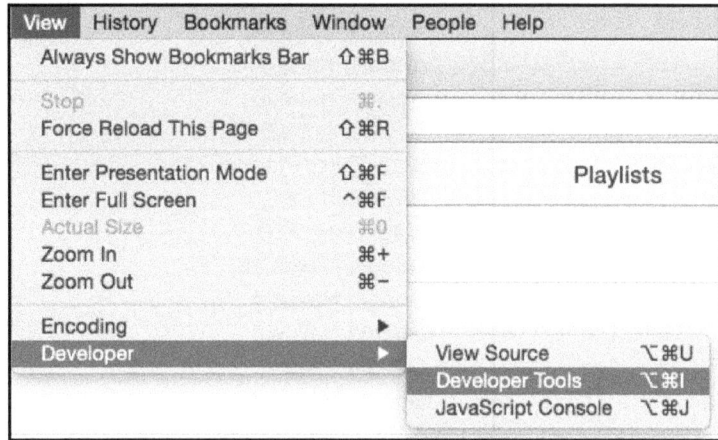

4. Click on the small mobile icon in the Chrome Developer Tools area, as illustrated:

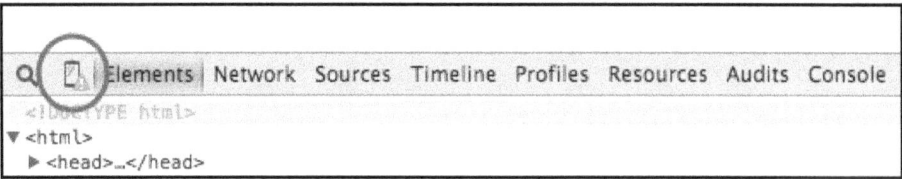

5. There will be a long list of devices to pick from, as shown:

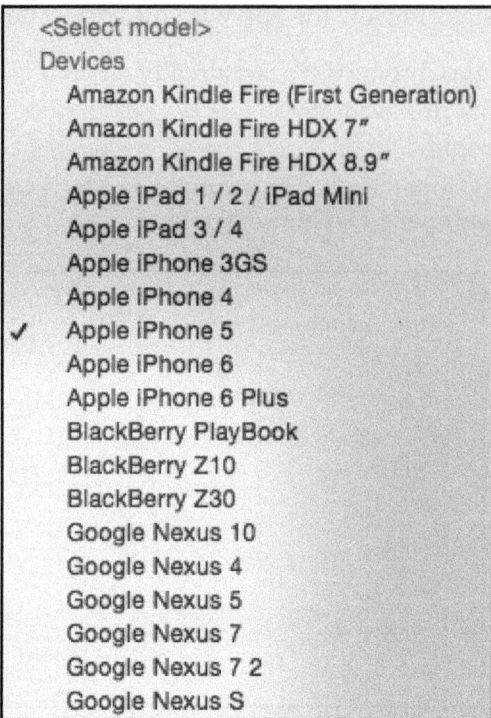

```
<Select model>
Devices
    Amazon Kindle Fire (First Generation)
    Amazon Kindle Fire HDX 7"
    Amazon Kindle Fire HDX 8.9"
    Apple iPad 1 / 2 / iPad Mini
    Apple iPad 3 / 4
    Apple iPhone 3GS
    Apple iPhone 4
✓   Apple iPhone 5
    Apple iPhone 6
    Apple iPhone 6 Plus
    BlackBerry PlayBook
    BlackBerry Z10
    BlackBerry Z30
    Google Nexus 10
    Google Nexus 4
    Google Nexus 5
    Google Nexus 7
    Google Nexus 7 2
    Google Nexus S
```

6. After selecting a device, you need to refresh the page to ensure that the UI is updated. Chrome should give you the exact view resolution of the device.

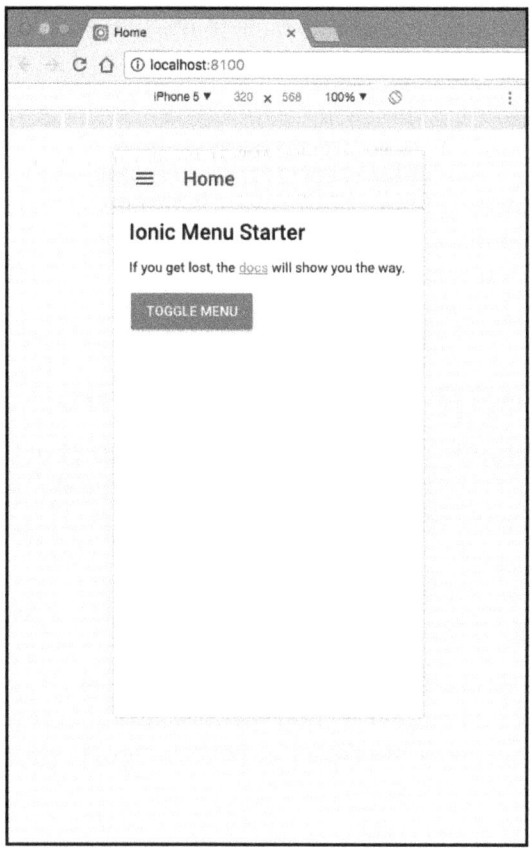

Most developers would prefer to use this method to code, as you can debug the app using Chrome Developer Tools. It works exactly like any other web application. You can create breakpoints or output variables to the console.

How it works...

Note that Ionic serve is actually watching everything under the /src folder and transpiring the TypeScript code into JavaScript under /www on the fly. This makes sense because there is no need for the system to scan through every single file when the probability of it changing is very small.

While the web server is running, you can go back to the IDE and continue coding. For example, let's open `page1.html` or any other template file and change the first line to this:

```
<ion-view view-title="Updated Playlists">
```

Go back to the web browser where Ionic opened the new page; the app interface will change the title bar right away without requiring you to refresh the browser. This is a very nice feature when there is a lot of back and forth between code changes and instantly checking how it works or looks in the app.

Viewing the app using the Ionic CLI

So far, you have been testing the web app portion of Ionic. Most of the time, you will need to actually run the app on a physical device or at least an emulator to see how the app behaves and whether all native features work.

Getting Ready

You will need to have the emulator installed. iOS emulator comes when you do npm install, `-g ios-sim`, and the Android emulator comes with Android Studio. To test the app on a physical device, you must connect the device to your computer via a USB connection.

How to do it...

1. Add the specific platform (such as iOS) and build the app using the following command line:

```
$ ionic cordova platform add ios
$ ionic cordova build ios
```

2. Note that you need to add the platforms to build the app. However, if you use the standard template from the Ionic CLI, it should already have the iOS platform included. To build and run for Android, you can replace iOS with Android.

3. To emulate the app using the `ios` emulator, use the following command line:

```
$ ionic cordova emulate ios
```

4. To run the app on the actual physical iPhone device, use the command line as shown:

```
$ ionic cordova run ios --device
```

Viewing the app using Xcode for iOS

You could run the app using Xcode (in Mac) as well.

How to do it...

1. Go to the /platforms/ios folder.
2. Look for the folder with .xcodeproj and open it in Xcode.
3. Click on the iOS device icon and select your choice of iOS simulator:

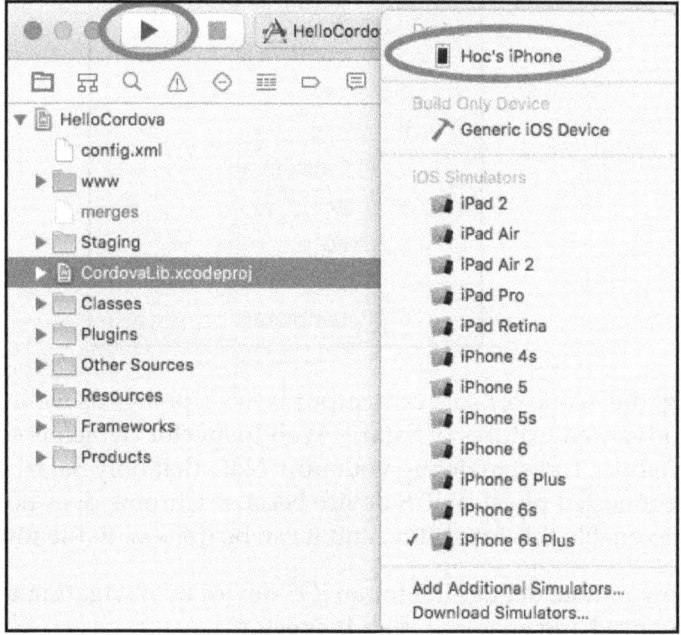

4. Click on the run button and you should be able to see the app running in the simulator.

There's more...

You can connect a physical device via a USB port and it will show up in the iOS Device list for you to pick it. Then, you can deploy the app directly on your device. Note that iOS Developer membership is required for this. This method is more complex than just viewing the app via a web browser.

However, it's a must when you want to test out your code regarding device features, such as cameras or maps. If you change the code in the /src folder and want to run it again in Xcode, you have to do Ionic Cordova build ios first, because the running code is in the **Staging** folder of your Xcode project, as illustrated:

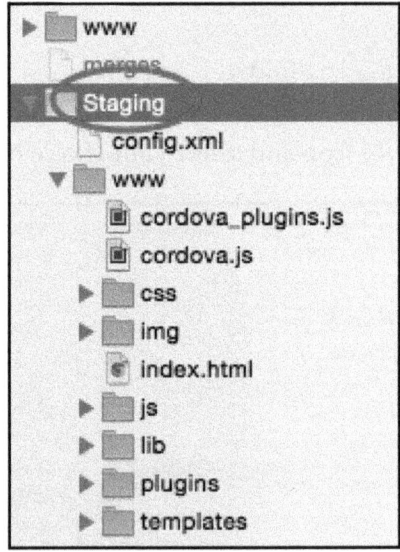

For debugging, the Xcode console can output JavaScript logs as well. However, you could use the more advanced features of Safari's **Web Inspector** (which is similar to Google Chrome's Developer Tools) to debug your app. Note that only Safari can debug a web app running on a connected physical iOS device because Chrome does not support this on a Mac. It's easy to enable this capability, and it can be done with the following steps:

1. Allow remote debugging for an iOS device by navigating to **Settings** | **Safari** | **Advanced** and enabling **Web Inspector**:

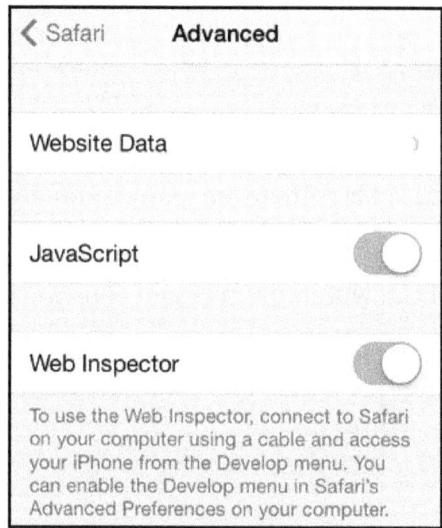

2. Connect the physical iOS device to your Mac via USB and run the app
3. Open the Safari browser
4. Select **Develop** | your device's name or **iOS Simulator** | **index.html**, as shown:

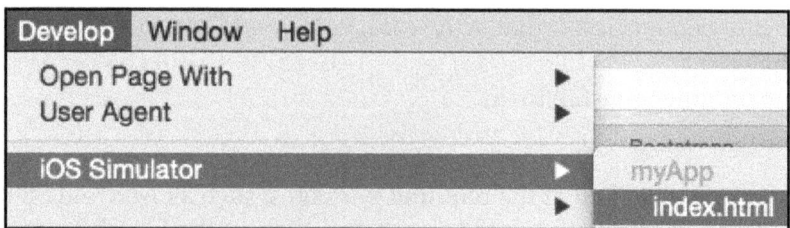

If you don't see the **Develop** menu in Safari, you need to navigate to **Preferences** | **Advanced** and check on **Show Develop menu in menu bar**.

Safari will open a new console just for that specific device, just as it's running within the computer's Safari.

Viewing the app using Genymotion for Android

While it's possible to install the Google Android simulator, many developers have an inconsistent experience on a Mac. There are many commercial and free alternatives that offer more convenience and a wide range of device support. Genymotion provides some unique advantages, such as allowing users to switch the Android model and version, supporting networking from within the app, and allowing SD card simulation.

In this section, you will learn how to set up an Android developer environment (on a Mac in this case) first. Then, you will install and configure Genymotion for mobile app development.

How to do it...

1. The first step is to set up the Android environment properly for development. Download and install Android Studio from
   `https://developer.android.com/studio/index.html`.

2. You might be asked to install other libraries if your machine doesn't have the correct dependencies. If that is the case, you should run `sudo apt-get install lib32z1 lib32ncurses5 lib32bz2-1.0 lib32stdc++6` from the command line to install them.

3. Run Android Studio.

4. You need to install all of the required packages, such as Android SDK. Just click **Next** twice on the setup wizard screen and click on the **Finish** button to start the packages' installation.

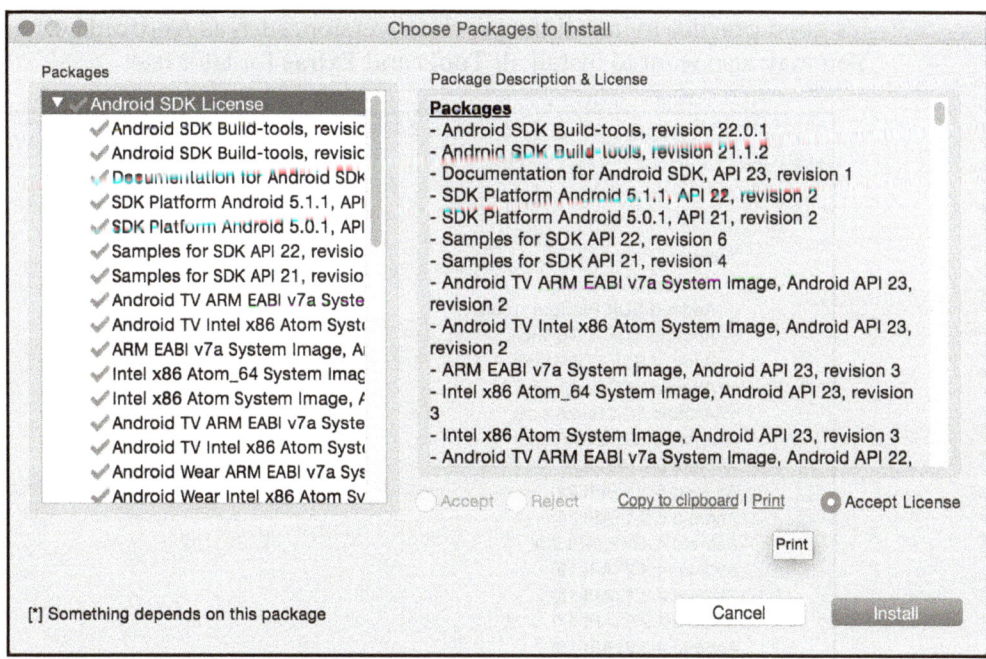

5. After the installation is complete, you need to install additional packages and other SDK versions. On the **Quick Start** screen, select **Configure**:

6. After this, select **SDKManager**, as shown:

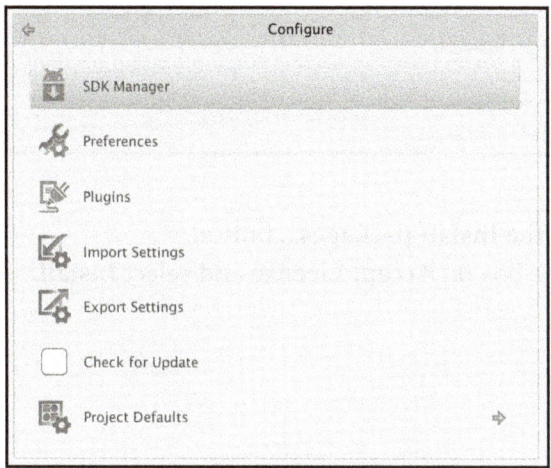

7. It's good practice to install the previous version, such as **Android5.0.1** and **5.1.1**. You may also want to install all **Tools** and **Extras** for later use:

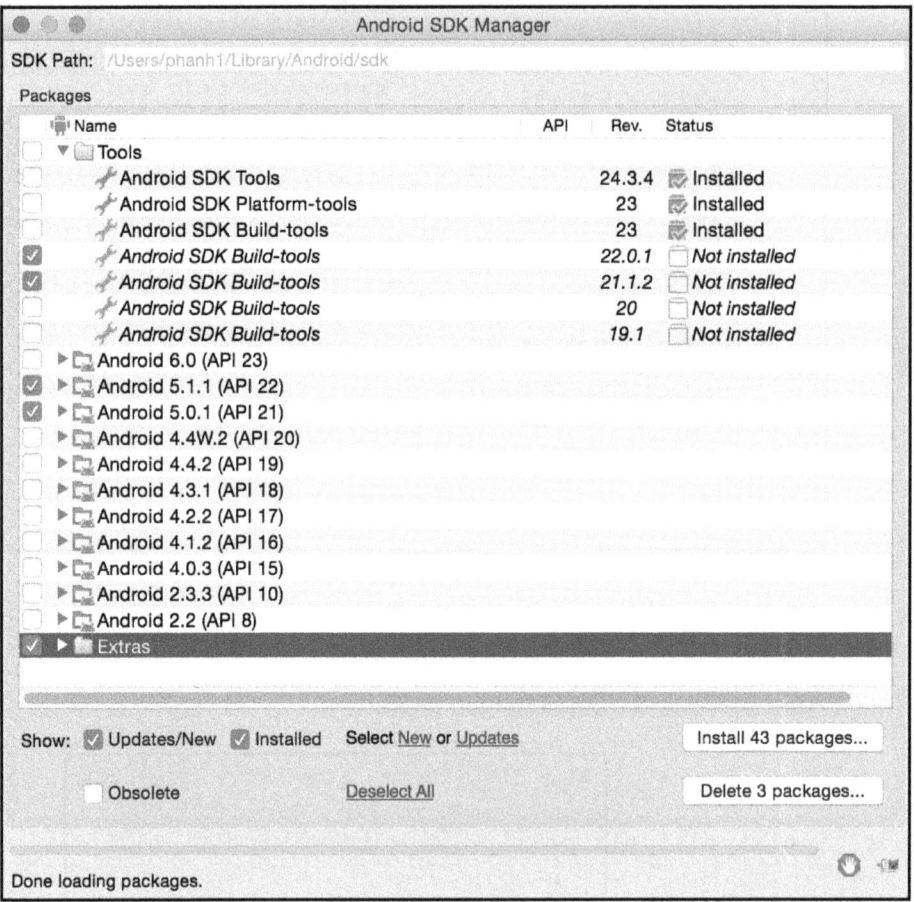

8. Click on the **Install packages...** button.
9. Check the box on **Accept License** and select **Install**.

10. The **SDK Manager** will give you an SDK path on the top. Make a copy of this path because you need to modify the environment path.

11. Go to the terminal and type the following command:

```
$ touch ~/.bash_profile; open ~/.bash_profile
```

12. This will open a text editor to edit your bash profile file. Insert the following the line, where `/YOUR_PATH_TO/android-sdk` should be the SDK Path that you copied earlier:

```
export ANDROID_HOME=/YOUR_PATH_TO/android-sdk
export PATH=$ANDROID_HOME/platform-tools:$PATH
export PATH=$ANDROID_HOME/tools:$PATH
```

13. Save and close that text editor.

14. Go back to the terminal and type:

```
$ source ~/.bash_profile
$ echo $ANDROID_HOME
```

15. You should see the output as your SDK path. This verifies that you have correctly configured the Android developer environment.

16. The next step is to install and configure Genymotion. Download and install Genymotion and Genymotion Shell from `sudo apt-get install lib32z1 lib32ncurses5 lib32bz2-1.0 lib32stdc++6`.

17. Run Genymotion.

18. Click on the **Add** button to start adding a new Android device, as illustrated:

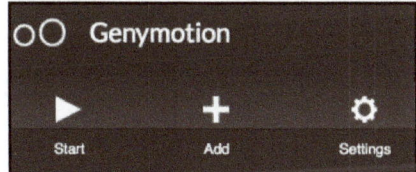

19. Select the device that you want to simulate. In this case, let's select **Samsung Galaxy S5**, as follows:

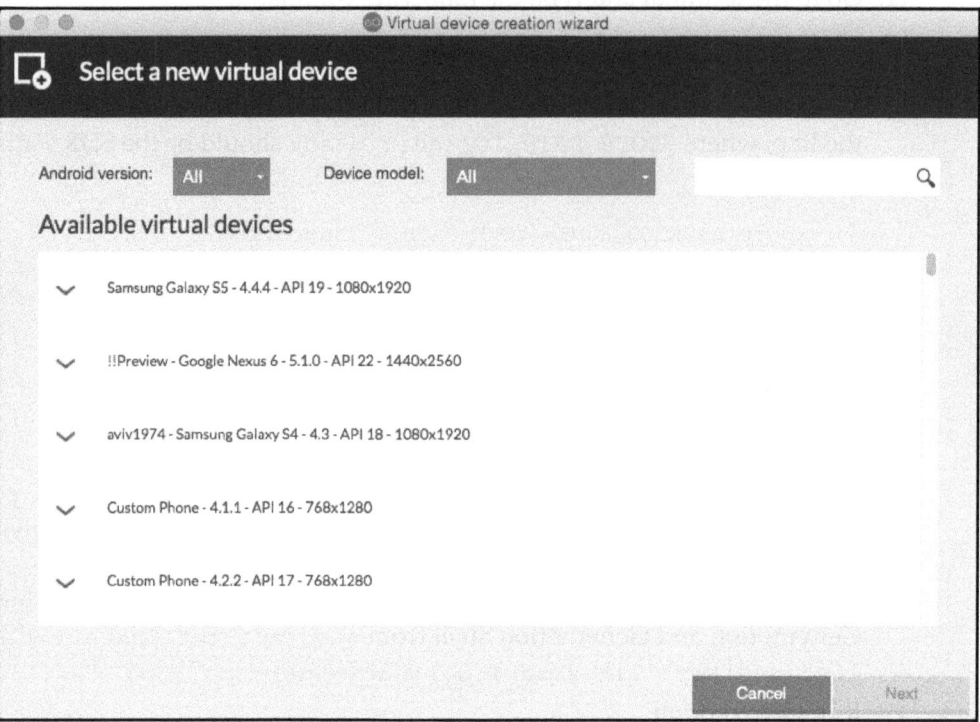

20. You will see the device being added to your virtual devices. Click on that device.
21. Then click on **Start**.

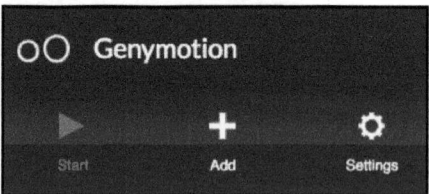

22. The simulator will take a few seconds to start and will show another window. This is just a blank simulator without your app running inside it yet.
23. Run Genymotion Shell.

24. From Genymotion Shell, you need to get a device list and keep the IP address of the device attached, which is the Samsung Galaxy S5. Type `devices list`.
25. Type `adb connect 192.168.56.101` (or whatever the IP address was that you saw earlier from the devices list command line),
26. Type `adb devices` to confirm that it is connected.
27. Type `Ionic Cordova platform` adds Android to add Android as a platform for your app.
28. Finally, type Ionic Cordova run android.
29. You should be able to see the Genymotion window showing your app.

Although there are many steps to take to get this working, it's a lot less likely that you have to go through the same process over. Once your environment is set up, all you need to do is to leave Genymotion running, while writing code. If there is a need to test the app on different Android devices, it's easy to add another virtual device in Genymotion and connect to it.

Viewing the app using Ionic View

Ionic View is an app viewer that you can download from the App Store or Google Play. When you are in the development process and the app is not complete, you don't want to submit it to either Apple or Google right away but limit access to your testers. Ionic View can help load your own app inside Ionic View and make it behave like a real app with some access to native device features. Additionally, Ionic View lets you use your app on an iOS device without any certification requirements.

Since Ionic View uses the Cordova `InAppBrowser` plugin to launch your app, all the device features have to be hacked to make it work. Currently, Ionic View only supports SQLite, battery, camera, device motion, device orientation, dialog/notification, geolocation, globalization, network information, vibration, keyboard, status bar, barcode scanner, and zip. It's a good idea to check the updated support list prior to using Ionic View to ensure that your app works properly.

How to do it...

There are two ways to use Ionic View. You can either upload your own app or load someone else's app ID. If you test your own app, follow these steps:

1. Download Ionic View from either the App Store or Google Play.

2. Make sure to register an account on `ionic.io`.

3. Go to your app's project folder.

4. Search for the Ionic upload.

5. Enter your credentials.

6. The CLI will upload the entire app and give you the app ID, which is **152909f7** in this case. You may want to keep this app ID to share with other testers later.

```
Uploading app...
Successfully uploaded (152909f7)

Share your beautiful app with someone:

$ ionic share EMAIL
```

7. Open the Ionic View app on the mobile device and log in if you haven't done so already.

8. Now, you should be able to see the app name on your **MY APPS** page. Go ahead and select the app name (**myApp** in this case), as illustrated:

9. Select **VIEW APP** to run the app, as shown:

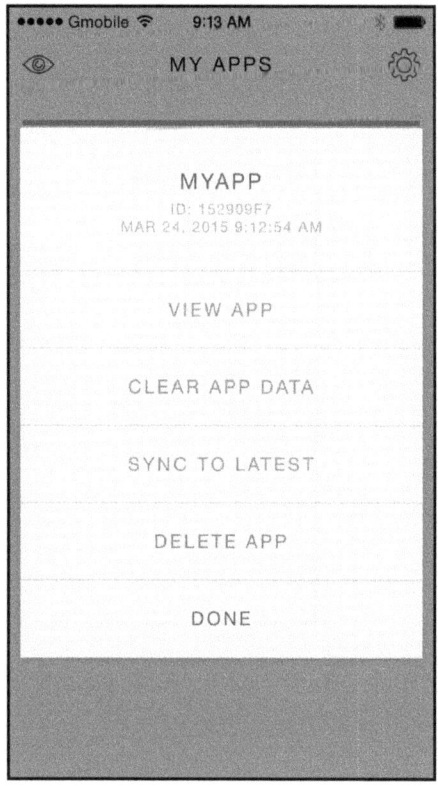

10. You will see that the app interface appears with initial instructions on how to exit the app. Since your app will cover the full screen of Ionic View, you need to swipe down using three fingers, as illustrated, to exit back to Ionic View:

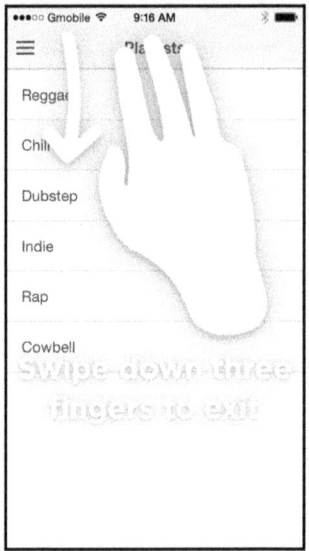

If there is no code update, the process is the same, except that you need to select **SYNC TO LATEST** from the menu.

There's more...

To summarize, there are several benefits of using Ionic View, some of which are as follows:

- It's convenient because there is only one command line to push the app
- Anyone can access your app by entering the app ID
- There is no need to have iOS Developer membership to start developing with Ionic. Apple has its own TestFlight app, which is very similar
- You can maintain an agile development process by having testers test the app as you develop it
- Ionic View supports a wide range of device features, and that support continues to grow

2
Adding Ionic Components

In this chapter, we will cover the following tasks related to using Ionic components:

- Adding multiple pages using tabs
- Adding left and right menu navigation
- Navigating multiple pages with state parameters
- Using menu, tags, and segment together in an app
- Using the Ionic grid to create a complex UI

Introduction

It's possible to write a simple app with a handful of pages. Ionic provides a lot of out-of-the-box components that allow simple plug and play operations. When an app grows, managing different views and their custom data at a specific time or triggered event can be very complex. Ionic comes with some changes to the handling of state and navigation. In Ionic 1, you could use UI-Router for advanced routing management mechanisms. In Ionic, `NavController` enables the push/pop implementation of the navigation.

Since Ionic introduces many new components, you have to understand how these components impact on your app's state hierarchy and when each state is triggered.

Adding multiple pages using tabs

This section will explain how to work with the Ionic tab interface and expand it to other use cases. The example used is very basic, with three tabs and some sample Ionic components in each tab. This is a very common structure that you will find in many apps. You will learn how Ionic structures the tab interface and how it translates to individual folders and files.

In this example, you will build three tabs, as follows:

- A tab showing a simple text-only page to explain where to place the components
- A tab showing a signup form
- A tab showing a horizontal slider box

Although the app is very straightforward, it will teach you a lot of key concepts in Angular and Ionic. Some of them are the component decorators, themes, and the TypeScript compiler process.

Here is a screenshot of the example app with the middle tab selected:

Getting ready

Since this is the first app you are building from scratch, you need to ensure that you have followed through Chapter 1, *Creating Our First App with Ionic*, to set up the environment and Ionic CLI. If you already had Ionic 1, it must be updated. For this, you can use the same command line as was used to install it, which is as follows:

```
$ sudo npm install -g cordova ionic ios-sim
```

How to do it...

The following are the instructions to create example app:

1. Create a new `PagesAndTabs` app using the `tabs` template and go into the `PagesAndTabs` folder to start Visual Studio Code, as shown:

```
$ ionic start PagesAndTabs tabs
$ cd PagesAndTabs
$ code .
```

2. The `blank` template only gives you a basic page. Open the `Finder` app in Mac or Windows Explorer in Windows to see the following folder structure:

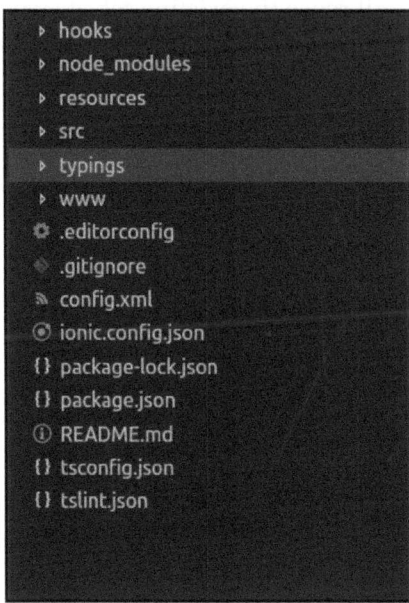

You will only modify what is in the /src folder and not /www, as in Ionic 1. Everything in the /src folder will be built and the /www folder will be created automatically. We will also reserve the folder names and filenames as much as possible, since the main goal here is to understand how the tab template works and the areas you can modify.

3. Open and edit the /src/pages/tabs/tabs.html template file with the following code:

```
<ion-tabs>
  <ion-tab [root]="tab1Root" tabTitle="One"
    tabIcon="water"></ion-tab>   <ion-tab [root]="tab2Root"
    tabTitle="Two"
    tabIcon="leaf"></ion-tab>   <ion-tab [root]="tab3Root"
    tabTitle="Three"
    tabIcon="flame"></ion-tab>
</ion-tabs>
```

The new template only updates the title and icons. This is because this example wants to reserve the naming of the tab root variables. You could add more tabs using <ion-tab>, as needed.

4. To add a page, you need to ensure that tab1Root points to an existing folder and template. Since you will reuse the existing tab structure, you can just modify the /src/pages/home/home.html **template, as shown, as this is your first page:**

```
<ion-header>
  <ion-navbar>
    <ion-title>One</ion-title>
  </ion-navbar>
</ion-header>

<ion-content padding>
  <h2>Welcome to Ionic!</h2>
  <p>
    This starter project comes with simple tabs-based layout for
    apps
    that are going to primarily use a Tabbed UI.
  </p>
  <p>
    Take a look at the <code>src/pages/</code> directory to add or
    change tabs, update any existing page or create new pages.
  </p>
</ion-content>
```

5. Also, in the same `/home` folder, edit `home.ts`, which corresponds to the same template, and enter the code here:

```
import { Component } from '@angular/core';
import { NavController } from 'ionic-angular';

@Component({
  selector: 'page-home',
  templateUrl: 'home.html'
})
export class HomePage {

  constructor(public navCtrl: NavController) {

  }

}
```

6. For the second page, `tab2Root`, you will follow a similar process by editing the `/src/pages/about/about.html` template as shown:

```
<ion-header>
  <ion-navbar>
    <ion-title>
      Two
    </ion-title>
  </ion-navbar>
</ion-header>

<ion-content>
  <ion-list>
    <ion-item>
      <ion-input type="text" placeholder="First Name"></ion-input>
    </ion-item>

    <ion-item>
      <ion-input type="text" placeholder="Last Name"></ion-input>
    </ion-item>

    <div padding>
      <button ion-button primary block>Create Account</button>
    </div>
  </ion-list>
</ion-content>
```

7. Edit `about.ts` in the same folder as in the preceding step:

```
import { Component } from '@angular/core';
import { NavController } from 'ionic-angular';

@Component({
  selector: 'page-about',
  templateUrl: 'about.html'
})
export class AboutPage {

  constructor(public navCtrl: NavController) {

  }

}
```

8. Finally, for the `tab3Root` page, you can change the template so that it will show a slider in `/src/pages/contact/contact.html`, as follows:

```
<ion-header>
  <ion-navbar>
    <ion-title>
      Three
    </ion-title>
  </ion-navbar>
</ion-header>

<ion-content>
  <ion-slides #mySlider index=0
(ionSlideDidChange)="onSlideChanged($event)">
    <ion-slide style="background-color: green">
      <h2>Slide 1</h2>
    </ion-slide>

    <ion-slide style="background-color: blue">
      <h2>Slide 2</h2>
    </ion-slide>

    <ion-slide style="background-color: red">
      <h2>Slide 3</h2>
    </ion-slide>

  </ion-slides>
</ion-content>
```

9. In the `/contact` folder, you need to edit `contact.ts` with the following code:

```
import { Component, ViewChild } from '@angular/core';
import { NavController, Slides } from 'ionic-angular';

@Component({
  selector: 'page-contact',
  templateUrl: 'contact.html'
})
export class ContactPage {
  @ViewChild('mySlider') slider: Slides;
  constructor(public navCtrl: NavController) {

  }
  onSlideChanged(e) {
    let currentIndex = this.slider.getActiveIndex();
    console.log("You are on Slide ", (currentIndex + 1));
  }

}
```

10. Go to your Terminal and type the following command line to run the app:

```
$ ionic serve
```

How it works...

There is actually a lot of new information and a lot of concepts in this simple app. At a higher level, this is how the app is structured:

- When you run the app, Cordova loads the `/www/index.html` file to open first. All of your code and templates are combined into one file, `/www/build/main.js`.
- The `/app` folder is where most of your logic belongs. It starts with `app.component.ts` as the Bootstrap file.
- Each subfolder under the `/pages` folder will represent a page, which is a new concept in Ionic. A page consists of an HTML template, TypeScript code, and an `.scss` file to customize that specific template only.
- The `/theme` folder will contain variables and customizations at a global level to override the default theme from Ionic.

Now, let's start with everything inside the `/app` folder.

The `app.component.ts` file only imports all the required pages and components to start the app. This example needs the following four imports by default:

```
import { Component } from '@angular/core';
import { Platform } from 'ionic-angular';
import { StatusBar } from '@ionic-native/status-bar';
import { SplashScreen } from '@ionic-native/splash-screen';
import { TabsPage } from '../pages/tabs/tabs';
```

You must always import `Component`, `Platform`, and `StatusBar` from Ionic, because that will give you the `@Component` decorator to Bootstrap your app. A decorator is placed in front of its class to provide metadata for the class. The following example shows that the `MyApp` class has the characteristics of a component with a `template` property:

```
@Component({
  templateUrl: 'app.html'
})
export class MyApp {
  rootPage:any = TabsPage;

  constructor(platform: Platform, statusBar: StatusBar, splashScreen:
  SplashScreen) {
    platform.ready().then(() => {
      // Okay, so the platform is ready and our plugins are available.
      // Here you can do any higher level native things you might need.
      statusBar.styleDefault();
      splashScreen.hide();
    });
  }
}
```

Since this is a simple example, you don't need to declare much except the template information. Similar to Ionic 1, you can use either `template` or `templateUrl` to point to a local file. In our case, it is `app.html` and it has the following content:

```
<ion-nav [root]="rootPage"></ion-nav>
```

Classes are another new concept in ES6. However, developers have been declaring classes in various programming languages, such as Java and C#. In ES6, you can use classes to be able to efficiently reuse code with better abstraction. A class could exist within that file context only. Consider the following example:

```
class Example {}
```

However, if you want to use that class somewhere else, you have to export:

```
export class Example {}
```

In a class, you can have the following:

- A variable, such as `this.a` or `this.b`
- A method, such as `doSomething()`
- A constructor that automatically executes (or initializes) when an object is created using the class

 More information about classes can be found at `https://developer.mozilla.org/en-US/docs/Web/JavaScript/Referenc` `e/Classes`.

Another nice thing about ES6 is the arrow function, as shown:

```
platform.ready().then(() => {

});
```

The preceding is the same as:

```
platform.ready().then(function() {

});
```

An example (by passing a parameter) is as follows:

```
var a1 = a.map( s => s.length );
```

The same code can be rewritten as shown:

```
var a1 = a.map(function(s){ return s.length });
```

 More information about the arrow function can be found at: `https://developer.mozilla.org/en-US/docs/Web/JavaScript/Referenc` `e/Functions/Arrow_functions`.

One important thing in `app.component.ts` is that you must declare a `root` page. You can see that from the template via `[root]="rootPage"`, and then again in the constructor via `this.rootPage = TabsPage`. The square brackets, `[]`, around `root` mean that it's a property of that DOM node. This is a new concept from Angular as it's trying to get rid of using a DOM property, such as `ngmodel` (which tends to result in lower performance). The assignment here is to tell Ionic 2 that you will use `TabsPage`, which was imported earlier, and assign that as a `root` page. Then, the `ion-nav` directive will look at its own `root` property to start rendering the page. There seem to be a lot of abstractions and boilerplate compared to Ionic 1. However, this practice is recommended to ensure better separation and scaling.

Once you understand how `app.component.ts` works, it's easier to grasp the concepts from the other pages. Let's take a look at the `/pages/tabs/tabs.ts` file, because that's where you define the `TabsPage` class. From this file, you need to import three other pages, which are the following:

```
import { Component } from '@angular/core';
import { HomePage } from '../home/home';
import { AboutPage } from '../about/about';
import { ContactPage } from '../contact/contact';
```

The template for this page is in `tabs.html`. However, you could also put the template in a string inside the `.ts` file, as follows:

```
@Component({
  template:
  ` <ion-tabs>
      <ion-tab [root]="tab1Root" tabTitle="One"
      tabIcon="water"></ion-tab><ion-tab [root]="tab2Root" tabTitle="Two"
      tabIcon="leaf"></ion-tab><ion-tab [root]="tab3Root"
      tabTitle="Three"
      tabIcon="flame"></ion-tab>
    </ion-tabs>`
})
```

ES6 also introduces a new feature, called a multiline template string. You probably realize that the preceding template string does not have any `join()` or string combine (+) operators. The reason is that you can use back-tick (` `` `) to allow a multiline template.

So, instead of doing this:

```
console.log("string text line 1\n"+
"string text line 2");
```

You can now do this:

```
console.log(`string text line 1
string text line 2`);
```

Below the page decorator, you need to export TabsPage (so that you can use it in app.component.ts) and tell the constructor to use tab1Root, tab2Root, and tab3Root as the roots for other pages in the tab navigation, as shown:

```
export class TabsPage {
  tab1Root: any = HomePage;
  tab2Root: any = AboutPage;
  tab3Root: any = ContactPage;
  constructor() {
  }
}
```

Ionic tab declaration is very similar to Ionic 1, shown as follows:

```
<ion-tabs>
    <ion-tab><ion-tab>
</ion-tabs>
```

You just have to make sure that the root property is pointing to another page.

tab1Root is actually very simple to understand, because it's a text page where you add your own content and design within the <ion-content> element, as shown:

```
<ion-content padding>
  <h2>Welcome to Ionic 2 Tabs!</h2>
  <p>
    This starter project comes with simple tabs-based layout for
    apps that are going to primarily use a Tabbed UI.
  </p>
</ion-content>
```

If you want to change the title, you can simply change the following line:

```
<ion-title>One</ion-title>
```

`tab2Root` and `tab3Root` are very similar in terms of how they are structured. Ionic gives you the convenience of binding to an event right in the `AboutPage` class, as shown:

```
import { Component } from '@angular/core';
import { NavController } from 'ionic-angular';

@Component({
  selector: 'page-about',
  templateUrl: 'about.html'
})
export class AboutPage {

  constructor(public navCtrl: NavController) {

  }

  ionViewWillEnter() {
    console.log('Enter Page 2');
  }
}
```

In the preceding example from `about.ts`, if the user enters `tab2Root`, it will call the `ionViewWillEnter()` function automatically. This is a significant improvement because, in Ionic 1, you had to use `$ionicView.enter` on the `$scope` variable. Again, the concept of `$scope` no longer exists in Angular.

For a scalable app, it's better to separate templates into different files and avoid co-mingling templates inside the JavaScript code. `templateUrl` must always point to the relative location of the `.html` file.

In `./src/pages/contact/contact.html`, you can use the slider box and bind to slide the change event, as shown:

```
<ion-header>
  <ion-navbar>
    <ion-title>
      Three
    </ion-title>
  </ion-navbar>
</ion-header>

<ion-content>
  <ion-slides #mySlider index=0
(ionSlideDidChange)="onSlideChanged($event)">
    <ion-slide style="background-color: green">
      <h2>Slide 1</h2>
```

```
    </ion-slide>

    <ion-slide style="background-color: blue">
      <h2>Slide 2</h2>
    </ion-slide>

    <ion-slide style="background-color: red">
      <h2>Slide 3</h2>
    </ion-slide>

  </ion-slides>
 </ion-content>
```

To get an event in Angular (or Ionic), you have to use parentheses, ( ), because the concept of `ng-click` or similar is no longer available. In this case, if the slide is changed based on `ionSlideDidChange`, the `ion-slides` directive will trigger the `onSlideChanged()` function in the `ContactPage` class.

You cannot really run the TypeScript directly without having TypeScript to transpile the code into JavaScript. This process happens automatically behind the scenes when you run `ionic serve`. Also, when you change some code in the project, Ionic will detect those changes and rebuild the files before updating the browser. There is no need to hit refresh every time.

See also

- The Mozilla Developer Network has very extensive documentation on ECMAScript 6, which you can find at the following link: `https://developer.mozilla.org/en-US/docs/Web/JavaScript/New_in_JavaScript/ECMAScript_6_support_in_Mozilla`.
- For Angular 2-specific information, you can read directly from the Angular 2 documentation at `https://angular.io/docs/ts/latest/index.html`.

Adding left and right menu navigation

Menu navigation is a very common component in many mobile apps. You can use the menu to allow users to change to different pages in the app, including login and logout. The menu could be placed on the left or right of the app. Ionic also lets you detect events and further customize the menu's look and feel.

This is a screenshot of the app you will develop:

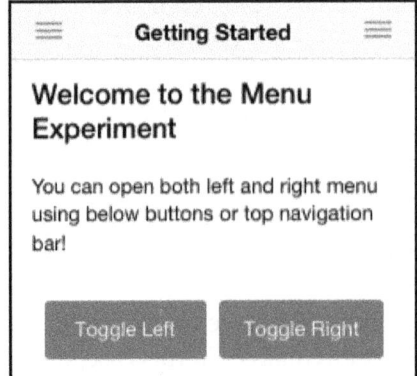

The app will have two pages and two menus. You can toggle either the left or right menu (but not both at the same time). In reality, it is much less likely that you will have both menus, but for the purposes of demonstration, this app will include both menus as the app will show the different properties of the menus that you can set. The left menu will change the page and the right menu will allow you to capture the exact item that is clicked on.

Getting ready

This app can run on your web browser, so there is no need to have a physical device available. Again, you only need to have Ionic available on your computer.

How to do it...

Here are the instructions to create example app:

1. Create a new `LeftRightMenu` app using the `sidemenu` template, as shown, and go to the `LeftRightMenu` folder:

```
$ ionic start LeftRightMenu sidemenu
$ cd LeftRightMenu
```

2. Check that your app folder structure is similar to the following:

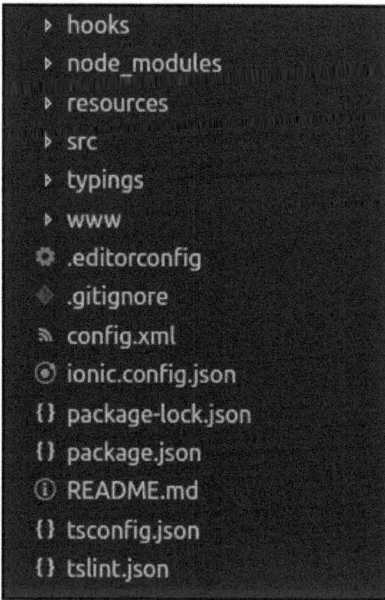

3. Edit `./src/app/app.component.ts` and replace it with the following code:

```typescript
import { Component, ViewChild } from '@angular/core';
import { Nav, Platform } from 'ionic-angular';
import { StatusBar } from '@ionic-native/status-bar';
import { SplashScreen } from '@ionic-native/splash-screen';

import { HomePage } from '../pages/home/home';
import { ListPage } from '../pages/list/list';

@Component({
  templateUrl: 'app.html'
})
export class MyApp {
  @ViewChild(Nav) nav: Nav;
  text: string = '';
  rootPage: any = HomePage;

  pages: Array<{title: string, component: any}>;

  constructor(public platform: Platform, public statusBar:
StatusBar, public splashScreen: SplashScreen) {
    this.initializeApp();
```

```
      // used for an example of ngFor and navigation
      this.pages = [
        { title: 'Home', component: HomePage },
        { title: 'List', component: ListPage }
      ];

    }

    initializeApp() {
      this.platform.ready().then(() => {
        // Okay, so the platform is ready and our plugins are
available.
        // Here you can do any higher level native things you might
need.
        this.statusBar.styleDefault();
        this.splashScreen.hide();
      });
    }

    openPage(page) {
      // Reset the content nav to have just this page
      // we wouldn't want the back button to show in this scenario
      this.nav.setRoot(page.component);
    }

    rightMenuClick(text) {
      this.text = text;
    }
  }
```

4. Open and edit the `./src/app/app.html` file with the following code:

```
<ion-menu id="leftMenu" [content]="content" side="left"
type="overlay">
  <ion-header>
    <ion-toolbar>
      <ion-title>Menu</ion-title>
    </ion-toolbar>
  </ion-header>

  <ion-content>
    <ion-list>
      <button menuClose ion-item *ngFor="let p of pages"
        (click)="openPage(p)">
        {{p.title}}
      </button>
    </ion-list>
  </ion-content>
```

```
</ion-menu>

<ion-menu id="rightMenu" [content]="content" side="right"
type="reveal">
  <ion-header>
    <ion-toolbar>
      <ion-title>Items</ion-title>
    </ion-toolbar>
  </ion-header>

  <ion-content>
   <ion-list>
    <button ion-item (click)="rightMenuClick('Item One')">
      Item One
    </button>
    <button ion-item (click)="rightMenuClick('Item Two')">
      Item Two
    </button>
   </ion-list>

   <ion-card *ngIf="text">
    <ion-card-content>
      You just clicked {{ text }}
    </ion-card-content>
   </ion-card>
  </ion-content>

</ion-menu>

<!-- Disable swipe-to-go-back because it's poor UX to combine STGB
with side menus -->
<ion-nav [root]="rootPage" #content swipeBackEnabled="false"></ion-
nav>
```

> There are two menus as siblings in this template. They are also at the same
> level as ion-nav and not a parent or child. This structure is important for
> menu navigation to work.

5. Now let's create two pages, for which you only have to modify the standard
   pages from the sidemenu template. Open and edit the
   ./src/app/pages/home/home.html template:

```
<ion-header>
  <ion-navbar>
    <ion-title>Getting Started</ion-title>
    <ion-buttons left>
```

```
        <button ion-button menuToggle="leftMenu">
          <ion-icon name="menu"></ion-icon>
        </button>
      </ion-buttons>

      <ion-buttons right>
        <button ion-button menuToggle="rightMenu">
          <ion-icon name="menu"></ion-icon>
        </button>
      </ion-buttons>
    </ion-navbar>
</ion-header>

<ion-content padding class="getting-started">
  <h3>Welcome to the Menu Experiment</h3>
  <p>
    You can open both left and right menu using below buttons or
top
    navigation bar!
  </p>
  <ion-row>
    <ion-col width-50>
      <button ion-button primary block menuToggle="leftMenu">Toggle
Left</button>
    </ion-col>
    <ion-col width-50>
      <button ion-button primary block
menuToggle="rightMenu">Toggle Right</button>
    </ion-col>
  </ion-row>
</ion-content>
```

6. In the same folder, open and edit the `.css` classes via `home.scss`, as shown:

```
page-home {
    .getting-started {
        p {
            margin: 20px 0;
            line-height: 22px;
            font-size: 16px;
        }
    }
    .bar-button-menutoggle {
        display: inline-flex;
    }
}
```

 Note that since you're using the `sidemenu` template, it already comes with a second page (for example, list). There is no need to modify that page in this specific example.

7. Open and edit the template for the second page at `./src/pages/list/list.html`, as shown:

```
<ion-header>
  <ion-navbar>
    <button ion-button menuToggle>
      <ion-icon name="menu"></ion-icon>
    </button>
    <ion-title>List</ion-title>
  </ion-navbar>
</ion-header>

<ion-content>
  <ion-list>
    <button ion-item *ngFor="let item of items"
(click)="itemTapped($event, item)">
      <ion-icon [name]="item.icon" item-left></ion-icon>
      {{item.title}}
      <div class="item-note" item-right>
        {{item.note}}
      </div>
    </button>
  </ion-list>
  <div *ngIf="selectedItem" padding>
    You navigated here from <b>{{selectedItem.title}}</b>
  </div>
</ion-content>
```

8. Go to your Terminal and run the app:

```
$ ionic serve
```

How it works...

Since this app is just an introduction to menu navigation, it will not manage page routing and state parameters. At a higher level, this is how the app flows:

- `app.ts` loads both of the `menu` templates in `app.html`.
- The left menu will trigger the `openPage()` function to open `PageTwo`.
- The right menu will trigger the `rightMenuClick()` function to change the `this.text` property and be displayed on the screen.

In the `app.html` template, the left menu has the following properties:

```
side="left" type="overlay"
```

However, the right menu has the following assigned instead:

```
side="right" type="reveal"
```

The `side` property will determine where on the screen the menu should show. There are two types of menus. The `overlay` option will leave the center page as it is, without moving. The `reveal` option will push the entire screen to show the menu. Which type you pick depends on the design of your app.

Each `ion-menu` directive must have `[content]="content"` declared because it will use the content area to bind swipe left or right. In this case, it is basically a local variable in `ion-nav`, as follows:

```
<ion-nav id="nav" [root]="rootPage" #content
swipeBackEnabled="false"></ion-nav>
```

The use of `ion-toolbar` inside `ion-menu` is optional if you want to have the title for your menu. The key to having a menu item displayed is to use `ion-list` and `ion-item`. You can loop through an array to display the menu items dynamically, as illustrated:

```
<ion-list>
  <button menuClose ion-item *ngFor="let p of pages"
  (click)="openPage(p)">
    {{p.title}}
  </button>
</ion-list>
```

`*ngFor` is a replacement for `ng-repeat` in Ionic 1. You need to use `let p` because it's the same as declaring a local variable named p. This is best practice for variable isolation. Otherwise, the concept is very similar to Ionic 1, as you can grab `p.title` for each item in the `pages` array.

On the right menu, instead of going to a different page via `nav.setRoot()`, you just set some text and dynamically display the text inside the menu, as shown:

```
<ion-card *ngIf="text">
  <ion-card-content>
    You just clicked {{ text }}
  </ion-card-content>
</ion-card>
```

So, if the `text` variable doesn't exist (which means that the user has not clicked on anything yet), the `ion-card` will not show anything via `*ngIf`.

For each page, you have to declare the same `ion-navbar`. Otherwise, you will lose the top navigation and buttons to the menus:

```
<ion-header>
  <ion-navbar>
    <ion-title>Getting Started</ion-title>

    <ion-buttons start>
      <button ion-button menuToggle="leftMenu">
        <ion-icon name="menu"></ion-icon>
      </button>
    </ion-buttons>
    <ion-buttons end>
      <button ion-button menuToggle="rightMenu">
        <ion-icon name="menu"></ion-icon>
      </button>
    </ion-buttons>
  </ion-navbar>
</ion-header>
```

Note that `leftMenu` and `rightMenu` must be the same `id` you used earlier, in the `app.html` template.

On the first page, there are two buttons to trigger the menus from within the content page as well, as shown:

```
<ion-row>
  <ion-col width-50>
    <button primary block menuToggle="leftMenu">Toggle
     Left</button>
  </ion-col>
  <ion-col width-50>
    <button primary block menuToggle="rightMenu">Toggle
     Right</button>
  </ion-col>
</ion-row>
```

These two buttons also call `menuToggle` to trigger the menu. The buttons are placed within the Ionic grid system. Since Ionic uses Flexbox, it is very simple to use—you just need to create `ion-col` and `ion-row`. The `width` property, with a number, will determine the width percentage.

See also

- For further usage of the Ionic menu, you can check out the following link:
  `http://ionicframework.com/docs/v2/components/#menus`.
- The API documentation for the Ionic menu is also available at:
  `http://ionicframework.com/docs/v2/api/components/menu/Menu/`.

Navigating multiple pages with state parameters

App navigation is an important topic because it's at the core of a user's experience. You want to manage the user's expectation of what will happen after they submit a form or after they go to a new tab. In addition, you may want to ensure that the user data is available on the correct page or in the correct state. This could also get more complicated when the requirement of a back navigation is involved.

This section will teach you how to work with `NavController` and `NavParams`, which are the two important base classes to manage all navigation for the app. This is a screenshot of the app you will develop:

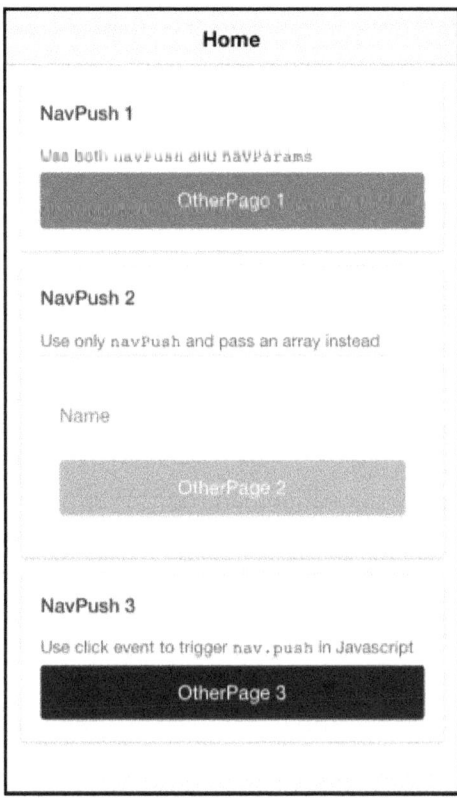

This app has three different examples of how to navigate to a different page and how to pass parameters. When you click on any button, it will show the second page, which is as follows:

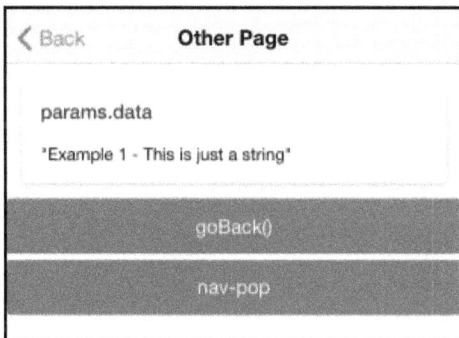

The second page, basically, captures parameters and displays them on the screen. It also gives you three different options to navigate back to the previous page.

In this example, you will learn the following:

- How to use `NavController` and `NavParams`
- How to use `[navPush]` and `[navParams]` directly in the template
- How to add two-way data binding in an input box
- How to use the pipe to convert a JSON object to a string and render it on the screen

Getting ready

You only need to have the Ionic CLI available to run this app.

How to do it...

Here are the instructions:

1. Create a new `Navigation` app using the blank template, as shown, and go into the `Navigation` folder:

```
$ ionic start Navigation blank
$ cd Navigation
```

2. Edit `./src/app/app.module.ts` with the following code:

```
import { BrowserModule } from '@angular/platform-browser';
import { ErrorHandler, NgModule } from '@angular/core';
import { IonicApp, IonicErrorHandler, IonicModule } from 'ionic-angular';
import { SplashScreen } from '@ionic-native/splash-screen';
import { StatusBar } from '@ionic-native/status-bar';

import { MyApp } from './app.component';
import { HomePage } from '../pages/home/home';
import { OtherPage } from '../pages/otherPage/otherPage';

@NgModule({
  declarations: [
    MyApp,
    HomePage,
```

```
      OtherPage
    ],
    imports: [
      BrowserModule,
      IonicModule.forRoot(MyApp)
    ],
    bootstrap: [IonicApp],
    entryComponents: [
      MyApp,
      HomePage,
      OtherPage
    ],
    providers: [
      StatusBar,
      SplashScreen,
      {provide: ErrorHandler, useClass: IonicErrorHandler}
    ]
})
export class AppModule {}
```

 The main reason you have to modify this file is to declare OtherPage as a dynamically loaded module via NgModule. You will have to declare OtherPage again in the home.ts file.

3. Edit ./src/app/pages/home/home.html:

```html
<ion-header>
  <ion-navbar>
    <ion-title>
      Home
    </ion-title>
  </ion-navbar>
</ion-header>

<ion-content padding>
  <ion-card>
    <ion-card-header>
      NavPush 1
    </ion-card-header>
    <ion-card-content>
      <p>Use both <code>navPush</code> and
      <code>navParams</code></p>
        <button ion-button block [navPush]="otherPage"
        [navParams]="myString">
          OtherPage 1
        </button>
```

```
          </ion-card-content>
        </ion-card>

      <ion-card>
       <ion-card-header>
       NavPush 2
       </ion-card-header>
        <ion-card-content>
          <p>Use only <code>navPush</code> and pass an array instead</p>
            <ion-list>
              <ion-item>
                <ion-label floating>Name</ion-label>
                Adding Ionic 2 Components 58
                <ion-input type="text" [(ngModel)]="myJSON.text"></ion-
                input>
              </ion-item>
            </ion-list>
            <div>
              <button ion-button block color="secondary"
              [navPush]="otherPage"
              [navParams]="myJSON">OtherPage 2</button>
            </div>
        </ion-card-content>
      </ion-card>

      <ion-card>
        <ion-card-header>
          NavPush 3
        </ion-card-header>
        <ion-card-content>
          <p>Use click event to trigger <code>nav.push</code> in
          Javascript </p>
          <button ion-button block color="dark"
          (click)="gotoOtherPage()">OtherPage 3</button>
        </ion-card-content>
      </ion-card>
    </ion-content>
```

4. Edit `./src/app/pages/home/home.ts` with the following code:

```
import { Component } from '@angular/core';
import { NavController } from 'ionic-angular';
import { OtherPage } from '../otherPage/otherPage';

@Component({
  selector: 'page-home',
  templateUrl: 'home.html'
})
```

```
export class HomePage {
  public myString: string = 'Example 1 - This is just a string';
  public myJSON: any = {text: ''};
  otherPage: any = OtherPage;
  constructor(public navCtrl: NavController) {

  }

  gotoOtherPage() {
    this.navCtrl.push(OtherPage, {text: 'Example 3 - This is an
object'});
  }

}
```

5. Create the `./src/app/pages/otherPage` folder

6. Create the `otherPage.html` file in the previously created `otherPage` folder:

```html
<ion-header>
  <ion-navbar>
    <ion-title>Other</ion-title>
  </ion-navbar>
</ion-header>

<ion-content>
 <ion-card *ngIf="navParams.data">
    <ion-card-header>
      navParams.data
    </ion-card-header>
    <ion-card-content>
    {{ navParams.data | json }}
    </ion-card-content>
 </ion-card>

 <button ion-button block (click)="goBack()">
    goBack()
 </button>

 <button ion-button block navPop>
    nav-pop
 </button>
</ion-content>
```

7. In the same folder, add `otherPage.ts` as well, with the following code:

```ts
import { Component } from '@angular/core';
import { NavController, NavParams } from 'ionic-angular';
```

```
@Component({
  selector: 'page-other',
  templateUrl: 'otherPage.html',
})
export class OtherPage {

  constructor(public navCtrl: NavController, public navParams:
NavParams) {
  }

  ionViewDidLoad() {
    console.log('ionViewDidLoad OtherPage');
  }
  goBack() {
    this.navCtrl.pop();
  }
}
```

8. Go to your Terminal and run the app:

```
$ ionic serve
```

 You can also generate new pages using Ionic CLI's generate commands. For example, to generate a new page you can use the following ionic command: `ionic generate page pageName`. Here, `pageName` is the name of the new page.

 You can not only generate pages but components, pipes, and many other things. Take a look at `https://ionicframework.com/docs/cli/generate/`.

How it works...

At a high level, this is how the app is structured:

- The app will Bootstrap via `app.ts` and load `home.html` as the `root` page
- Everything in the `/home` folder is your first page
- Everything in the `/otherPage` folder is your second page
- These two pages communicate using `NavParams` (or `navParams` from the template)

Let's take a look at `home.ts`. You must import both `NavController` and `NavParams`:

```
import { NavController, NavParams } from 'ionic-angular';
```

For your constructor, you need to do a few things, which are as follows:

```
public myString: string = 'Example 1 - This is just a string';
public myJSON: any = {text: ''};
otherPage: any = OtherPage;

constructor(public navCtrl: NavController) {
}
```

The `this.navCtrl` variable will reference the imported `NavController`. You are supposed to bring it in like this in order to use the navigation feature internally. `myString` and `myJSON` are just variables that you will pass in the parameter to the second page. You also have to bring in the class for `OtherPage` and make it accessible to `navPush`, later in your template.

The `gotoOtherPage()` method, as shown, does one simple thing: it pushes the page to the current navigation:

```
gotoOtherPage() {
  this.navCtrl.push(OtherPage, {text: 'Example 3 - This is an
    object'});
}
```

By doing so, your app will switch to `OtherPage` right away, and this will also include the parameters.

The `home.html` template for the first page demonstrates the following three scenarios:

- You can use `[navPush]` and `[navParams]` directly inside the template. You just need to pass the internal object of the class handling this page. So, in this case, you have to pass `otherPage` and not `OtherPage` (notice the uppercase O):

  ```
  <button block [navPush]="otherPage"
  [navParams]="myString">OtherPage 1</button>
  ```

- You can also pass a JSON object as a param into `[navPush]`:

  ```
  <button ion-button block color="secondary"
  [navPush]="otherPage" [navParams]="myJSON">OtherPage
  2</button>
  ```

- The third scenario is to navigate to a new page manually, as shown, using a method implemented inside the page class:

```
<button block dark (click)="gotoOtherPage()">OtherPage 3</button>
```

 Unlike Angular 1 or Ionic 1, you cannot use `ng-model` to do two-way binding anymore. The new syntax will be `[(ngModel)]` for any input element instead.

In your second page, you just need to make `NavController` and `NavParams` available in the class from the constructor.

Let's take a look at your `otherPage.js` file:

```
constructor(public navCtrl: NavController, public params: NavParams) {
}
```

The template for the second page (that is, `otherPage.html`) is very simple. First, the navigation bar on the top is to enable the default back button:

```
<ion-header>
  <ion-navbar>
    <ion-title>Other</ion-title>
  </ion-navbar>
</ion-header>
```

The back button is an automatic mechanism in Ionic, so you don't have to worry about when it will be shown.

The following code will display the variable content if the state parameter exists:

```
<ion-card *ngIf="params.data">
  <ion-card-header>
    params.data
  </ion-card-header>
  <ion-card-content>
    {{ params.data | json }}
  </ion-card-content>
</ion-card>
```

The `ion-card` leverages `*ngIf` to decide whether this DOM should be rendered or not. Since `params.data` could be a JSON object, you need to convert it to a string to display it on the screen. Angular 1 has filters, but Angular renamed this feature as pipes. However, the basic concept is the same. The `{{ params.data | json }}` code basically tells Angular to apply the `json` function to `params.data` and render the output.

You could go back to the previous page using the `nav.pop()` function, as shown:

```
<button block (click)="goBack()">
  goBack()
</button>
```

Alternatively, you could go back using a directive `navPop` and put that inside your button, as shown:

```
<button block navPop>
  nav-pop
</button>
```

So, those are the possibilities within the Ionic navigation features.

See also

For more information, refer to the official Ionic documentation for `NavController` and `NavParams` at the following links:

- https://ionicframework.com/docs/api/navigation/NavController/
- https://ionicframework.com/docs/api/navigation/NavParams/

To read more about how Angular pipes work, you can review the following page for the previous example on JSON pipes at: `https://angular.io/api/common/JsonPipe`

Using menu, tabs, and segment together in an app

In the previous examples, we used tabs and menu for the navigation. We used them in two different applications. But, sometimes, we might want to use both tabs and menu in a single application. In this example, we will use tabs, menu, and segment. The second page of the app will look something like the following screenshot:

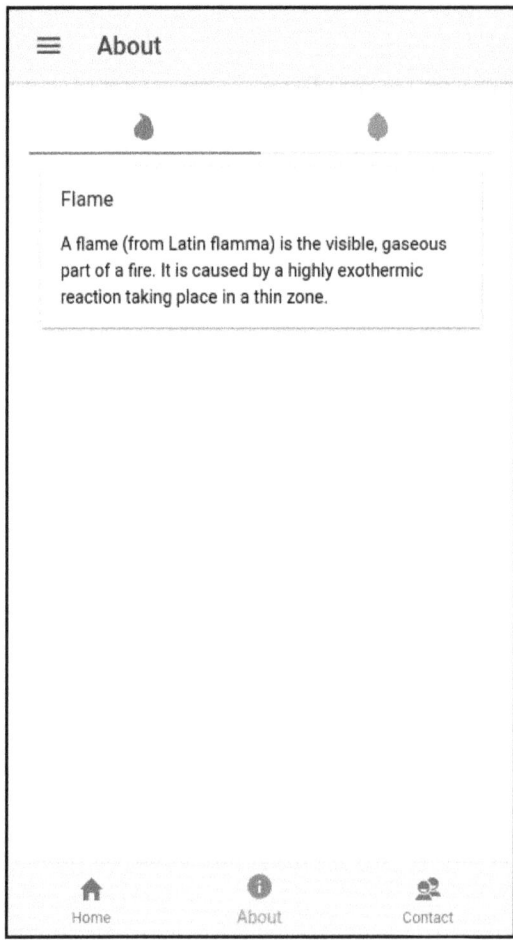

If you take a closer look at the preceding screenshot, you will see that there is hamburger menu button, three tabs at the bottom, and two tabs like buttons just after the page title. These two buttons are actually called segment buttons. They are similar to tabs in UX, but they are very different in their workings. You will see later on in the code how they are different.

Getting ready

You need the Ionic CLI and a web browser to run this app.

How to do it...

Here are the instructions to create example app:

1. Create a new `MenuTabsSegment` app using the `tabs` template, as shown, and go into the `MenuTabsSegment` folder:

```
$ ionic start MenuTabsSegment tabs
$ cd MenuTabsSegment
```

2. Edit `./src/app/app.html` with the following code:

```
<ion-menu [content]="content">
  <ion-header>
    <ion-toolbar>
      <ion-title>Menu</ion-title>
    </ion-toolbar>
  </ion-header>
  <ion-content>
    <ion-list>
      <button ion-item menuToggle>
        Close Menu
      </button>
    </ion-list>
  </ion-content>
</ion-menu>

<ion-nav #content [root]="rootPage"></ion-nav>
```

3. Edit `./src/app/pages/about/about.ts` with the following code:

```
import { Component } from '@angular/core';
import { NavController } from 'ionic-angular';

@Component({
  selector: 'page-about',
  templateUrl: 'about.html'
})
export class AboutPage {
  seg:string = "flame";
  constructor(public navCtrl: NavController) {

  }

}
```

4. Edit `./src/app/pages/about/about.html` with the following code:

```
<ion-header>
  <ion-navbar>
    <button ion-button menuToggle icon-only>
      <ion-icon name='menu'></ion-icon>
    </button>
    <ion-title>
      About
    </ion-title>
  </ion-navbar>
</ion-header>

<ion-content padding>
  <ion-segment [(ngModel)]="seg" color="danger">
      <ion-segment-button value="flame">
        <ion-icon name="flame"></ion-icon>
      </ion-segment-button>
      <ion-segment-button value="leaf">
        <ion-icon name="leaf"></ion-icon>
      </ion-segment-button>
  </ion-segment>

  <div *ngIf="seg === 'flame'">
    <ion-card>
      <ion-card-header>
        Flame
      </ion-card-header>
      <ion-card-content>
        A flame (from Latin flamma) is the visible, gaseous part of
```

```
                a fire. It is caused by a highly exothermic reaction taking
       place in
                a thin zone.
              </ion-card-content>
            </ion-card>
          </div>

          <div *ngIf="seg == 'leaf'">
            <ion-card>
            <ion-card-header>
              Leaf
            </ion-card-header>
            <ion-card-content>
              A leaf is an organ of a vascular plant and is the principal
              lateral appendage of the stem.
            </ion-card-content>
          </ion-card>
        </div>
      </ion-content>
```

How it works...

So far, we have used both menu and tabs, but in different applications. In this example, we are using both of them in a single application. Let's take a look at our app.html again:

```
<ion-menu [content]="content">
  <ion-header>
    <ion-toolbar>
      <ion-title>Menu</ion-title>
    </ion-toolbar>
  </ion-header>
  <ion-content>
    <ion-list>
      <button ion-item menuToggle>
        Close Menu
      </button>
    </ion-list>
  </ion-content>
</ion-menu>

<ion-nav #content [root]="rootPage"></ion-nav>
```

You will notice that we are using `ion-menu` to show a menu. We are also initializing Ionic navigation with `rootPage`. If you check `app.component.ts`, you will see that we are initializing `rootPage` to be equal to `TabsPage`, as shown here:

```
rootPage:any = TabsPage;
```

This is the key to using both a side menu and tabs on a single page:

Furthermore, we have added a segment on the second page of our application in `about.html`. The reason why I used segment alongside menu and tabs is that segment is very similar to tabs in terms of user experience. The user clicks on it and they see a different view/content, based on segment. But it is very much different from the tabs in Ionic. See the code following fragment from `about.html`:

```
<ion-segment [(ngModel)]="seg" color="danger">
      <ion-segment-button value="flame">
        <ion-icon name="flame"></ion-icon>
      </ion-segment-button>
      <ion-segment-button value="leaf">
        <ion-icon name="leaf"></ion-icon>
      </ion-segment-button>
   </ion-segment>
```

The preceding HTML code is for rendering the `segment` container and `segment` buttons. We link the segment with a `seg` property in our `AboutPage` class via `ngModel`. When the user clicks on any segment button, the property `seg` is initialized to the value of the segment button. In this example, the `seg` property can have a value of `flame` or `leaf`. Based on that value, we show content to the user in the other fragment of `about.html`, as shown in the following code block:

```
<div *ngIf="seg === 'flame'">
    <ion-card>
      <ion-card-header>
        Flame
      </ion-card-header>
      <ion-card-content>
        A flame (from Latin flamma) is the visible, gaseous part of a
        fire.
        It is caused by a highly exothermic reaction taking place in a
        thin zone.
      </ion-card-content>
    </ion-card>
  </div>

  <div *ngIf="seg === 'leaf'">
```

```
<ion-card>
  <ion-card-header>
    Leaf
  </ion-card-header>
  <ion-card-content>
    A leaf is an organ of a vascular plant and is the principal
    lateral appendage of the stem.
  </ion-card-content>
</ion-card>
</div>
```

You should also keep in mind that when you load the AboutPage, the value of the seg property will be undefined. So, in order to make a default selection, we have to initialize the value of the seg property in About.ts, as shown here:

```
seg:string = "flame";
```

See also

Take a look at Ionic's MenuController documentation at `https://ionicframework.com/docs/api/components/app/MenuController/`. It has really good examples of how you can use multiple menus in the same app.

Using the Ionic grid to create a complex UI

Since this chapter is about Ionic components, I will mention that one of my favorite components is the Ionic grid—a really useful component to lay out your application. Based on Flexbox, it is very similar to Bootstrap's grid. The documentation on the Ionic grid says:

"The grid is composed of three units—a grid, row(s) and column(s). Columns will expand to fill their row and will resize to fit additional columns. It is based on a 12 column layout with different breakpoints based on the screen size. The number of columns and breakpoints can be fully customized using Sass."

We will create a complex UI structure with very minimal code. The app will look like the following image:

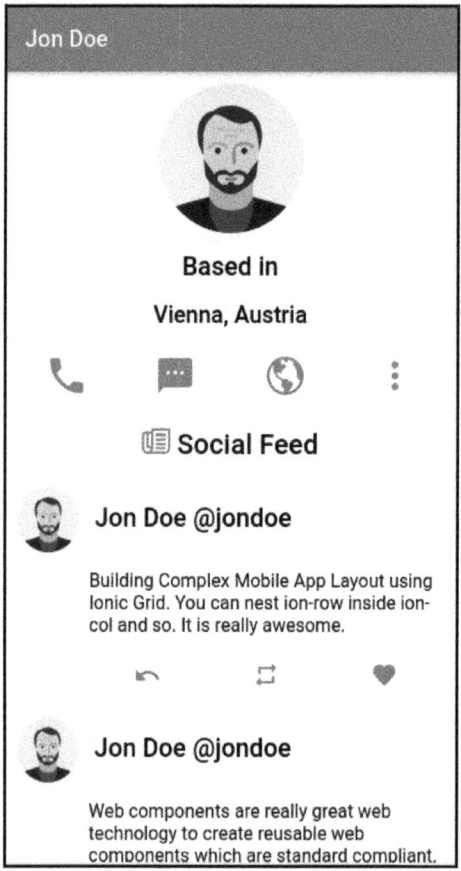

Getting ready

Just like the previous examples, you just need the Ionic CLI to work on and run this example app.

How to do it...

Here are the instructions to create the example app:

1. Create a new `IonicGrid` app using the `blank` template, as shown, and go into the `IonicGrid` folder:

```
$ ionic start IonicGrid blank
$ cd IonicGrid
```

2. Edit `./src/app/pages/home.ts` with the following code:

```
import { Component } from '@angular/core';
import { NavController } from 'ionic-angular';

@Component({
  selector: 'page-home',
  templateUrl: 'home.html'
})
export class HomePage {
  socialFeed:Array<any>;
  constructor(public navCtrl: NavController) {
    this.socialFeed = [
      { post: 'Building Complex Mobile App Layout using Ionic Grid.
You can
        nest ion-row inside ion-col and so. It is really awesome.'},
      { post: 'Web components are really great web technology to
create
        reusable web components which are standard compliant.'},
      { post: 'Nothing is in my mind. I am just writing to make
sure there
        are at least 3 rows in feed'}
    ]
  }

}
```

3. Edit `./src/app/pages/home/home.html` with the following code:

```
<ion-header>
  <ion-navbar color="danger">
    <ion-title>
      Jon Doe
    </ion-title>
  </ion-navbar>
</ion-header>
```

```
<ion-content>
 <ion-grid>
   <ion-row text-center id="info-row">
     <ion-col>
       <ion-avatar>
         <img src="assets/img/avatar.png">
       </ion-avatar>
       <h3>Based in</h3>
       <h4>Vienna, Austria</h4>
     </ion-col>
   </ion-row>

   <ion-row text-center id="contact-icons">
     <ion-col><ion-icon name="call" color="danger"></ion-icon>
</ion-col><ion-col><ion-icon name="text" color="danger"></ion-icon>
</ion-col><ion-col><ion-icon name="globe" color="danger"></ion-
icon>
</ion-col><ion-col><ion-icon name="more" color="danger"></ion-icon>
</ion-col></ion-row>

   <h2 text-center><ion-icon name="paper" color="danger"></ion-
icon>
   Social Feed</h2>
   <ion-row class="social-row" *ngFor="let feed of socialFeed">
     <ion-col col-2>
      <ion-avatar>
         <img src="assets/img/avatar.png">
      </ion-avatar>
     </ion-col>
     <ion-col col-10>
      <ion-row>
        <ion-col><h3>Jon Doe @jondoe</h3></ion-col>
      </ion-row>
      <ion-row>
        <p>{{feed.post}}</p>
      </ion-row>

      <ion-row text-center class="social-interaction-row">
        <ion-col><ion-icon name="undo" color="danger"></ion-icon>
      </ion-col>
        <ion-col><ion-icon name="repeat" color="danger"></ion-icon>
      </ion-col>
        <ion-col><ion-icon name="heart" color="danger"></ion-icon>
      </ion-col>
      </ion-row>

     </ion-col>
   </ion-row>
```

```
    </ion-grid>
  </ion-content>
```

4. Edit `./src/app/pages/home/home.scss` with the following code:

```scss
page-home {
    #info-row {
        ion-col {
            ion-avatar img{
                margin: 0 auto;
                border-radius:50%;
            }
        }
    }
    #contact-icons {
        ion-icon {
            font-size:40px;
        }
    }

    .social-row {
        ion-avatar {
            margin-top: 0.8rem;
        }
        p {
            font-size:1.6rem;
        }
        .social-interaction-row {
            font-size: 20px;
        }
    }
}
```

How it works...

In the Ionic grid, there are three types of components. The first is `ion-grid`, the second is `ion-row`, and the third is `ion-col`. `ion-grid` acts as a container for `ion-row` and `ion-col`. It takes the full width of the parent. `ion-row` is for creating rows in the grid. It takes the full width of `ion-grid`. `ion-col` is used to create a column inside `ion-row`. As I said in the chapter earlier, it is a 12-column grid. So, you can have a maximum of twelve columns in a row, without having a line break.

Now, let's understand how we structured our example.

Our `home.html` page is a kind of profile page for a dummy social network site. We have an avatar of the user, their location, name, various contact icons, and then the social feed.

This is how the avatar and location of the user look inside the app:

The following is the code for this:

```
<ion-row text-center id="info-row">
    <ion-col>
      <ion-avatar>
        <img src="assets/img/avatar.png">
      </ion-avatar>
      <h3>Based in</h3>
      <h4>Vienna, Austria</h4>
    </ion-col>
</ion-row>
```

It is very straightforward. We have a row with one column. That column has an avatar and the location of the user. Note that we have saved the avatar image in the `assets/img` folder.

Next is the contact icons. They look like the following in our app:

```
<ion-row text-center id="contact-icons">
    <ion-col><ion-icon name="call" color="danger"></ion-icon></ion-col><ion-col><ion-icon name="text" color="danger"></ion-icon></ion-col><ion-col><ion-icon name="globe" color="danger"></ion-icon></ion-col><ion-col><ion-icon name="more" color="danger"></ion-icon></ion-col></ion-row>
```

This is also straightforward. But the thing that we learn from this example is that if you have multiple `ion-col` inside `ion-row`, the Ionic grid automatically divides the width equally between each `ion-col`. This is because `ion-row` is a flex parent and `ion-col` are flex children.

Finally, we have the social feed, which looks like the following:

The code for the social feed is as follows:

```
<ion-row class="social-row" *ngFor="let feed of socialFeed">
    <ion-col col-2>
     <ion-avatar>
        <img src="assets/img/avatar.png">
     </ion-avatar>
    </ion-col>
    <ion-col col-10>
     <ion-row>
        <ion-col><h3>Jon Doe @jondoe</h3></ion-col>
     </ion-row>
     <ion-row>
        <p>{{feed.post}}</p>
     </ion-row>

     <ion-row text-center class="social-interaction-row">
        <ion-col><ion-icon name="undo" color="danger"></ion-icon></ion-col>
        <ion-col><ion-icon name="repeat" color="danger"></ion-icon>
     </ion-col>
        <ion-col><ion-icon name="heart" color="danger"></ion-icon>
     </ion-col>
     </ion-row>
```

```
      </ion-col>
    </ion-row>
```

There are three things to learn from this example:

- You can force the width of `col` using the `col-width*` attribute. We replace the `width*` with a value from 1-12 and that column will take only `width*/12` of the space in the `ion-row`.
- We can nest `ion-row` inside `ion-col`, and so on. You will notice that we have an `ion-col` that takes 10/12 of the width of `ion-row`. Inside that `ion-column`, we have a child `ion-row` element, which shows the user's post, and one more `ion-row` to show three icons for social sharing and interaction.
- Each child `ion-row` will take the full width of its `ion-col` parent.

The following image shows this structure with an explanation:

See also

- For more information about the Ionic grid, take a look at the Ionic documentation at: `https://ionicframework.com/docs/api/components/grid/Grid/`.
- If you want to see how Flexbox works in general, take a look at this very good introduction to it at: `https://css-tricks.com/snippets/css/a-guide-to-flexbox/`.

3
Extending Ionic with Angular Building Blocks

In this chapter, we will cover the following tasks related to creating custom components, directives, and filters with Angular:

- Creating a custom pizza ordering component
- Creating a custom username input directive
- Creating a custom pipe
- Creating a shared service to provide data to multiple pages
- Reusing an existing page as an HTML element

Introduction

Most of Ionic's out-of-the-box features are actually prebuilt components. In this section, you will learn how to create your own custom component using the HTML template, which contains Ionic components as well.

Components actually define Angular. A component is no more than just a class with self-describing features. For example, `<ul>` is a component that you are already familiar with. Previously, you used various Ionic components, such as `<ion-list>` and `<ion-item>`. A component is a decorator (that is, `@Component`) to add metadata to a class to describe the following:

- **selector**: This is the name that is to be used in the DOM (for example, `<my-component>`)
- **template or templateUrl**: This refers to the way the component is rendered

- **directives**: This refers to a list of directive dependencies you plan to use inside the component
- **providers**: This is a list of providers (that is, services) you plan to use inside the component

Of course, there are many other options, but the preceding four options are the most common ones.

Creating a custom pizza ordering component

In this section, you will build an app to demonstrate a custom component with its private variables and template. Observe the following screenshot of a pizza ordering component:

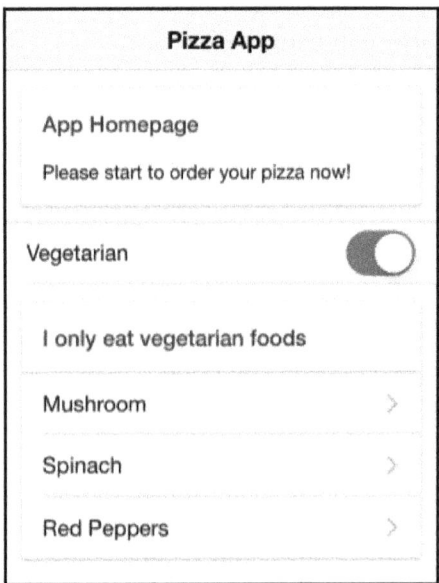

The user will not notice which area is part of the page, as opposed to being a self-contained component. Your custom component here is the only area where the list is *listening* to the **Vegetarian** check box:

Getting ready

This app example could work either in a browser or on a physical device.

How to do it...

Perform the following instructions:

1. Create a new MyComponent app using the blank template, as shown, and go into the MyComponent folder:

```
$ ionic start MyComponent blank
$ cd MyComponent
```

2. Open the ./src/pages/home/home.html file and replace the content with the following code:

```
<ion-header>
  <ion-navbar>
    <ion-title>
      Pizza App
    </ion-title>
  </ion-navbar>
</ion-header>
```

```
<ion-content padding>
  <ion-card>
    <ion-card-header>
      App Homepage
    </ion-card-header>
    <ion-card-content>
      Please start to order your pizza now!
    </ion-card-content>
  </ion-card>
  <my-component></my-component>
</ion-content>
```

This is your root page containing `<my-component>`, which will be defined later.

3. Open `./app/pages/home/home.ts` for editing globally with the following code:

```
import { Component } from '@angular/core';
import { NavController } from 'ionic-angular';

@Component({
  selector: 'page-home',
  templateUrl: 'home.html'
})
export class HomePage {

  constructor(public navCtrl: NavController) {

  }

}
```

You simply have to declare `MyComponent` as a dependency. A component is basically just a directive with a template, (assuming you are familiar with the directive concept of Angular 1).

4. Now, let's create the component by first creating a directive, as illustrated in the following code:

```
$ mkdir ./src/components
```

5. Create a `foo.ts` file in the `components` directory that you just created, as shown in the following code:

```
import { Component } from '@angular/core';

@Component({
  selector: 'my-component',
  templateUrl: 'foo.html'
})
export class MyComponent {
  public data: any = {myToggle: true};

  constructor() {}
  isClicked(val) {
    console.log('Vegetarian: ' + val);
  }

}
```

6. Create `foo.html` in the `./src/components` folder, as follows:

```
<ion-list>
  <ion-item>
    <ion-label>Vegetarian</ion-label>
    <ion-toggle (click)="isClicked(data.myToggle)"
[(ngModel)]="data.myToggle"></ion-toggle>
  </ion-item>
  <ion-card *ngIf="data.myToggle">
    <ion-card-header>
      I only eat vegetarian foods
    </ion-card-header>
    <ion-list>
      <button ion-item>
        Mushroom
      </button>
      <button ion-item>
        Spinach
      </button>
      <button ion-item>
        Red Peppers
      </button>
    </ion-list>

  </ion-card>

  <ion-card *ngIf="!data.myToggle">
    <ion-card-header>
```

```
      I love meat
    </ion-card-header>
    <ion-list>
      <button ion-item>
        Beef
      </button>
      <button ion-item>
        Chicken
      </button>
      <button ion-item>
        Sausage
      </button>

    </ion-list>
  </ion-card>

</ion-list>
```

7. Modify `./src/app/app.module.ts`, as illustrated, so that you can declare `MyComponent`. Observe the following code:

```
import { BrowserModule } from '@angular/platform-browser';
import { ErrorHandler, NgModule } from '@angular/core';
import { IonicApp, IonicErrorHandler, IonicModule } from 'ionic-angular';
import { SplashScreen } from '@ionic-native/splash-screen';
import { StatusBar } from '@ionic-native/status-bar';

import { MyApp } from './app.component';
import { HomePage } from '../pages/home/home';
import { MyComponent } from '../components/foo/foo';

@NgModule({
  declarations: [
    MyApp,
    HomePage,
    MyComponent
  ],
  imports: [
    BrowserModule,
    IonicModule.forRoot(MyApp)
  ],
  bootstrap: [IonicApp],
  entryComponents: [
    MyApp,
    HomePage,
    MyComponent
```

```
      ],
      providers: [
        StatusBar,
        SplashScreen,
        {provide: ErrorHandler, useClass: IonicErrorHandler}
      ]
    })
    export class AppModule {}
```

8. Go to your Terminal and run the app using the following command:

```
$ ionic serve
```

How it works...

You may wonder why it's necessary to create a component just to toggle a list of pizza topping options. The answer is that this is just a demonstration of how you can compartmentalize your app using a component. The key things that you have done are as follows:

- You created a custom component, called <my-component>, which can be used anywhere, including outside your app.
- The data within your component is completely private. This means that nobody else can access it without calling a method within your component's class.
- You can add or change behaviors within your component without impacting on other areas outside the component.

To create a component, you need to ensure that you import the @Component decorator, as shown, from Angular itself (and not from Ionic):

```
import { Component } from '@angular/core';

@Component({
  selector: 'my-component',
  templateUrl: 'foo.html'
})
```

In your `component` template, everything is local to what is inside the `component` class. So, you can bind the click event using `click`, as shown in the following code:

```
<ion-item>
  <ion-label>Vegetarian</ion-label>
  <ion-toggle (click)="isClicked(data.myToggle)"
    [(ngModel)]="data.myToggle"></ion-toggle>
</ion-item>
```

Just as in Angular 1, you need to use `[(ngModel)]` to declare that you want `data.myToggle` to be your model. The `[(..)]` part is to tell Angular 2 that this is a two-way binding.

There are two lists of pizza toppings. The first one is as follows:

```
<ion-card *ngIf="data.myToggle">
  <ion-card-header>
    I only eat vegetarian foods
  </ion-card-header>

  <ion-list>
    <button ion-item>
      Mushroom
    </button>
    <button ion-item>
      Spinach
    </button>
    <button ion-item>
      Red Peppers
    </button>
  </ion-list>
</ion-card>
```

The second list of pizza toppings is as shown:

```
<ion-card *ngIf="!data.myToggle">
  <ion-card-header>
    I love meat
  </ion-card-header>

  <ion-list>
    <button ion-item>
      Beef
    </button>
    <button ion-item>
      Chicken
    </button>
```

```
      <button ion-item>
        Sausage
      </button>
    </ion-list>
  </ion-card>
```

To toggle the visibility of each list based on the `data.myToggle` model, you can use `*ngIf`, which is very similar to `ng-if` from Angular 1.

See also

To see more information about components in the Angular documentation, you can visit `https://angular.io/docs/ts/latest/guide/architecture.html#!#component`.

Creating a custom username input directive

Since you have gone through the process of creating a component in the preceding section, you may wonder what the difference is between a component and a directive. If you have some experience with Angular 1, you may notice that it had no definition of a component. Starting in Angular 2, there are the following three kinds of directive:

Kind	Description
Components	They have a template and a class associated with the component (that is, `ion-input`)
Structural directives	They change the DOM structure within the scope of where it is (that is, `*ngIf` or `*ngFor`)
Attribute directives	They change the appearance of the current DOM by intercepting its display or events

You may have a mix of both structural and attribute characteristics in the same directive. In this section, you will learn how to create an attribute directive that can prevent certain characters from being input in the **Username**, as well as showing another DOM node (where it says **You are typing username**) by toggling its visibility. Observe the following screenshot of the app:

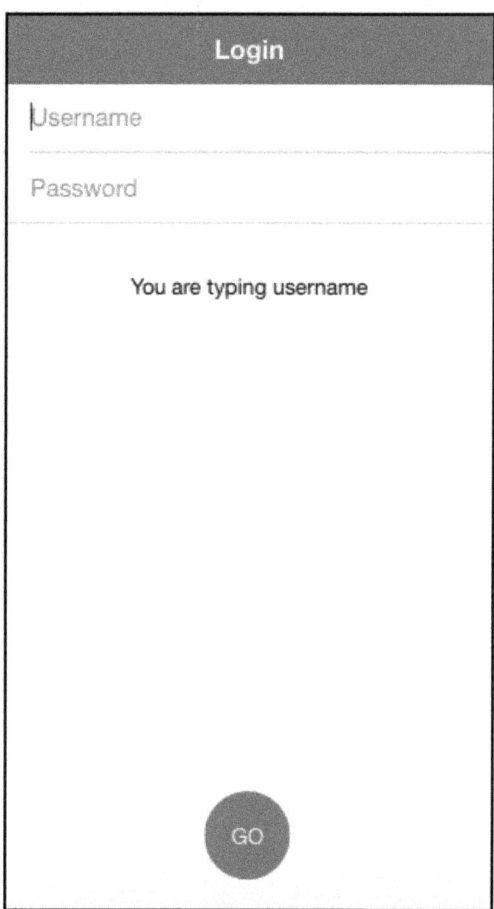

The **GO** button is there just for cosmetic purposes, and you will not need to write any code for it.

Getting ready

This app example could work either in a browser or on a physical device.

How to do it...

Observe the following instructions:

1. Create a new `MyIonicInputDirective` app using the `blank` template, as shown, and go into the `MyIonicInputDirective` folder:

```
$ ionic start MyIonicInputDirective blank
$ cd MyIonicInputDirective
```

2. Open the `./src/app/pages/home/home.html` file and replace the content with the following code:

```
<ion-header>
  <ion-navbar color="danger">
    <ion-title>
      Login
    </ion-title>
  </ion-navbar>
</ion-header>

<ion-content padding>
  <ion-list>
    <ion-item>
      <ion-input type="text" placeholder="Username"
[(ngModel)]="username" [myIonicInput]="myStyles"></ion-input>
    </ion-item>
    <ion-item>
      <ion-input type="password" placeholder="Password"></ion-input>
    </ion-item>
  </ion-list>
  <p *ngIf="myStyles.showUsername" class="hint">
    You are typing username
  </p>
  <ion-fab bottom center>
    <button ion-fab>GO</button>
  </ion-fab>
</ion-content>
```

As mentioned earlier, the **GO** button is just an example of the new floating button feature from Ionic. All you need to do is include `bottom` and `center` in order to position it. These are actually good examples of attribute directives.

3. Open `home.ts`, in the same folder as in the preceding step, to edit and insert the following code:

```
import { Component } from '@angular/core';
import { NavController } from 'ionic-angular';

@Component({
  selector: 'page-home',
  templateUrl: 'home.html'
})
export class HomePage {
  private myStyles = { showUsername: false };
  constructor(public navCtrl: NavController) {

  }
}
```

4. Create the `./src/directives` folder, as shown in the following command:

$ mkdir ./src/directives

5. Create the `my-ionic-input.ts` file in the `directives` folder and copy in the following code:

```
import { Directive, Input, ElementRef, OnInit } from
'@angular/core';
@Directive({
  selector: '[myIonicInput]', // Attribute selector
  host: {
    '(mouseenter)': 'onMouseEnter()',
    '(mouseleave)': 'onMouseLeave()'
    // '(keypress)': 'onKeyPress'
  }
})
export class MyIonicInputDirective {
  @Input('myIonicInput') myStyles: any;
  constructor(private el: ElementRef) {
    el.nativeElement.onkeypress = function(e) {
      console.log(e);
      if ('~!@#$%^&*()-='.includes(String.fromCharCode(e.keyCode)))
{
        e.preventDefault();
        return;
```

```
          }
        }
      }

    ngOnInit() {
      console.log(this.myStyles);
    }

    onMouseEnter() {
      this.myStyles.showUsername = true;
    }
    onMouseLeave(e) {
      this.myStyles.showUsername = false;
    }

    // onKeyPress will not work with ion-input directly
    // because the actual input element is a child of ion-input
    // onKeyPress() {
    // console.log("onKeyPress");
    // }
  }
```

6. Open and edit `./src/app/app.module.ts` to declare your new directive, as follows:

```
import { BrowserModule } from '@angular/platform-browser';
import { ErrorHandler, NgModule } from '@angular/core';
import { IonicApp, IonicErrorHandler, IonicModule } from 'ionic-
angular';
import { SplashScreen } from '@ionic-native/splash-screen';
import { StatusBar } from '@ionic-native/status-bar';

import { MyApp } from './app.component';
import { HomePage } from '../pages/home/home';
import { MyIonicInputDirective } from '../directives/my-ionic-
input';

@NgModule({
  declarations: [
    MyApp,
    HomePage,
    MyIonicInputDirective
  ],
  imports: [
    BrowserModule,
    IonicModule.forRoot(MyApp)
  ],
```

```
        bootstrap: [IonicApp],
        entryComponents: [
          MyApp,
          HomePage
        ],
        providers: [
          StatusBar,
          SplashScreen,
          {provide: ErrorHandler, useClass: IonicErrorHandler}
        ]
    })
    export class AppModule {}
```

7. Go to your Terminal and run the app, as shown:

```
$ ionic serve
```

How it works...

The homepage template (home.html) is very typical with ion-list and ion-item, which contain your input elements. However, there are two important things to take note of. Firstly, there is an attribute, called myIonicInput, in the ion-input component. Observe the following code:

```
<ion-item >
  <ion-input type="text" placeholder="Username"
    [(ngModel)]="username" [myIonicInput]="myStyles"></ion-input>
</ion-item>
```

Secondly, the myStyles object is now used to toggle the visibility of the <p> element, as shown:

```
<p *ngIf="myStyles.showUsername" class="hint">
  You are typing username
</p>
```

This myStyles object is actually a private variable in your HomePage class in the home.ts file, as follows:

```
export class HomePage {
  private myStyles: Object = {showUsername: false};
}
```

With TypeScript, you could assign a type (that is, an object) to a variable with a default value. You may also note that `MyIonicInputDirective` should be declared for a dependency to be injected into the template directives.

To create a basic directive, you must import at least `Directive` and `ElementRef` in order to manipulate the DOM. However, since this `Directive` has input (that is, `myStyles`), you should also import `Input` in your `my-ionic-input.ts`, as illustrated in the following code:

```
import {Directive, ElementRef, Input} from '@angular/core';
```

You have `selector` and `host` metadata in your directive, as shown:

```
@Directive({
  selector: '[myIonicInput]',
  host: {
    '(mouseenter)': 'onMouseEnter()',
    '(mouseleave)': 'onMouseLeave()'
    // '(keypress)': 'onKeyPress'
  }
})
```

The `myIonicInput` selector will be queried from the DOM and will trigger *actions* on that DOM node. For event detection on the DOM, you have to map the event name to the `class` method. For example, the `mouseenter` event will trigger a call to the `onMouseEnter()` method in the directive's class, which is `MyIonicInputDirective`.

Now, let's look more closely at the directive's class:

```
export class MyIonicInputDirective {
  @Input('myIonicInput') myStyles: any;
  constructor(private el: ElementRef) {
    el.nativeElement.onkeypress = function(e) {
      console.log(e);
      if ('~!@#$%^&*()-
      ='.includes(String.fromCharCode(e.keyCode))) {
        e.preventDefault();
        return;
      }
    }
  }
  onMouseEnter() {
    this.myStyles.showUsername = true;
  }
  onMouseLeave(e) {
    this.myStyles.showUsername = false;
```

```
    }

    // onKeyPress will not work with ion-input directly because the
      actual input element is a child of ion-input
    // onKeyPress() {
    //    console.log("onKeyPress");
    // }
  }
```

The @Input decorator is used to declare that you will bring in a variable from the template. This is the reason why you must have the square brackets [myIonicInput]="myStyles". Otherwise, myStyles would just be a string instead of an expression referring to the myStyles object from the HomePage class.

Another interesting thing to note here is the code inside constructor. ElementRef is pointing to the same DOM at which you placed your attribute directive. You want to modify the behavior of the keyboard using el.nativeElement.onkeypress so that special characters won't be allowed. If the user enters a special character, it will trigger e.preventDefault() and nothing will happen. The keyboard event is basically discarded. You may wonder why we cannot just use the keypress event and map it to onKeyPress, which was intentionally commented out. The reason is that you are placing the myIonicInput directive on top of ion-input. But the actual <input> DOM is just a child of ion-input. Therefore, if you listen to the keypress event on the parent ion-input, you won't be able to bind it.

The onMouseEnter and onMouseLeave methods are self-explanatory because they just toggle the myStyles.showUsername variable. Again, this myStyles object is just a reference back to the myStyles of HomePage. So, if you change the variable here, it will change at the home page's level as well.

See also

- For more information about Angular 2 directives, you can refer to the official documentation at
  https://angular.io/docs/ts/latest/guide/attribute-directives.html
- Since this is the first section in which TypeScript appears, it might be helpful to go through the handbook for more details:
  http://www.typescriptlang.org/docs/tutorial.html

Creating a custom pipe

Pipes are also a feature of Angular and are not specific to Ionic. If you are familiar with Angular 1, a *pipe* is exactly the same thing as a *filter*. The main reason you might want to use pipes is to display data in a different format in the view. You don't want to change the actual value in the component. This makes things very convenient because you don't have to decide on the specific format within the code while leaving flexibility in the view layer. Here is a list of some useful built-in pipes (from `https://angular.io/docs/ts/latest/api/#!?apiFilter=pipe`):

- `AsyncPipe`
- `DatePipe`
- `NumberPipe`
- `SlicePipe`
- `DecimalPipe`
- `JsonPipe`
- `PercentPipe`
- `UpperCasePipe`
- `LowerCasePipe`
- `CurrencyPipe`
- `ReplacePipe`

In this section, you will learn how to create a custom pipe using the `@Pipe` decorator. The following is a screenshot of the app:

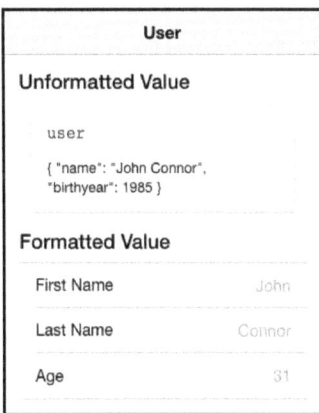

While the app interface is very simple, the purpose of this example is to show you how to create a pipe to extract object data.

Getting ready

There is no need to test on a physical device because the Angular pipe will work just fine in the web browser.

How to do it...

Observe the following instructions:

1. Create a new `CustomPipe` app using the `blank` template, as shown, and go to the `CustomPipe` folder:

```
$ ionic start CustomPipe blank
$ cd CustomPipe
```

2. Open the `./src/pages/home/home.html` file and modify the content with the following code:

```
<ion-header>
  <ion-navbar>
    <ion-title>
      User
    </ion-title>
  </ion-navbar>
</ion-header>
<ion-content padding>
  <h4>Unformatted Value</h4>
  <ion-card>
    <ion-card-header>
      <code>user</code>
    </ion-card-header>
    <ion-card-content>
      {{ user | json }}
    </ion-card-content>
  </ion-card>
  <h4>Formatted Value</h4>
  <ion-list>
    <ion-item>
      <ion-label fixed>First Name</ion-label>
      <ion-note item-right>{{ user | userExtract : "firstname"
```

```
}}</ion-note>
    </ion-item>
    <ion-item>
      <ion-label fixed>Last Name</ion-label>
      <ion-note item-right>{{ user | userExtract : "lastname"
}}</ion-note>
    </ion-item>
    <ion-item>
      <ion-label fixed>Age</ion-label>
      <ion-note item-right>{{ user | userExtract : "age" }}
      </ion-note>
    </ion-item>
  </ion-list>
</ion-content>
```

You can quickly see that the template uses the `userExtract` pipe to render the correct information.

3. Then, replace the content of `./src/pages/home/home.ts` with the following code:

```
import { Component } from '@angular/core';
import { NavController } from 'ionic-angular';

@Component({
  selector: 'page-home',
  templateUrl: 'home.html'
})
export class HomePage {

  private user: any;
  constructor(public navCtrl: NavController) {
    this.user = {
      name: 'John Connor',
      birthyear: 1985
    };

    console.log(this.user);
  }

}
```

You don't have the `custom-pipe.ts` file yet, so you need to create it next.

4. Create the `./src/utils` folder by using the following command:

    ```
    $ mkdir ./utils/utils
    ```

    You can call this folder anything. However, since pipes are sometimes considered *utility* functions, let's call it `utils`.

5. Create the `custom-pipe.ts` file in the `utils` folder and copy the following code:

    ```
    import { Pipe, PipeTransform } from '@angular/core';

    @Pipe({ name: 'userExtract' })
    export class UserExtractPipe implements PipeTransform {
        transform(value: any, arg): any {
            let newVal: any;
            if (arg == "firstname") {
                newVal = value.name ? value.name.split(' ')[0] : '';
            } else if (arg == "lastname") {
                newVal = value.name ? value.name.split(' ').splice(-
                    1) : '';
            } else if (arg == "age") {
                var currentTime = new Date();
                newVal = value.birthyear ? currentTime.getFullYear()
                    - value.birthyear : 0;
            }
            return newVal;
        }
    }
    ```

6. Add `UserExtractPipe` to `./src/app/app.module.ts` by replacing it with the following code:

    ```
    import { BrowserModule } from '@angular/platform-browser';
    import { ErrorHandler, NgModule } from '@angular/core';
    import { IonicApp, IonicErrorHandler, IonicModule } from 'ionic-
    angular';
    import { SplashScreen } from '@ionic-native/splash-screen';
    import { StatusBar } from '@ionic-native/status-bar';

    import { MyApp } from './app.component';
    import { HomePage } from '../pages/home/home';
    import { UserExtractPipe } from '../utils/custom-pipe';

    @NgModule({
      declarations: [
        MyApp,
    ```

```
        HomePage,
        UserExtractPipe
      ],
      imports: [
        BrowserModule,
        IonicModule.forRoot(MyApp)
      ],
      bootstrap: [IonicApp],
      entryComponents: [
        MyApp,
        HomePage
      ],
      providers: [
        StatusBar,
        SplashScreen,
        {provide: ErrorHandler, useClass: IonicErrorHandler}
      ]
    })
    export class AppModule {}
```

7. Go to your Terminal and run the app, as follows:

```
$ ionic serve
```

How it works...

You can use an Angular pipe in the view to simply convert or transform any value to a desired value. There are no limitations to how you structure the pipe. Angular automatically detects the | sign in the template and turns the value in front of it to an input. To create a pipe, you must import the decorator and provide a name (see custom-pipe.ts), as shown:

```
import { Pipe, PipeTransform } from '@angular/core';

@Pipe({name: 'userExtract'})
```

The input from the template is the following value parameter:

```
transform(value: any, arg) : any {
```

The value returned by the transform method will be the output to the view, as shown in the following code:

```
return newVal;
```

In this example, you are taking a parameter for the pipe to process, as illustrated in the following code:

```
if (arg == "firstname") {
  newVal = value.name ? value.name.split(' ')[0] : '';

} else if (arg == "lastname") {
  newVal = value.name ? value.name.split(' ').splice(-1) : '';
} else if (arg == "age") {
  var currentTime = new Date();
  newVal = value.birthyear ? currentTime.getFullYear() -
   value.birthyear : 0;
}
```

For example, this is what you had in the `home.html` template:

```
<ion-item>
  <ion-label fixed>First Name</ion-label>
  <ion-note item-right>{{ user | userExtract : "firstname"
   }}</ion-note>
</ion-item>
```

Each parameter is placed after a colon (`:`). Then, within your `@Pipe` class, you can refer to it using `arg`. The rest of the code is very simple, as already shown in the preceding section. Observe the following:

- If it's `firstname`, take the first word
- If it's `lastname`, take the last word
- If it's `age`, subtract the current year from the birth year

Of course, you could have more complicated scenarios with pipes. However, the overall recommendation is to keep things simple in the view to ensure rendering performance. If you need to do heavy processing, it's best to handle it as a separate variable.

See also

To understand more about Angular pipes, you can check out the official documentation at `https://angular.io/docs/ts/latest/guide/pipes.html`

Creating a shared service to provide data to multiple pages

When you develop an app that involves a lot of pages and communication to the backend, you will need to have a way to communicate across pages and components. For example, you may have a service to request user data from the backend and store it in a common local service. Then, you will need to provide a way for the user to update their user data and see the update in real time. When the user navigates to different pages, the same information will be pulled and rendered too, without making multiple trips to the backend. This is a very common scenario that requires the use of the @Injectable decorator in Angular.

Observe the following screenshot of the app you will build:

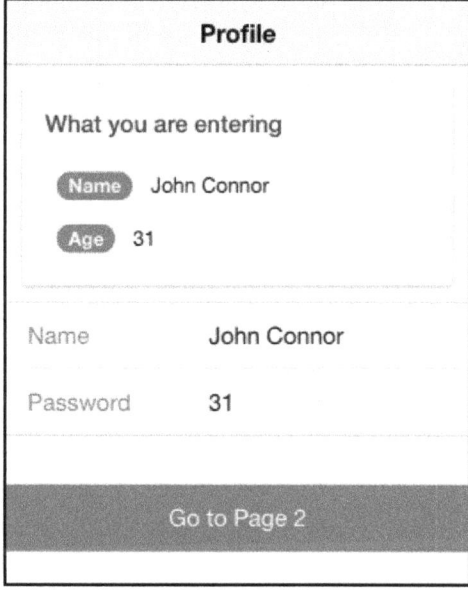

The user can fill out the form and see updates on it in real time. Then, they can move to the next page (**Go to Page 2**) and see the following screenshot:

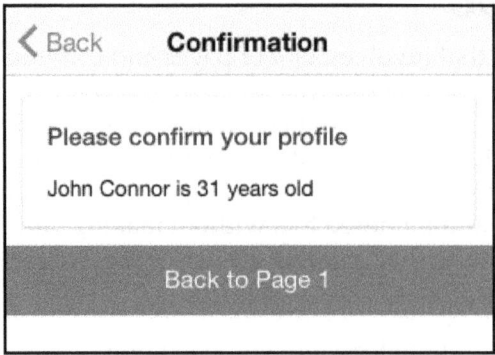

This page uses the same service as the preceding page and references the same date with the name and age. You will learn the following topics in this section:

- Creating a service using @Injectable
- Sharing a service across multiple pages
- Detecting changes using getters and setters inside the service

Getting ready

This app example could work either in a browser or on a physical device.

How to do it...

Observe the following instructions:

1. Create a new SharedService app using the blank template as shown and go to the SharedService folder:

```
$ ionic start SharedService blank
$ cd SharedService
```

2. You will need to make several changes in the directory because you have two pages and a common service for both. Let's start by modifying the `./src/app/app.component.ts` file so that the `rootPage` is pointing to `Page1`:

```
import { Component } from '@angular/core';
import { Platform } from 'ionic-angular';
import { StatusBar } from '@ionic-native/status-bar';
import { SplashScreen } from '@ionic-native/splash-screen';

import { Page1 } from '../pages/page1/page1';

@Component({
  templateUrl: 'app.html'
})
export class MyApp {
  rootPage:any = Page1;

  constructor(platform: Platform, statusBar: StatusBar,
splashScreen: SplashScreen) {
    platform.ready().then(() => {
      // Okay, so the platform is ready and our plugins are
available.
      // Here you can do any higher level native things you might
need.
      statusBar.styleDefault();
      splashScreen.hide();
    });
  }
}
```

3. Create `./src/pages/page1`, as shown in the following code:

$ mkdir ./src/pages/page1

4. Create your first template, `page1.html`, in the `page1` folder with the following code:

```
<ion-header>
    <ion-navbar>
        <ion-title>
            Profile
        </ion-title>
    </ion-navbar>
</ion-header>

<ion-content>
    <ion-card>
```

```
        <ion-card-header>
            What you are entering
        </ion-card-header>
        <ion-card-content>
            <ion-badge item-right>Name</ion-badge> {{ user.name }}
            <br><br>
            <ion-badge item-right>Age</ion-badge> {{ user.age }}
        </ion-card-content>
    </ion-card>
    <ion-list>
        <ion-item>
            <ion-label fixed>Name</ion-label>
            <ion-input type="text" [(ngModel)]="user.name">
        </ion-input>
        </ion-item>
        <ion-item>
            <ion-label fixed>Password</ion-label>
            <ion-input type="number" [(ngModel)]="user.age">
        </ion-input>
        </ion-item>
    </ion-list>
    <button ion-button full block (click)="goToPage2()">Go to Page
2</button>
</ion-content>
```

5. Create page1.ts in the page1 folder, as follows:

```
import { Component } from '@angular/core';
import { NavController } from 'ionic-angular';
import { UserService } from '../../services/user';
import { Page2 } from '../page2/page2';
@Component({
    selector: 'page-one',
    templateUrl: 'page1.html'
})
export class Page1 {
    private user: any;
    private nav: any;
    constructor(public navCtrl: NavController, user:
        UserService, nav: NavController) {
        console.log(user.name);
        this.user = user;
        this.nav = nav;
    }
    goToPage2() {
        this.nav.push(Page2);
    }
}
```

 The file extension is `.ts`, and not `.js`, because you are going to use some TypeScript-specific features, such as getters and setters.

6. Similarly, create the `page2` folder using the following command:

```
$ mkdir ./src/pages/page1
```

7. Add the `page2.html` template in the `page2` folder as well, as follows:

```
<ion-header>
  <ion-navbar>
    <ion-title>
      Confirmation
    </ion-title>
  </ion-navbar>
</ion-header>

<ion-content class="home">
  <ion-card>
    <ion-card-header>
      Please confirm your profile
    </ion-card-header>
    <ion-card-content>
      {{ user.name }} is {{ user.age }} years old
    </ion-card-content>
  </ion-card>
  <button ion-button full block (click)="goToPage1()">Back to Page
1</button>
</ion-content>
```

This is your second page with the same `name` and `age` information.

8. Create `page2.ts` in the `page2` folder with the following code:

```
import { Component } from '@angular/core';
import { NavController } from 'ionic-angular';
import { UserService } from '../../services/user';
import { Page1 } from '../page1/page1';
@Component({
  selector: 'page-two',
  templateUrl: 'page2.html'
})
export class Page2 {
  private user: any;
  private nav: any;
```

```
        constructor(public navCtrl: NavController, user:
          UserService, nav: NavController) {
          console.log(user.name);
          this.user = user;
          this.nav = nav;
        }
        goToPage1() {
          this.nav.push(Page1);
        }
      }
```

9. Create the `services` folder with the following command:

$ mkdir ./src/services

10. Put `UserService` in the `user.ts` file, in the `services` folder, as shown:

```
      import { Injectable } from '@angular/core';
      @Injectable()
      export class UserService {
          private _name: string;
          private _age: number;
          constructor() {
              this._name = 'John Connor';
              this._age = 31;
          }
          get name() {
              return this._name;
          }
          set name(newVal) {
              console.log('Set name = ' + newVal);
              this._name = newVal;
          }
          get age() {
              return this._age;
          }
          set age(newVal) {
              console.log('Set age = ' + newVal);
              this._age = newVal;
          }
      }
```

11. Open and edit `./src/app/app.module.ts` so that you can inject `UserService` as a global provider and declare `Page1` and `Page2`:

```
import { BrowserModule } from '@angular/platform-browser';
import { ErrorHandler, NgModule } from '@angular/core';
import { IonicApp, IonicErrorHandler, IonicModule } from 'ionic-
angular';
import { SplashScreen } from '@ionic-native/splash-screen';
import { StatusBar } from '@ionic-native/status-bar';

import { MyApp } from './app.component';
;
import { Page1 } from '../pages/page1/page1';
import { Page2 } from '../pages/page2/page2';
import { UserService } from '../services/user';

@NgModule({
  declarations: [
    MyApp,
    Page1,
    Page2
  ],
  imports: [
    BrowserModule,
    IonicModule.forRoot(MyApp)
  ],
  bootstrap: [IonicApp],
  entryComponents: [
    MyApp,
    Page1,
    Page2
  ],
  providers: [
    StatusBar,
    SplashScreen,
    UserService,
    {provide: ErrorHandler, useClass: IonicErrorHandler}
  ]
})
export class AppModule {}
```

12. Verify that your folder structure looks like the following screenshot:

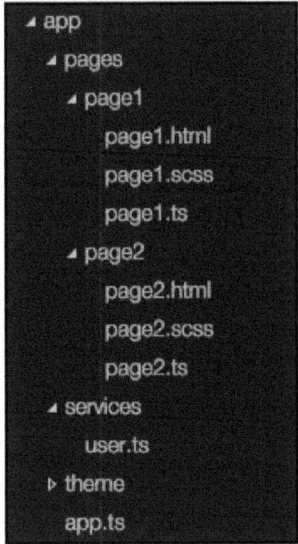

13. Go to your Terminal and run the app with the following command:

```
$ ionic serve
```

You can move from page 1 to page 2 and then back, and the data will persist across the pages.

How it works...

In general, if you want to use a common service across multiple pages, you must inject it at the highest level. In this example, you put UserService as a dependency at the start of app.module.ts, as follows:

```
providers: [UserService]
```

After that, other pages within the app can start using this common service without having to reinject it. The main reason is that, whenever you inject a service or class, it will instantiate a new object, which ends up erasing all of the existing data in the memory. If you want the data to persist across the pages, it should be in the parent app to avoid reinjection.

To use the `UserService` on each page, you just need to import it, as illustrated in the following code:

```
import { UserService } from '../../services/user';
```

The way to bring in the service is to put the referencing in the constructor (`page1.ts`), as shown:

```
constructor(user: UserService, nav: NavController) {
  console.log(user.name);
  this.user = user;
  this.nav = nav;
}
```

This will pass down `UserService` reference to a local private variable of the page (in this case, `this.user`).

From a template standpoint, there is no difference between using `{{ user.name }}` and `{{ user.age }}` to inject data.

Now, let's take a look at `UserService`:

```
import {Injectable} from '@angular/core';

@Injectable()
export class UserService {
  private _name: string;
  private _age: number;
  constructor() {
    this._name = 'John Connor';
    this._age = 31;
  }
  get name() {
    return this._name;
  }
  set name(newVal) {
    console.log('Set name = ' + newVal);
    this._name = newVal;
  }
  get age() {
    return this._age;
  }
  set age(newVal) {
    console.log('Set age = ' + newVal);
    this._age = newVal;
  }
}
```

Actually, there are several things going on here. Firstly, you need to import `Injectable` from
`@angular/core`.

 Don't forget the parentheses in `@Injectable()`.

Secondly, if you want to use getters and setters, you need to make separate variables, called `_name` and `_age`, to store the data. Then, you can use the get/set method to do additional processing when other pages access or set the variables in this common class. If you change the `name` or `age` from `Page 1`, you can see the following logs in the console:

```
Set name = John Conno
Set age = 3

>
```

This feature is very beneficial since you can use this as a replacement for `watch` or `observable`. If you recall from Angular 1, you have to use `$scope.$watch` for a similar approach.

See also

- For more information about Angular 2 services, visit the official documentation at `https://angular.io/docs/ts/latest/tutorial/toh-pt4.html`
- You can get great instructions on many techniques for component communication at `https://angular.io/docs/ts/latest/cookbook/component-communication.htm l`

Reusing an existing page as an HTML element

So far, we have used Ionic pages using Ionic's navigation system. In this recipe, we're going to extend the existing page so that we can use it as an HTML element/component in the application. The following is the first page of the application:

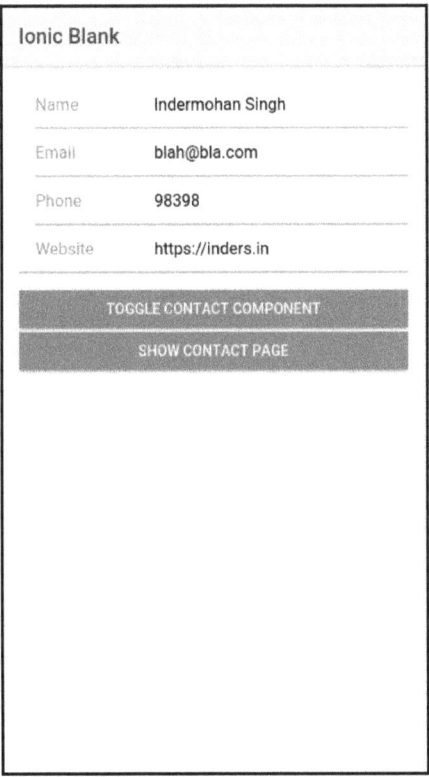

When you click on **SHOW CONTACT PAGE**, it shows the contact page with the information from the previous page as shown in the following screenshot:

We will reutilize this contact page as an HTML element in the application.

Getting ready

In this recipe, we are using web functionalities, so we only need a web browser to run the application.

How to do it...

Follow these instructions:

1. Create a new app named PageComponent using the blank template, as shown in the following code block and go to the PageComponent folder:

```
$ ionic start PageComponent blank
$ cd PageComponent
```

2. Open the ./src/app/pages/home/home.html file and replace the content with the following code:

```html
<ion-header>
  <ion-navbar>
    <ion-title>
      Ionic Blank
    </ion-title>
  </ion-navbar>
</ion-header>

<ion-content padding>
  <ion-list>
      <ion-item>
        <ion-label fixed>Name</ion-label>
        <ion-input type="text" value="" [(ngModel)]="user.name">
      </ion-input>
      </ion-item>
      <ion-item>
        <ion-label fixed>Email</ion-label>
        <ion-input type="text" [(ngModel)]="user.email">
      </ion-input>
      </ion-item>

      <ion-item>
        <ion-label fixed>Phone</ion-label>
        <ion-input type="text" [(ngModel)]="user.phone">
      </ion-input>
      </ion-item>

      <ion-item>
        <ion-label fixed>Website</ion-label>
        <ion-input type="text" [(ngModel)]="user.website">
      </ion-input>
      </ion-item>
  </ion-list>
```

```
        <button full ion-button (click)="toggleContact()">
        TOGGLE CONTACT COMPONENT</button>
        <button full ion-button (click)="openContact()">SHOW CONTACT
    PAGE</button>
        <page-contact [userInput]="user" *ngIf="showContact">
        </page-contact>

    </ion-content>
```

3. Open the `./src/pages/home/home.ts` file and replace the content with the following:

```
import { Component } from '@angular/core';
import { NavController } from 'ionic-angular';
import { ContactPage } from "../contact/contact";
@Component({
 selector: 'page-home',
 templateUrl: 'home.html'
})
export class HomePage {
 user:any = {};
 showContact:Boolean = false;
 constructor(public navCtrl: NavController) {}

 openContact() {
   this.navCtrl.push(ContactPage, { user: this.user });
 }
 toggleContact() {
   this.showContact = !this.showContact;
 }
}
```

4. Now create a folder, `./src/pages/contact`, and in the folder, create `contact.html` and add the following content:

```
<ion-header *ngIf="!userInput">
    <ion-navbar>
        <ion-title>
            Contact Page
        </ion-title>
    </ion-navbar>
</ion-header>

<ion-content>
    <ion-card>
        <ion-card-header>
            User Contact
```

```
        </ion-card-header>
        <ion-card-content>
            <ion-grid>
                <ion-row>
                    <ion-col>Name</ion-col>
                    <ion-col>{{user.name}}</ion-col>
                </ion-row>

                <ion-row>
                    <ion-col>Email</ion-col>
                    <ion-col>{{user.email}}</ion-col>
                </ion-row>

                <ion-row>
                    <ion-col>Phone</ion-col>
                    <ion-col>{{user.phone}}</ion-col>
                </ion-row>

                <ion-row>
                    <ion-col>Website</ion-col>
                    <ion-col>{{user.website}}</ion-col>
                </ion-row>
            </ion-grid>
        </ion-card-content>
    </ion-card>

</ion-content>
```

5. In the same folder, create a file named `contact.ts` and add the following content to it:

```
import { Component, Input, OnChanges } from '@angular/core';
import { NavController, NavParams } from 'ionic-angular';

@Component({
  selector: 'page-contact',
  templateUrl: 'contact.html'
})
export class ContactPage {
  user:any = {};
  @Input() userInput;
  constructor(public navCtrl: NavController, private
params:NavParams) {
      this.user = params.get('user');
  }

  ngOnChanges() {
```

```
        if(this.userInput) {
            this.user = this.userInput;
        }
    }
}
```

6. Now open `./src/app/app.modules.ts` and add `ContactPage` in `NgModule`'s `declarations` and the `entryComponents` list, as shown in the following code:

```
import { BrowserModule } from '@angular/platform-browser';
import { ErrorHandler, NgModule } from '@angular/core';
import { IonicApp, IonicErrorHandler, IonicModule } from 'ionic-angular';
import { SplashScreen } from '@ionic-native/splash-screen';
import { StatusBar } from '@ionic-native/status-bar';

import { MyApp } from './app.component';
import { HomePage } from '../pages/home/home';
import { ContactPage } from '../pages/contact/contact';

@NgModule({
  declarations: [
    MyApp,
    HomePage,
    ContactPage
  ],
  imports: [
    BrowserModule,
    IonicModule.forRoot(MyApp)
  ],
  bootstrap: [IonicApp],
  entryComponents: [
    MyApp,
    HomePage,
    ContactPage
  ],
  providers: [
    StatusBar,
    SplashScreen,
    {provide: ErrorHandler, useClass: IonicErrorHandler}
  ]
})
export class AppModule {}
```

7. Now go to the Terminal and run the app using the following command:

```
$ ionic serve
```

How it works...

We already used multiple Ionic pages in the navigation, so we know that push/pop navigation works. Let's take a closer look at how we define an Ionic Page as follows:

```
@Component({
  selector: 'page-contact',
  templateUrl: 'contact.html'
})
export class ContactPage {}
```

You can see that an Ionic page is actually an Angular component, and we already know that we can use components as an HTML element using their `selector`. In the preceding example, selector of the page is `page-contact`. So technically we can use the selector in HTML. But it becomes a problem if our page is getting data from the previous page using `NavParams`. Let's take a look at the constructor of `ContactPage`, shown in the following code block:

```
constructor(public navCtrl: NavController, private params:NavParams) {
    this.user = params.get('user');
}
```

In the code, we are getting the user's information from the previous page using Ionic's navigation. So, if we want to use this component as an HTML element, we need to pass this data to the component somehow.

This is where `@Input` decorator is particularly useful. The `@Input` decorator allows us to pass data to the `component` as an input. So, we have `@Input() userInput` as an input to the component. This `userInput` has the same value as the user from `NavParams` shown in the preceding code. The only difference is `userInput` will have a value when we use the page component as an HTML element and `params.get('user')` will have a value when we use this component via Navigation Controlller.

The following is the first page of the app:

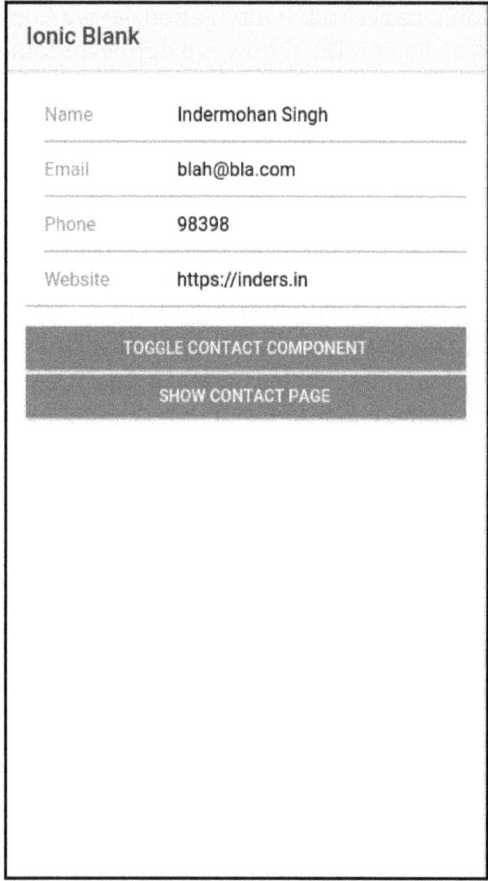

When the user enters information in the input fields and then clicks on **SHOW CONTACT PAGE**, it opens the ContactPage, as shown in the following screenshot:

It is important to note that we might not want to show the header bar of the Ionic page when we are using it as an HTML component in other pages. If you take a look at contact.html, you will see that we hide the page's header when we use it as an HTML component, as follows:

```
<ion-header *ngIf="!userInput">
    <ion-navbar>
        <ion-title>
            Contact Page
        </ion-title>
    </ion-navbar>;
</ion-header>
```

So, what we are saying is, only show the header when `userInput` is empty. This `userInput` is given as input via `@Input`, as described in the chapter. So, if you take a look at the `home.html` file, you will add the following code to show `ContactPage` inside `HomePage`:

```
<page-contact [userInput]="user" *ngIf="showContact">
</page-contact>
```

When we click on the **TOGGLE CONTACT COMPONENT**, it shows the same `Contact Page` inside `HomePage`, as shown in the following screenshot:

See also

- Read more about Angular components at `https://angular.io/api/core/Component`.
- Angular components have a life cycle and events related to it. We can hook up to any life cycle events such as destroy or initialize. Read more about life cycle hooks at `https://angular.io/guide/lifecycle-hooks`.

Validating Forms and Making HTTP Requests

4

In this chapter, we will cover the following tasks related to creating form input validation, mocked API calls, and payment pages using Stripe:

- Creating a complex form with input validation
- Creating reactive forms in Ionic
- Retrieving data via a mocked API using a static JSON file
- Integrating with Stripe for online payment

Introduction

All mobile apps require taking user input and sending it to a backend server. A simple example is filling out a form, such as a user registration or contact form. The information is validated against a set of rules before being sent to the backend. Also, there are many other scenarios where the information is captured based on user behavior from the app, such as where they touch or how much time they spend on a certain page. Regardless, you will run into many sending- and retrieving-data scenarios.

This chapter will cover the following three basic examples:

- How to validate user inputs, such as text, number, and required versus not required, and communicate data to another page
- How to render data without having an actual backend
- How to process payments using Stripe

All of these are actually available natively in Angular 2. However, since Angular 2 has a lot of changes compared to Angular 1 in terms of processing data and working with the backend server, it's worth covering these topics in detail.

Creating a complex form with input validation

In this section, you will build an app to demonstrate form validation using `ngForm` and `ngControl`. Here is a screenshot of the form:

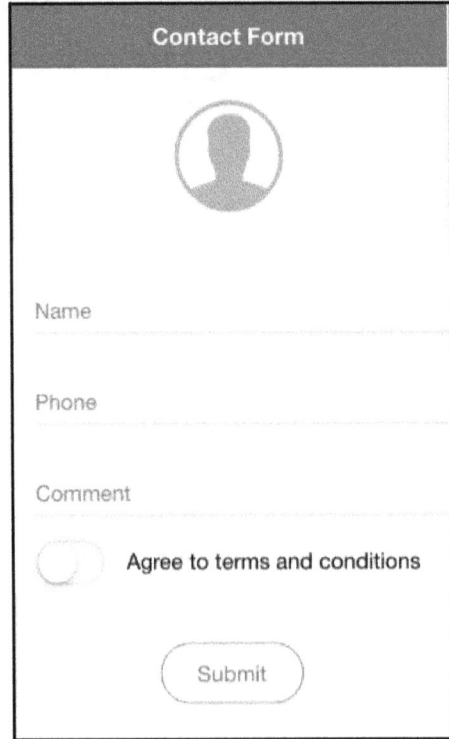

If the user tries to submit without providing valid information, the form will show the following error:

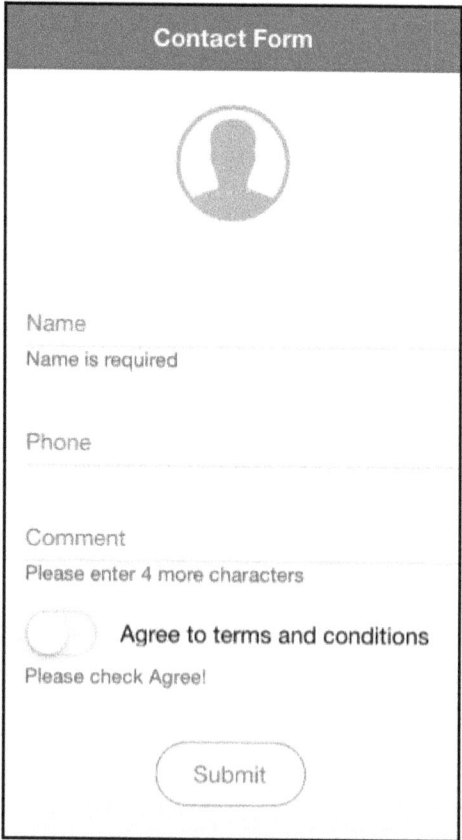

Basically, the **Name** field is required. The **Phone** field is the number type, but is optional. The **Comment** field is required and the user must enter at least four characters. Of course, this is just for demonstration of the input length. The user, finally, must agree to the terms and conditions via the toggle input.

After a successful validation, the user will be taken to the second screen with a summary of the previous screen, as illustrated in the following screenshot:

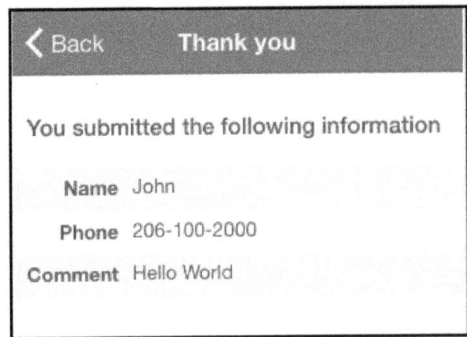

Getting ready

This app example could work either in a browser or on a physical device. However, you can optionally connect your physical device to verify the **Phone** field for number keypad.

How to do it...

1. Create a new `MyFormValidation` app using the `blank` template, as shown, and go to the `MyFormValidation` folder:

```
$ ionic start MyFormValidation blank
$ cd MyFormValidation
```

2. Open the `./src/app/app.module.ts` file and replace the content with the following code:

```
import { BrowserModule } from '@angular/platform-browser';
import { ErrorHandler, NgModule } from '@angular/core';
import { IonicApp, IonicErrorHandler, IonicModule } from 'ionic-angular';
import { SplashScreen } from '@ionic-native/splash-screen';
import { StatusBar } from '@ionic-native/status-bar';

import { MyApp } from './app.component';
import { HomePage } from '../pages/home/home';
import { ThankyouPage } from '../pages/thankyou/thankyou';
import { MyFormService } from '../services/myform';
```

```
@NgModule({
  declarations: [
    MyApp,
    HomePage,
    ThankyouPage
  ],
  imports: [
    BrowserModule,
    IonicModule.forRoot(MyApp)
  ],
  bootstrap: [IonicApp],
  entryComponents: [
    MyApp,
    HomePage,
    ThankyouPage
  ],
  providers: [
    StatusBar,
    SplashScreen,
    MyFormService,
    {provide: ErrorHandler, useClass: IonicErrorHandler}
  ]
})
export class AppModule {}
```

You may realize that there is a common service to be used in the app, called
`MyFormService` here. This example also has a second page, called
`ThankyouPage`.

3. Now, let's create the service by first creating a directory, as shown:

```
$ mkdir ./src/services
```

4. Create the `myform.ts` file in the component's directory that you just created,
   as follows:

```
import { Injectable } from '@angular/core';

@Injectable()
export class MyFormService {
    public name: string = '';
    public phone: number;
    public comment: string = '';
}
```

This example will keep the service component simple for demonstration purposes.

5. Open and edit the `./src/pages/home/home.html` template, as shown:

```
<ion-header>
  <ion-navbar color="primary">
    <ion-title>
      Contact Form
    </ion-title>
  </ion-navbar>
</ion-header>

<ion-content>
  <p class="center">
    <ion-icon class="large lighter" primary name="contact"></ion-icon>
  </p>

  <form #f="ngForm" novalidate (ngSubmit)="onSubmit(f)">
    <ion-list>
      <ion-item>
        <ion-label floating>Name</ion-label>
        <ion-input type="text" name="name" required
        [(ngModel)]="data.name"></ion-input>
      </ion-item>
      <div [hidden]="f.controls.name && (f.controls.name.valid ||
      (f.controls.name.pristine && !isSubmitted))" class="note
danger">
        Name is required
      </div>

      <ion-item>
        <ion-label floating>Phone</ion-label>
        <ion-input type="tel" name="phone"
[(ngModel)]="data.phone">
        </ion-input>
      </ion-item>

      <ion-item>
        <ion-label floating>Comment</ion-label>
        <ion-input type="text" required minlength=4 name="comment"
        [(ngModel)]="data.comment">
        </ion-input>
      </ion-item>
      <div *ngIf="(isSubmitted && f.controls.comment &&
      f.controls.comment.pristine) || ((f.controls.comment) &&
```

```
        (f.controls.comment.dirty && f.controls.comment.errors))"
class="note
      danger">
        Please enter {{ 4 - (f.controls.comment.errors.minlength ?
        f.controls.comment.errors.minlength.actualLength : 0) }}
more
        characters
      </div>
      <ion-item class="tos">
        <ion-toggle item-left [(ngModel)]="data.tos" name="tos"
        type="button" (click)="noSubmit($event)"></ion-toggle>
        <ion-label item-right>Agree to terms and conditions
        </ion-label>
      </ion-item>
      <div [hidden]="(!isSubmitted) || (f.controls.tos &&
data.tos)"
        class="note danger">
        Please check Agree!
      </div>
    </ion-list>
    <div class="center">
      <button ion-button type="submit" round
outline>Submit</button>
    </div>
  </form>
</ion-content>
```

This is probably the most complicated part of the form validation process because there are many places where you have to embed validation logic for the input.

6. Open and replace the content of the `./src/pages/home/home.scss` file with the following code:

```
page-home {
    .center {
        text-align: center;
    }
    ion-icon.large {
        font-size: 7em;
    }
    ion-icon.lighter {
        opacity: 0.5;
    }
    ion-list > .item:first-child {
        border-top: 0;
    }
    ion-list > .item:last-child, ion-list > ion-itemsliding:last-
```

```
child .item
   {
       border-bottom: 0;
   }
   .tos {
       padding-top: 10px;
       ion-toggle {
           padding-left: 0px;
       }
       .item-inner {
           border-bottom: 0;
       }
   }
   .item ion-toggle {
       padding-left: 0;
   }
   .note.danger {
       padding-left: 16px;
       color: #d14;
   }
}
```

7. Open `./src/pages/home/home.ts` for editing with the following code:

```
import { Component } from '@angular/core';
import { NavController } from 'ionic-angular';
import { ThankyouPage } from '../thankyou/thankyou';
import { MyFormService } from '../../services/myform';

@Component({
  selector: 'page-home',
  templateUrl: 'home.html'
})
export class HomePage {
  private data: any;
  private isSubmitted: Boolean = false;
  constructor(public nav: NavController, private formData:
    MyFormService) {
    this.nav = nav;
    this.formData = formData;
    this.data = {
      name: '',
      phone: '',
      comment: '',
      tos: false
    }
  }
  onSubmit(myForm) {
```

```
          this.isSubmitted = true;
          console.log('onSubmit');
          console.log(myForm);
          if ((myForm.valid) && (myForm.value.tos)) {
            this.formData.name = this.data.name;
            this.formData.phone = this.data.phone;
            this.formData.comment = this.data.comment;
            this.nav.push(ThankyouPage);
          }
        }
        noSubmit(e) {
          e.preventDefault();
        }
      }
```

You may note that there isn't much validation code in the JavaScript part. This means that the template takes care of a lot of the validations. There is also an `import` command for a `thankyou` page, which you will have to create next.

8. Now, let's create the `thankyou` folder, as follows:

$ mkdir ./src/pages/thankyou

9. Create a `thankyou.ts` file in the `Component`'s directory that you just created, as shown:

```
import { Component } from '@angular/core';
import { MyFormService } from '../../services/myform';
@Component({
    selector: 'page-thankyou',
    templateUrl: 'thankyou.html'
})
export class ThankyouPage {
    constructor(private formData: MyFormService) {
        this.formData = formData;
    }
}
```

This page just renders the data from the `MyFormService` service, so you can keep it very simple.

10. Create `thankyou.html` in the `./src/pages/thankyou` folder, as illustrated:

```
<ion-header>
    <ion-navbar color="secondary">
        <ion-title>
            Thank You
```

```
            </ion-title>
        </ion-navbar>
    </ion-header>
    <ion-content>
        <h6 class="padding">
            You submitted the following information
        </h6>
        <div class="my-table">
            <ion-row>
                <ion-col width-25 class="my-label">Name</ion-col>
                <ion-col width-75>{{ formData.name }}</ion-col>
            </ion-row>
            <ion-row>
                <ion-col width-25 class="my-label">Phone</ion-col>
                <ion-col width-75>{{ formData.phone }}</ion-col>
            </ion-row>
            <ion-row>
                <ion-col width-25 class="my-label">Comment</ion-col>
                <ion-col width-75>{{ formData.comment }}</ion-col>
            </ion-row>
        </div>
    </ion-content>
```

11. Create `thankyou.scss` in the `./src/pages/thankyou` folder, as shown:

```
page-thankyou {
    h6.padding {
        color: #4C555A;
        padding: 10px;
    }
    .my-label {
        text-align: right;
        font-weight: bold;
    }
    .my-table {
        ion-row {
            color: #4C555A;
            padding: 0;
            height: 30px;
        }
        ion-row + ion-row {
            margin-top: 0;
        }
        ion-row:nth-child(odd) ion-col {
            background: #F9FAFB;
        }
    }
}
```

12. Go to your Terminal and run the app with the following command:

```
$ ionic serve
```

How it works...

Let's start with the `home.html` file, where most of the validation code is located. If you look at the structure of this page, it's very typical. You have `<ion-navbar>` with `<ion-title>`. The `<form>` element must be inside the `<ion-content>` area.

 It's a requirement to use the `<form>` element for Angular validation to work. Otherwise, there will be no `submit` event and you cannot catch errors for each input.

`form` has the following attributes:

```
<form #f="ngForm" novalidate (ngSubmit)="onSubmit(f)">
```

To assign a local variable on the fly, you use the `#` sign. This means that you want the `f` variable to refer to `ngForm`, which is automatically created by Angular. This is a special object that contains everything related to the current form. You are advised to use `novalidate` to bypass the default HTML5 validation because you are using Angular for validation instead. Otherwise, the `form` will acquire conflicts. The `(ngSubmit)` is pretty much an event to trigger the `onSubmit(f)` function whenever the `button` with `type=submit` is touched or clicked. When you submit the form, it will pass the `f` variable along so that you can process the object inside the `onSubmit` method.

The `form` template consists of just `<ion-list>` and `<ion-item>`. You just need to know how to validate each input and display the error. Let's use the `Name` field as the first example. This is the `<ion-input>` for `Name`:

```
<ion-input type="text" name="name" required [(ngModel)]="data.name"></ion-
input>
```

The following is the error displayed:

```
<div [hidden]="f.controls.name && (f.controls.name.valid ||
(f.controls.name.pristine && !isSubmitted))" class="note danger">
  Name is required
</div>
```

To validate, you must assign `name` a local variable name. This is to refer to that input using `f.controls.name` in other areas. Recall that the `f` variable has been declared previously as the `ngForm` object. Here is a view of how the `ngForm` is structured:

```
▼ NgForm {ngSubmit: EventEmitter, form: ControlGroup} 
  ▶ control: ControlGroup
  ▼ controls: Object
    ▶ comment: Control
    ▶ name: Control
    ▶ phone: Control
    ▶ tos: Control
    ▶ __proto__: Object
    dirty: true
    errors: null
  ▶ form: ControlGroup
  ▶ formDirective: NgForm
  ▶ ngSubmit: EventEmitter
  ▶ path: Array[0]
    pristine: false
    touched: false
    untouched: true
    valid: true
  ▶ value: Object
  ▶ __proto__: ControlContainer
```

You can view this using the Chrome Developer console because the code actually gives this output when you submit the form.

The error message `Name is required` will be hidden when either of the following conditions takes place:

- The form has not been submitted yet. Otherwise, people will see the error message right away before they even type in something. This is not a good user experience. To check for this, you have to use a temporary Boolean, called `isSubmitted`. The `f.controls.name.pristine` variable means that the input has not been modified. The opposite of this would be `f.controls.name.dirty`.
- The `f.controls.name.valid` variable is `true`. However, you cannot check this right away because, if the input is empty, the `name` object does not exist yet. That's why you need to check for the existence of `f.controls.name` before checking for the `valid` Boolean.

There is no need to check the phone requirement; so, you just need to assign `name` and a model, as shown:

```
<ion-input type="tel" name="phone" [(ngModel)]="data.phone"></ion-input>
```

For the `comment` field, you need to validate using both `required` and `minlength=4`, as follows:

```
<ion-input type="text" required minlength=4 name="comment"
[(ngModel)]="data.comment"></ion-input>
```

You may think `required` is unnecessary because, if the length is zero, Angular will trigger an error flag. However, that is not true. When the user doesn't enter anything in the input, the input will have no length because the variable doesn't exist. That's why you need to check for both scenarios.

The error message for the `comment` field is quite interesting because it shows the number of characters the user needs to enter, as shown in the following code:

```
<div *ngIf="(isSubmitted && f.controls.comment &&
 f.controls.comment.pristine) || ((f.controls.comment) &&
 (f.controls.comment.dirty && f.controls.comment.errors))"
 class="note danger"> Please enter {{ 4 -
(f.controls.comment.errors.minlength
 ?
 f.controls.comment.errors.minlength.actualLength : 0) }} more
 characters
</div>
```

The main idea here is that you only want to show this `div` when the form is submitted and it's pristine via `f.controls.comment.pristine`. This means that the user has not entered anything in the form. You also want to show the message when the form is dirty and has errors via `f.controls.comment.errors`. If you inspect the console, you can see a list of many detailed errors under the `f.controls.comment.errors` object. In order to tell the user how many characters they have left to enter, you have to first check `f.controls.comment.errors.minlength` because, if that variable doesn't exist, there is no error or the `comment` input is empty. If you do not check for this, you will get a parse error later on.

In your `home.ts` file, the `onSubmit` method must toggle the `isSubmitted` Boolean to `true`, as shown in the following code snippet:

```
onSubmit(myForm) {
   this.isSubmitted = true;
   console.log('onSubmit');
```

```
    console.log(myForm);
    if ((myForm.valid) && (myForm.value.tos)) {
      this.formData.name = this.data.name;
      this.formData.phone = this.data.phone;
      this.formData.comment = this.data.comment;
      this.nav.push(ThankyouPage);
    }
  }
```

Then, you have to do a general check for `myForm.valid` and `myForm.value.tos`. You may wonder why we are checking for `tos` here instead of validating it inside the template. The reason is that there is no way to validate a toggle button in Angular since it doesn't make sense to do so as it cannot be `required`. Therefore, you have to do a custom validation here to make sure it's `true` in the form. This means that the user has checked the **Agree to terms and conditions** toggle.

> Refer to the W3 website, at `https://www.w3.org/TR/2011/WD-html5-20110525/the-button-element.html`, for information about the default behavior of the `button` element.

The `thankyou` page is very self-explanatory because you just parse the `formData` object in the template by getting the data from the `MyFormService` service.

See also

Check out the following links for more information:

- For more information about `form` from the Angular 2 documentation, you can visit `https://angular.io/docs/ts/latest/guide/forms.html` and `https://angular.io/docs/ts/latest/api/forms/index/NgForm-directive.html`
- The Ionic documentation has its own page specifically for Ionic input components, which is at `https://ionicframework.com/docs/v2/resources/forms/`
- It also has a good list of HTML5 input types that you can use for validation or keyboard enforcement, which you can find at `http://ionicframework.com/html5-input-types/`

Creating reactive forms in Ionic

In the previous example, we have created a complex form with validations. If you notice carefully, we used angular validations inside our template file, particularly in `home.html`. These type of forms are called as template driven form, where most of the work is done on template side. This is something very similar to what we had in AngularJS.

There is another type of form in Angular, called the reactive form. The difference is, in reactive forms, we used validations and other configuration inside the class of the component, instead of in the template. The following is the definition from Angular Docs:

> *"With reactive forms, you create a tree of Angular form control objects in the component class and bind them to native form control elements in the component template."*

We will create a registration form, which looks like the following:

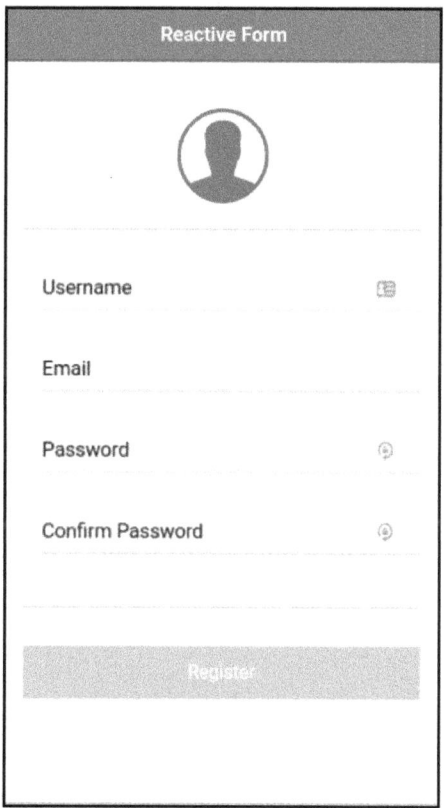

Getting ready

Since we are using forms, we only require a web browser to run this recipe.

How to do it...

1. Open Terminal (or Command Prompt) and create a new app named
   ReactiveForm based on blank template and go into the folder as follows:

```
$ ionic start ReactiveForm blank
$ cd ReactiveForm
```

2. Open home.html and replace the file with following content:

```
<ion-header>
<ion-navbar color="primary">
<ion-title>
Reactive Form
</ion-title>
</ion-navbar>
</ion-header>

<ion-content padding>
<p class="center">
<ion-icon class="large lighter" primary name="contact"></ion-icon>
</p>
<form [formGroup]="registerForm" (ngSubmit)="onSubmit()"
novalidate>
<ion-list>
<ion-item>
<ion-label floating>Username</ion-label>
<ion-input type="text" formControlName="username"></ion-input>
</ion-item>
<ion-item>
<ion-label floating>Email</ion-label>
<ion-input type="email" formControlName="email"></ion-input>
</ion-item>

<ion-item>
<ion-label floating>Password</ion-label>
<ion-input type="password" formControlName="pass"></ion-input>
</ion-item>

<ion-item>
<ion-label floating>Confirm Password</ion-label>
```

```
<ion-input type="password" formControlName="repass"></ion-input>
</ion-item>

<ion-item text-wrap class="error">
<div *ngIf="registerForm.controls['username'].dirty &&
registerForm.controls['username'].invalid">
Username should at least have 10 Characters.
</div>
<div *ngIf="registerForm.controls['email'].dirty &&
registerForm.controls['email'].invalid">
Email is incorrect.
</div>
<div *ngIf="registerForm.controls['pass'].dirty &&
registerForm.controls['pass'].invalid">
Password should be 8 Character long.
</div>
<div *ngIf="registerForm.controls['repass'].dirty &&
registerForm.controls['repass'].invalid">
Choose same password in confirm password field.
</div>
</ion-item>
</ion-list>
<button ion-button full type="submit"
[disabled]="registerForm.invalid">Register</button>
</form>
</ion-content>
```

3. Open the `home.scss` file and replace the content with the following:

```
page-home {
 .center {
 text-align: center;
 }
 ion-icon.large {
 font-size: 7em;
 }
 ion-icon.lighter {
 opacity: 0.5;
 }
 .error {
 color: red;
 }
}
```

4. Open the `home.ts` file and replace the content with the following:

```
import { Component } from '@angular/core';
import { FormBuilder, FormGroup, Validators } from
'@angular/forms';
import { NavController, AlertController } from 'ionic-angular';
import { confirmPassword } from "../../app/confirmPassword";

@Component({
  selector: 'page-home',
  templateUrl: 'home.html'
})
export class HomePage {
  registerForm:FormGroup;

  constructor(public navCtrl: NavController, private
fb:FormBuilder,
    private alertCtrl: AlertController) {
    this.registerForm = this.fb.group({
      username: ['', [Validators.required,
Validators.minLength(10)]],
      email: ['', [Validators.required, Validators.email]],
      pass: ['', [Validators.required, Validators.minLength(8)]],
      repass: ['', [Validators.required, Validators.minLength(8)]],
    }, {
      validator: confirmPassword('pass', 'repass')
    });
  }

  onSubmit() {
    this.alertCtrl.create({
      title: 'Your inputs are:',
      message: JSON.stringify(this.registerForm.value),
      buttons: ['Dismiss']
    })
    .present();
    console.log(this.registerForm);
  }

}
```

Since, in our example, we have the registration form with the password and confirm password fields, we will be creating a custom validator for making sure that both fields have some values.

5. Create a file named `confirmPassword.ts` in /app folder. Then add the following content inside it:

```
import { FormGroup } from '@angular/forms';

export function confirmPassword(passwordKey: string,
passwordConfirmationKey: string) {
    return (group: FormGroup) => {
      let passwordInput = group.controls[passwordKey],
          passwordConfirmationInput =
          group.controls[passwordConfirmationKey];
      if (passwordInput.value !== passwordConfirmationInput.value)
{
          return passwordConfirmationInput.setErrors({notEquivalent:
true})
      }
      else {
          return passwordConfirmationInput.setErrors(null);
      }
    }
  }
```

6. Make sure your `app.module.ts` has the following content:

```
import { BrowserModule } from '@angular/platform-browser';
import { ErrorHandler, NgModule } from '@angular/core';
import { IonicApp, IonicErrorHandler, IonicModule } from 'ionic-
angular';
import { SplashScreen } from '@ionic-native/splash-screen';
import { StatusBar } from '@ionic-native/status-bar';

import { MyApp } from './app.component';
import { HomePage } from '../pages/home/home';

@NgModule({
  declarations: [
    MyApp,
    HomePage
  ],
  imports: [
    BrowserModule,
    IonicModule.forRoot(MyApp)
  ],
  bootstrap: [IonicApp],
  entryComponents: [
    MyApp,
    HomePage
```

```
      ],
      providers: [
        StatusBar,
        SplashScreen,
        {provide: ErrorHandler, useClass: IonicErrorHandler}
      ]
    })
    export class AppModule {}
```

7. Open the Terminal and run the following command :

```
$ ionic serve
```

How it works...

Since this recipe uses reactive forms, let's first take a look at home.ts, which initializes and sets up our form.

In the HomePage class, we have registerForm:FormGroup property, which is the collection of FormControl. Each FormControl is bound to the native FormControl in our template. In order to create FormGroup, we can do something like the following:

```
this.myForm = new FormGroup({
  first: new FormControl('Nancy', Validators.minLength(2)),
  last: new FormControl('Drew'),
});
```

In the preceding example, we are creating a FormGroup named myForm. The FormGroup constructor takes an object as input, which is the collection of FormControl. Each key in this object refers to some native FormControl in the template. The value in the key pair is a FormControl object. The FormControl constructor takes the initial value and a validator or array of validators as input. The template will look something like this:

```
<form formGroup="myForm" novalidate>
  <input type="text" formControlName="first"/>
  <input type="text" formControlName="last" />
</form>
```

Here, formControlName is set to the key of FormControl; for example, first. formGroup is set to the name of the group; in this example, it is myForm.

However, this method becomes complicated if we have nested `FormGroup`. To ease this process, Angular provides a better API via `FormBuilder`. `FormBuilder` is class, which allow us to create `FormGroup` via a really nice API. Take a look:

```
this.registerForm = this.fb.group({
 username: ['', [Validators.required, Validators.minLength(10)]],
 email: ['', [Validators.required, Validators.email]],
 pass: ['', [Validators.required, Validators.minLength(8)]],
 repass: ['', [Validators.required, Validators.minLength(8)]],
 }, {
 validator: confirmPassword('pass', 'repass')
});
```

`this.fb` is an instance of `FormBuilder` and has a `group` method to create `FormGroup`. It takes an object with a key-value pair. The key is used with `formControlName` to bind to the native element in the template and the value is an array with the initial value of the native element and a list of validators. For example, `username` has `required` and `minLength(10)` validators; similarly, other fields have validations too. You may notice that there is no `FormControl` constructor here. This is the abstraction provided by `FormBuilder`.

You can also pass group-level validator as a second input to the `group` method of `FormBuilder`. In the preceding example, we are using a custom `confirmPassword` validator with inputs `pass` and `repass`. These are keys inside the first object and refer to input fields; the validator makes sure that they are equal.

Our custom validator is created in the `confirmPassword.ts` file, as follows:

```
export function confirmPassword(passwordKey: string,
passwordConfirmationKey: string) {
 return (group: FormGroup) => {
    let passwordInput = group.controls[passwordKey],
    passwordConfirmationInput = group.controls[passwordConfirmationKey];
    if (passwordInput.value !== passwordConfirmationInput.value) {
       return passwordConfirmationInput.setErrors({notEquivalent: true})
    }
    else {
       return passwordConfirmationInput.setErrors(null);
    }
 }
}
```

It is just a function that takes two string type arguments. These are the names of the two fields that we want to compare. It compares the values in both fields and sets the validation on the repass (a.k.a confirm password) field accordingly.

In home.html, we have form element which looks like following:

```
<form [formGroup]="registerForm" (ngSubmit)="onSubmit()" novalidate>
```

[formGroup] is set to registerForm, and when the user clicks on the **submit** button, it fires the onSubmit method.

Each input is configured as follows:

```
<ion-item>
  <ion-label floating>Username</ion-label>
  <ion-input type="text" formControlName="username"></ion-input>
</ion-item>
```

We also show error messages, since we use validators in our form. Here is how we show validation error messages. We check whether the field is dirty or invalid and then show the appropriate error. formName.controls['controlName'] is the syntax to get control. Here, formName is the name of formGroup and controlName is the name of the control:

```
<ion-item text-wrap class="error">
 <div *ngIf="registerForm.controls['username'].dirty &&
registerForm.controls['username'].invalid">
 Username should at least have 10 Characters.
 </div>
 <div *ngIf="registerForm.controls['email'].dirty &&
registerForm.controls['email'].invalid">
 Email is incorrect.
 </div>
 <div *ngIf="registerForm.controls['pass'].dirty &&
registerForm.controls['pass'].invalid">
 Password should be 8 Character long.
 </div>
 <div *ngIf="registerForm.controls['repass'].dirty &&
registerForm.controls['repass'].invalid">
 Choose same password in confirm password field.
 </div>
 </ion-item>
```

Errors look something like this:

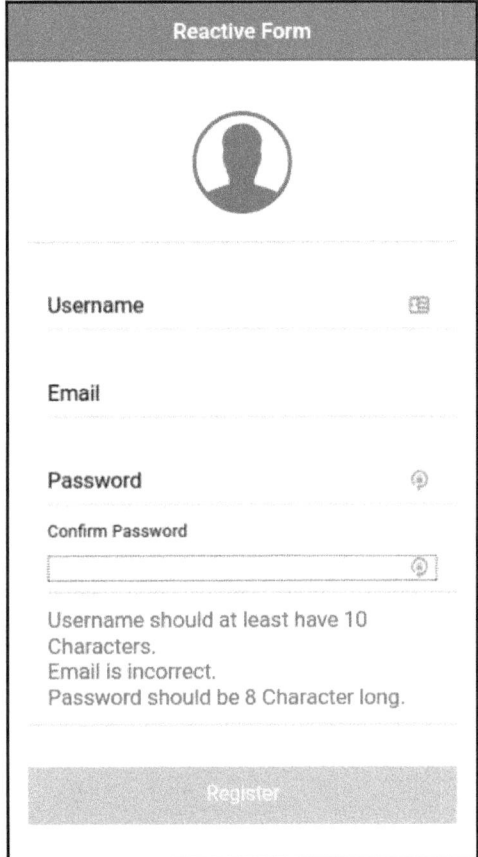

At last, we have **Register** button, which has following code:

```
<button ion-button full type="submit"
[disabled]="registerForm.invalid">Register</button>
```

We disable the button when the form is invalid. When the user clicks on it, it calls the onSubmit method and we show an alert box with the user's input, as shown in the following code:

```
onSubmit() {
  this.alertCtrl.create({
      title: 'Your inputs are:',
      message: JSON.stringify(this.registerForm.value),
      buttons: ['Dismiss']
```

```
})
.present();
 console.log(this.registerForm);
}
```

The alert message looks like the following:

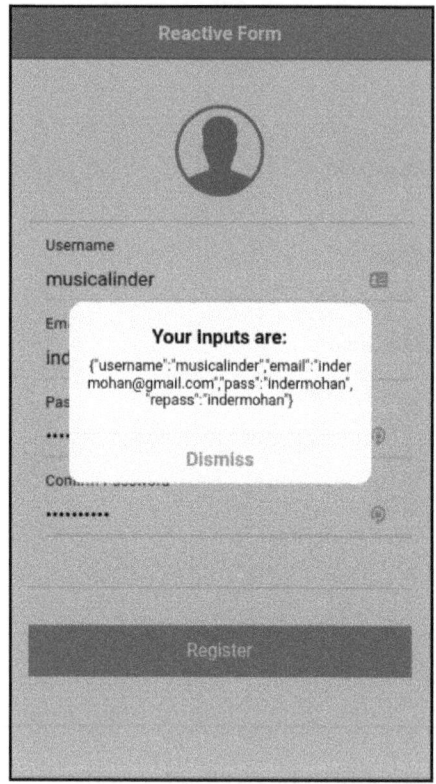

See also

- For further reading about reactive forms, go to Angular's Guide on reactive forms at `https://angular.io/guide/reactive-forms`
- There is an excellent article written by Todd Moto on reactive forms at `https://toddmotto.com/angular-2-forms-reactive`

Retrieving data via a mocked API using a static JSON file

As a frontend and app developer, you are often working with a team where someone else is responsible for the backend APIs. However, it's not always possible to have the backend available when you are developing the frontend. You have to simulate the backend in scenarios where the final backend APIs are not ready.

In this recipe, you will learn how to call a REST API using the `HttpClient` service. The API endpoint will be just a static JSON located on your local machine. You will also learn how to leverage placeholder images to meet design requirements. The app will show a list of image feeds and a description, as shown in the following screenshot:

Getting ready

This app example would work either in a browser or on a physical device. However, the fake backend server must be running on your local computer.

How to do it...

1. First, let's quickly create the fake backend server. You must install `http-server` for this:

```
$ sudo npm install -g http-server
```

2. Create a folder to store your `.json` file. Let's call it `MockRest`, as shown:

```
$ mkdir MockRest
$ cd MockRest
```

3. Create the `test.json` file and fill in the following content for the REST response:

```
[
  {
    "title": "What a beautiful song",
    "category": "objects",
    "description": "Music is a moral law. It gives soul to the
universe, wings to the mind, flight to the imagination, and charm
and gaiety to life and to everything."
  },
  {
    "title": "The world we live in",
    "category": "nature",
    "description": "Look deep into nature, and then you will
understand everything better."
  },
  {
    "title": "Life experiences",
    "category": "people",
    "description": "People who know little are usually great
talkers, while
    men who know much say little."
  }
]
```

Basically, whenever you send a REST request, you should receive the preceding content as the response. As your backend developer updates the REST response, you can always change the content of the test.json file accordingly.

4. Start your backend server by calling http-server from the Terminal in the MockRest folder, as shown:

```
$ http-server --cors=Access-Control-Allow-Origin
```

Go to your browser and visit http://localhost:8080/test.json to verify that you can see the JSON content. If not, you probably have a port conflict with another web server. You need to ensure that there is no other application using port 8080. After completing your backend, open another Terminal window, create a new MyRestBackend app using the blank template, and go to the MyRestBackend folder, as shown:

```
$ ionic start MyRestbackend blank
$ cd MyRestbackend
```

 You must not stop the backend server or create an Ionic project inside the MockRest folder. They are two independent project folders

5. Open the home.html file and replace the content with the following code:

```
<ion-header>
  <ion-navbar>
    <ion-title>
      Home
    </ion-title>
  </ion-navbar>
</ion-header>

<ion-content padding>
  <ion-card #myCard *ngFor="let item of quotes.data">
    <img [src]='"https://source.unsplash.com/category/" +
item.category + "/600x390"' [height]="myCard.clientWidth * 390 /
600" />
    <ion-card-content>
      <ion-card-title>
        {{ item.title }}
      </ion-card-title>
      <p>
        {{ item.description }}
```

```
        </p>
      </ion-card-content>
    </ion-card>
  </ion-content>
```

This example uses free photos from `https://source.unsplash.com/` because you can easily query to get random photos that meet your need.

6. Open `home.ts` and edit it with the following code:

```
import { Component } from '@angular/core';
import { NavController } from 'ionic-angular';
import { QuoteService } from '../../services/quote';

@Component({
  selector: 'page-home',
  templateUrl: 'home.html'
})
export class HomePage {
  constructor(public navCtrl: NavController, public
quotes:QuoteService) {
    this.quotes = quotes;
    this.quotes.getQuotes();
  }
}
```

You have not created the `QuoteService` service yet. However, you probably know that this service will call the fake backend server to get the JSON content using the `getQuotes()` method.

7. Do a small modification of the stylesheet `home.scss`, as follows:

```
page-home {
    ion-card {
        img {
            background-color: #f4f4f4;
        }
    }
}
```

8. Create the `./src/services` folder with the following command:

```
$ mkdir ./src/services
```

9. Create the `quote.ts` file in the `services` folder and copy the following code:

```
import { Injectable } from '@angular/core';
import { HttpClient } from '@angular/common/http';
@Injectable()
export class QuoteService {
    private http: any;
    public data: any;
    constructor(http: HttpClient) {
        this.http = http;
    }
    getQuotes() {
        this.http.get("http://localhost:8080/test.json")
            .subscribe(res => {
                this.data = res;
                console.log(this.data, this.http);
            }, error => {
                console.log(error);
            });
    }
}
```

10. Open and edit `./src/app/app.module.ts` to declare `QuoteService`, as shown:

```
import { BrowserModule } from '@angular/platform-browser';
import { ErrorHandler, NgModule } from '@angular/core';
import { HttpClientModule } from '@angular/common/http';
import { IonicApp, IonicErrorHandler, IonicModule } from 'ionic-
angular';
import { SplashScreen } from '@ionic-native/splash-screen';
import { StatusBar } from '@ionic-native/status-bar';

import { MyApp } from './app.component';
import { HomePage } from '../pages/home/home';
import { QuoteService } from '../services/quote'
@NgModule({
  declarations: [
    MyApp,
    HomePage
  ],
  imports: [
    BrowserModule,
    HttpClientModule,
    IonicModule.forRoot(MyApp)
  ],
  bootstrap: [IonicApp],
```

```
        entryComponents: [
          MyApp,
          HomePage
        ],
        providers: [
          StatusBar,
          SplashScreen,
          QuoteService,
          {provide: ErrorHandler, useClass: IonicErrorHandler}
        ]
      })
      export class AppModule {}
```

11. Go to your Terminal and run the app, as illustrated:

     `$ ionic serve`

12. You will note that the page is empty and the **Console** shows the following error:

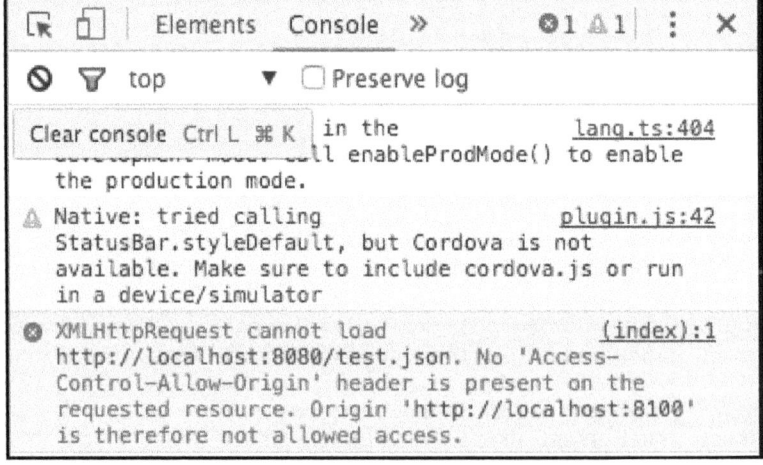

This means that your browser (in this case, Chrome) does not allow calling REST API from `http://localhost:8100` to `http://localhost:8080`. You need to install the Allow-**Control-Allow-Origin** (**CORS**) plugin, such as `https://chrome.google.com/webstore/detail/allow-control-allow-origi/nlfbmbojpeacfghkpbjhddihlkkiljbi?hl=en`, for Chrome. After that, turn on CORS, as shown in the following screenshot:

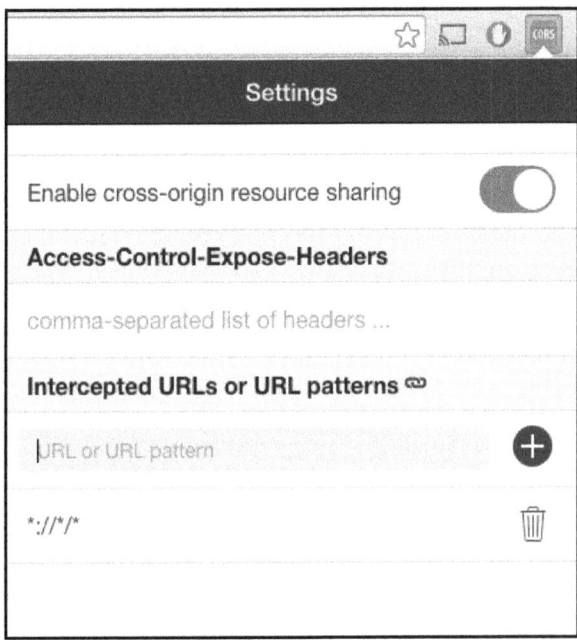

Refresh your browser to see the updated app.

How it works...

Your fake backend simply returns any file in the current `MockRest` folder. As you get more sample responses from the backend developer, you can copy them into this folder to provide additional backend endpoints.

 This section does not provide examples of how to handle POST and complex scenarios where the responses depend on request parameters. You may want to keep the code to handle temporary cases as simple as possible since they are not production code. The recommendation is to return the same content for each POST request as well.

Let's take a look at `quote.ts`, because it's the main place where the `Http` request is made. First, you need to import `Injectable` and `Http`, which you can do as follows:

```
import {Injectable} from '@angular/core';
import {Http} from '@angular/http';
```

The `@Injectable` decorator is used to allow other pages and components to use `QuoteService` as a dependency. The `Http` service (or class) is provided by Angular (not Ionic) and this is similar to the `$http` provider in Angular 1. However, instead of returning a promise, `Http` will return an **observable** object so that you can *subscribe* to it. The `getQuotes()` method, shown as follows, is the most important part of this file:

```
getQuotes() {
  this.http.get("http://localhost:8080/test.json")
    .subscribe(res => {
      this.data = res.json();
      console.log(this.data);
    }, error => {
      console.log(error);
    });
}
```

The `this.http` object must be injected from the constructor. Then, it will trigger GET via `this.http.get()`, just like the `$http` provider. However, there is no `.then()` function but in Angular 2; you have to `subscribe` to the object. A new feature of ES6 is the arrow function, as you see via `res => {}`. This is similar to the lambda function in other languages (for example, Python). There is no need to declare the name of the function and you don't have to type function each time. In addition, it automatically passes the parameter (`res` in this case) and the `this` context inside the function.

 You can read more about the arrow function from TypeScript documentation at
`https://www.typescriptlang.org/docs/handbook/functions.html`.

The REST response from your fake backend will be assigned to `this.data` of the `QuoteService` service, as shown:

```
this.data = JSON.parse(res._body);
```

If you see the browser console, it will look similar to the following screenshot:

```
                                                                              quote.ts:17
▼ [Object, Object, Object] 🔢
  ▼ 0: Object
      category: "objects"
      description: "Music is a moral law. It gives soul to the universe, wings to the mind, flight to the imagination,
      title: "What a beautiful song"
    ▶ __proto__: Object
  ▼ 1: Object
      category: "nature"
      description: "Look deep into nature, and then you will understand everything better."
      title: "The world we live in"
    ▶ __proto__: Object
  ▼ 2: Object
      category: "people"
      description: "People who know little are usually great talkers, while men who know much say little."
      title: "Life experiences"
    ▶ __proto__: Object
    length: 3
  ▶ __proto__: Array[0]
```

Another nice trick in the `home.html` template is to display a gray placeholder for the photos instead of pushing down the content when the photos are downloaded and rendered, as shown in the following code snippet:

```
<ion-card #myCard *ngFor="let item of quotes.data">
    <img [src]='"https://source.unsplash.com/category/" + item.category +
"/600x390"' [height]="myCard.clientWidth * 390 / 600"/>
```

The following screenshot shows a quick example before the photos are loaded:

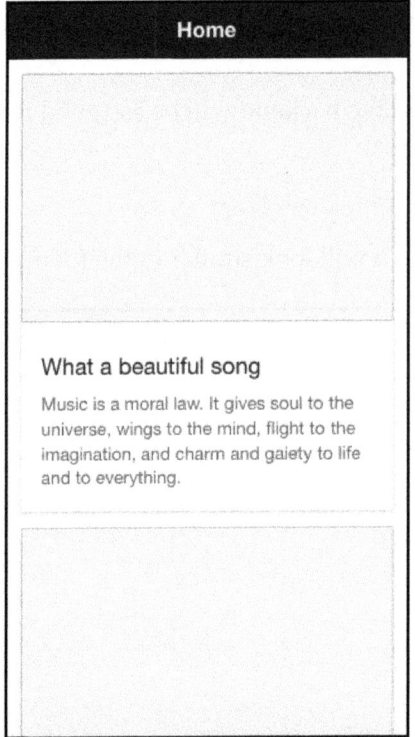

In order to tell the `<img>` tag to have an exact size, you have to do a height calculation using `[height]="myCard.clientWidth * 390 / 600"`. This is because the photo is 600 x 390. The `myCard` object is a local object created from `ion-card`. This `myCard` object will have access to all properties of the `ion-card` DOM, including the width via `clientWidth`. You have probably noted that this is just pure JavaScript and has nothing to do with Ionic or Angular itself.

See also

For more information about the Angular `Http` provider, you can visit the official documentation at `https://angular.io/docs/ts/latest/api/http/index/HttpModule-class.html`.

Integrating with Stripe for online payment

In this section, you will learn how to integrate with a real backend service for the payment process. Earning revenue is an important aspect of creating an app. While there are many other methods of collecting payment, Stripe is a common payment system and can integrate very well with Ionic. In addition, there is no need to provide a high level of security and compliance (that is, PCI) since you will not be storing the credit card information.

Your app will not process via a real payment method because you can use a public test key from Stripe. The app will ask for a few fields to create a token. Observe the following screenshot of the app:

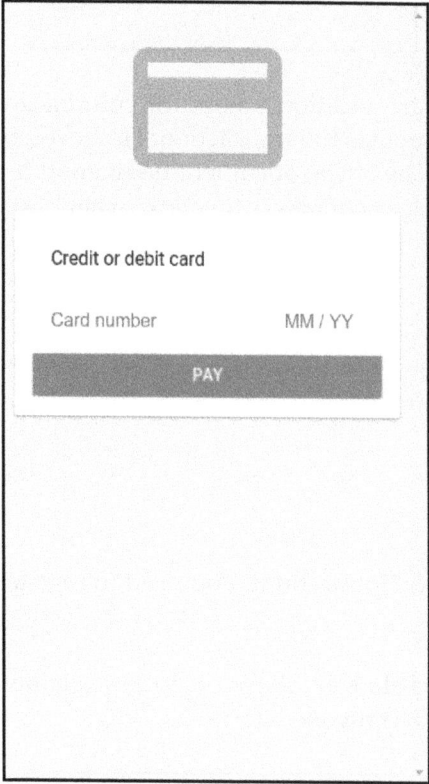

If you touch the **Pay** button, it will take you to the next screen where you will get the payment token, as shown in the following screenshot:

Your token is

tok_1800GeC0qcSH6gqQmAbApXpY

 Actually, there are additional steps for your backend to call Stripe to authorize and process the transaction. However, it's not within the scope of this section. The Stripe document has a good tutorial page on Node.js at `https://stripe.com/docs/api/node#authentication`.

Getting ready

There is no need to test in a physical device because Ionic and Stripe will work just fine in the web browser.

How to do it...

1. If you don't have a Stripe account, you need to register on `https://stripe.com`.

2. Log in and go to `https://dashboard.stripe.com/account/apikeys`.

3. Copy your **Publishable Key**, shown as follows, somewhere because you need to use it for your JavaScript code later:

Publishable key	pk_test_Yo9GMmHGYYawPef2mJkhcKoa

4. Now, go back to the Terminal and create a new `StripePayment` app using the `blank` template, as follows, and go into the `StripePayment` folder:

```
$ ionic start StripePayment blank
$ cd StripePayment
```

5. Open the `./src/index.html` file and insert the line shown somewhere in the `<body>` tab as follows:

```
<script type="text/javascript"
src="https://js.stripe.com/v3/"></script>
```

This is to load the `Stripe` object globally in your app. This is not the recommended method with Angular because anything that is used within a component must be imported via the `import` instruction. However, at the time of writing this book, angular-stripe is unavailable for Angular. So, there is no way to do this properly. The preceding method will work just fine.

6. Open the `./src/pages/home/home.html` file and modify the content with the following code:

```
<ion-content class="gray-bg">
  <p class="center">
    <ion-icon class="icon-large" name="card"></ion-icon>
  </p>
  <ion-card>
    <ion-card-content>
      <ion-card-header>
        Credit or debit card
      </ion-card-header>
        <ion-item>
          <div #cardElement>
            <!-- a Stripe Element will be inserted here. -->
          </div>
        </ion-item>
        <button ion-button full (click)="onSubmit()">Pay</button>
    </ion-card-content>
  </ion-card>
</ion-content>
```

Stripe only needs the credit card number, CVC, and expiration to create a token for charging. The customer name and address are optional; so, you don't need to include them here.

7. Then, replace the content of `./src/pages/home/home.ts` with the following code:

```
import { Component, ViewChild } from '@angular/core';
import { NavController } from 'ionic-angular';
import { ThankyouPage } from '../thankyou/thankyou'
declare var Stripe: any;
@Component({
  selector: 'page-home',
  templateUrl: 'home.html'
})
export class HomePage {
  private token: string = '';
  private card:any;
  private elements:any;
  private stripe:any;
  @ViewChild('cardElement') cardElement;
  constructor(public nav: NavController) {
    this.nav = nav;
    this.stripe = Stripe('YOUR STRIPE PUBLIC KEY HERE');
    this.elements = this.stripe.elements();
  }

  ngOnInit() {
    const style = {
      base: {
        fontSize: '16px',
        lineHeight: '24px',
        marginBottom: '10px'
      },
    };
    this.card = this.elements.create('card', {style});
    this.card.mount(this.cardElement.nativeElement);
  }
  onSubmit() {
    this.stripe.createToken(this.card)
    .then((data) => {
      this.stripeResponseHandler(data);
    });
  }

  stripeResponseHandler(response) {
    if (response.error) {
      // Show the errors on the form
      console.log('error');
      console.log(response.error.message);
    } else {
```

```
        // response contains id and card, which contains additional
card
        //details
        this.token = response.token.id;
        // Insert the token into the form so it gets submitted to the
server
        console.log('success');
        console.log('Sending token param:');
        console.log(this.token);
        this.nav.push(ThankyouPage, { token: this.token });
      }
    }
  }
```

You need to change your Test Publishable Key here by replacing YOUR STRIPE PUBLIC KEY HERE in Stripe Constructor with your own key that you copied earlier.

8. Edit ./src/pages/home/home.scss with the following code:

```
.page-home {
    .center {
        text-align: center;
    }
    .gray-bg {
        background-color: #f4f4f7;
    }
    .icon-large {
        font-size: 150px;
        color: #387ef5;
        opacity: 0.5;
    }
}
```

9. Create the thankyou page that shows the token ID by making a new folder, called ./src/pages/thankyou, as shown:

```
$ mkdir ./src/pages/thankyou
```

10. Create the thankyou.html file in the thankyou folder and copy the following code:

```
<ion-content class="green-bg">
  <h4 class="center">
    Your token is
  </h4>
  <p class="center">
```

```
        <code>
          {{ token }}
        </code>
      </p>
    </ion-content>
```

In reality, there is no need to show the token ID to the user. This is just an example to get the token ID to charge.

11. Create the `thankyou.ts` file in the `thankyou` folder and copy the following code:

```
import { Component } from '@angular/core';
import { NavController, NavParams } from 'ionic-angular';

@Component({
  selector: 'thank-you',
  templateUrl: 'thankyou.html'
})
export class ThankyouPage {
  private token: string = '';
  constructor(public nav: NavController, public params:
   NavParams) {
    this.token = this.params.get('token');
    console.log('Getting token param:');
    console.log(this.token);
  }

}
```

12. Create the `thankyou.scss` file to modify the theme using the following code:

```
thank-you {
    .green-bg {
        color: black;
        background-color: #32db64;
    }
    h4.center {
        padding-top: 150px;
    }
    .center {
        text-align: center;
    }
}
```

13. Open and edit `./src/app/app.module.ts` to declare `ThankyouPage` as follows:

```
import { NgModule } from '@angular/core';
import { IonicApp, IonicModule } from 'ionic-angular';
import { MyApp } from './app.component';
import { HomePage } from '../pages/home/home';
import { ThankyouPage } from '../pages/thankyou/thankyou'

@NgModule({
  declarations: [
    MyApp,
    HomePage,
    ThankyouPage
  ],
  imports: [
    IonicModule.forRoot(MyApp)
  ],
  bootstrap: [IonicApp],
  entryComponents: [
    MyApp,
    HomePage,
    ThankyouPage
  ],
  providers: []
})
export class AppModule {}
```

14. Go to your Terminal and run the app:

```
$ ionic serve
```

15. For the purpose of testing, you can use `4242424242424242` as the credit card number, `123` as `cvc`, and `12/2017` as the expiration.

How it works...

This is the Stripe charging process:

1. The user fills in the payment form and clicks on the **Submit** button.
2. The frontend (your Ionic app) will call API to Stripe using the `Stripe` object and send along all the payment information.
3. Stripe will return a token ID, which is basically a way to confirm that everything is correct and you can charge the card now.

4. The frontend will use the token ID to send to its backend (without the credit card information) to authorize the charge.
5. The backend will call another Stripe API to say *I'm going to charge now*. Stripe will return the `success` event to the backend at this point.
6. The backend will then return the `success` event to the frontend.
7. The frontend should render a new page, such as the `thankyou` page.

As discussed previously, this chapter will not cover the backend portion of this app because it doesn't focus on Ionic. You can build the backend using any language, such as Node.js, PHP, or Python.

Let's take a look at `home.ts` because the majority of Stripe API processing is located there. First, you need to do a `declare`, as illustrated, because `Stripe` is a global object that was included in the `index.html`:

```
declare var Stripe: any;
```

If you don't do a `declare`, the app will still run but you will get an error from TypeScript.

We are using Stripe Elements, which is pre-built set of UI Elements for payment. When our `home.ts` page is loaded, we initialize our Payment form using `ngOnInit` LikeCycle hook. Take a look at following code, inside `ngOnInt`:

```
this.card = this.elements.create('card', {style});
this.card.mount(this.cardElement.nativeElement);
```

We are creating a Stripe element card with a given style and then mounting that card to HTML element inside template using `this.card.mount`.

If you take a look at `home.html`, you will see something like this:

```
<div #cardElement>
 <!-- a Stripe Element will be inserted here. -->
</div>
```

We created a `div` in `home.html` with `#cardElement` local variable, and in `home.ts` we used `@ViewChild` decorator to get hold of it, and then mounted the `Stripe Element` UI on it. Mounting means creating an input field for card number, date of expiry, and CVV. `Stripe Element` also comes with its own validations and error messages.

When the user submits the form, it will trigger the following method:

```
onSubmit() {
    this.stripe.createToken(this.card)
    .then((data) => {
      this.stripeResponseHandler(data);
    });
  }
```

When you call `Stripe.card.createToken`, the Stripe object will trigger an API call in the background to `https://stripe.com/` with the information filled by the user via form. This functionality is accomplished by the following code in your `home.html`:

```
<button type="button" ion-button bottom block
  (click)="onSubmit()">Pay</button>
```

Once Stripe returns your token ID, it will call the
`this.stripeResponseHandler(response)` function:

```
    stripeResponseHandler(response) {
      if (response.error) {
        // Show the errors on the form
        console.log('error');
        console.log(response.error.message);
      } else {
        // response contains id and card, which contains additional card
details
        this.token = response.token.id;
        // Insert the token into the form so it gets submitted to the server
        console.log('success');
        console.log('Sending token param:');
        console.log(this.token);
        this.nav.push(ThankyouPage, { token: this.token });
      }
    }
```

The `response.token.id` will have your token ID from Stripe. Otherwise, you can handle the error using `response.error.message`. In this example, since it only passes the token ID to the next page, you can simply send it as a parameter `{token: this.token}`:

```
this.nav.push(ThankyouPage, {token: this.token});
```

In your `thankyou.ts`, you can access the parameter `token` using the following code:

```
this.params.get('token');
```

See also

- To understand more about Stripe API, you can check out the official documentation at `https://stripe.com/docs/stripe.js`
- To know more about Strip elements, you can take a look at `https://stripe.com/elements`
- There are more examples from other languages that you can experiment with at `https://stripe.com/docs/examples`

Adding Animation 5

In this chapter, we will cover the following tasks related to adding animation and interaction to the app:

- Embedding fullscreen inline video as background
- Creating physics-based animation using `Dynamics.js`
- Animating the slide component by binding gesture to animation state
- Adding background CSS animation to the login page

Introduction

User experience is crucial for the initial traction of users. When your early adopters use the app for the first time, they will have a better impression, which creates trust and increases retention. App animation will also provide interactive feedback for the users so that they know what to do or can take action based on very gentle visual hints.

Native apps used to have an advantage over web-based hybrid apps because of animation performance. However, frameworks such as Ionic and Angular have closed the gap in performance a lot in the recent years. Web animation is also easier to learn and code since many frontend developers are familiar with JavaScript and CSS.

In this chapter, you will learn how to do basic animation using video and CSS. Then, you will start utilizing physics-based animation to create interesting interactivity. Moreover, you could even bind the gesture frame by frame so that your animation happens instantly during a swipe event.

Embedding full screen inline video as background

Today, there are many apps that leverage video as an animated background for the introduction screen. This makes the app more interesting and creative. The users feel that they are welcomed to the app. This tactic is great to impress new users and encourage them to return.

This section will teach you how to add a video with autoplay in the background:

You will also learn how to use `animate.css` to add custom animation to the app header text.

Getting ready

This app example could work either in the browser or on a physical device. However, it's optional that you connect your physical device to verify that the animation plays correctly in the background.

How to do it...

The following are the instructions to add a video with autoplay in the background:

1. Create a new `VideoIntro` app using the `blank` template, as follows, and navigate to the `VideoIntro` folder:

   ```
   $ ionic start VideoIntro blank
   $ cd VideoIntro
   ```

2. You will need to have your video ready at this point. However, for this example, let's download a free video from a public website that does not require a license. Navigate to `http://www.coverr.co`.

3. You can download any video. The example in this app uses the `Blurry-People.mp4` clip. Download it to your computer:

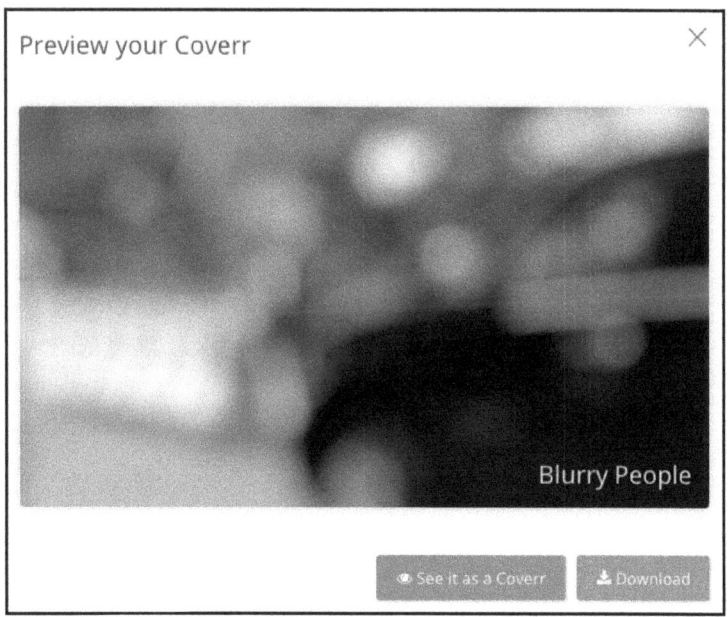

4. Save the videos in `./src/assets/`:

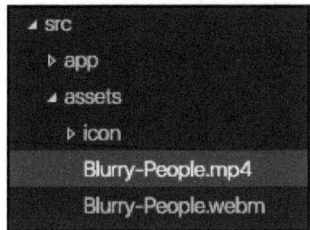

5. Open the `./src/index.html` file and replace the content with the following code:

```html
<!DOCTYPE html>
<html lang="en" dir="ltr">
<head>
  <meta charset="UTF-8">
  <title>Ionic App</title>
  <meta name="viewport" content="width=device-width,
    initial-scale=1.0, minimum-scale=1.0, maximum-scale=1.0,
    user-scalable=no">
  <meta name="format-detection" content="telephone=no">
  <meta name="msapplication-tap-highlight" content="no">

  <link rel="icon" type="image/x-icon"
    href="assets/icon/favicon.ico">
  <link rel="manifest" href="manifest.json">
  <meta name="theme-color" content="#4e8ef7">

  <!-- Google Fonts -->
  <link href='https://fonts.googleapis.com/css?family=Lobster'
rel='stylesheet' type='text/css'>
  <!-- cordova.js required for cordova apps -->
  <script src="cordova.js"></script>

  <!-- un-comment this code to enable service worker
  <script>
    if ('serviceWorker' in navigator) {
      navigator.serviceWorker.register('service-worker.js')
        .then(() => console.log('service worker installed'))
        .catch(err => console.log('Error', err));
    }
  </script>-->

  <link href="build/main.css" rel="stylesheet">
  <link rel="stylesheet"
```

```
href="https://cdnjs.cloudflare.com/ajax/libs/
animate.css/3.5.2/animate.min.css">

</head>
<body>

  <!-- Ionic's root component and where the app will
  load -->
  <ion-app></ion-app>

  <!-- The polyfills js is generated during the build
  process -->
  <script src="build/polyfills.js"></script>

  <!-- The bundle js is generated during the build
  process -->
  <script src="build/main.js"></script>

</body>
</html>
```

Basically, the main difference with the original `index.html` file is that you want to include the `Google Lobster` font for the heading text and `animate.css` for animation.

6. For the `main` template, you can modify the `./src/pages/home.html` file and replace it with the following code:

```
<ion-content class="home">
  <div class="fullscreen-bg">
    <video class="fullscreen-bg__video" autoplay loop
    muted webkit-playsinline><source src="assets/Blurry-
People.mp4"
      type='video/mp4; codecs="h.264"'><source src="assets/Blurry-
      People.webm"
      type="video/webm">
    </video>
  </div>
  <div class="center animated zoomIn">
    <h1>Beautiful App</h1>
    <h2>Fast. Easy. Cheap.</h2>
  </div>
</ion-content>
```

There are only two important items on this page: the video and the header with the subheader.

7. Open and edit the `./src/pages/home/home.scss` file in the same folder using the following code:

```scss
page-home {
    .home {
        font-family: 'Lobster', cursive;
        color: white;
        text-shadow: 1px 0 0 gray, -1px 0 0 gray, 0 1px 0 gray, 0
-1px 0 gray, 1px 1px gray, -1px -1px 0 gray, 1px -1px 0 gray, -1px
1px 0 gray;
        h1 {
            font-size: 5rem;
        }
    }
    .fullscreen-bg {
        position: fixed;
        top: 0;
        right: 0;
        bottom: 0;
        left: 0;
        overflow: hidden;
        z-index: -100;
    }
    .fullscreen-bg__video {
        position: absolute;
        top: 0;
        left: 0;
        height: 100%;
    }
    .center {
        top: 50%;
        transform: translateY(-50%);
        position: absolute !important;
        text-align: center;
        width: 100%;
    }
}
```

All animation is done using CSS; thus, you don't need to write any code for the JavaScript file.

8. Open the `config.xml` file, and add the following line within the `<widget>` tag:

```
<preference name="AllowInlineMediaPlayback" value="true"/>
```

9. Go to your terminal and run the app with the following command:

```
$ ionic serve
```

How it works...

Let's start with the `home.html` file because that is the only page where you added the animation:

```
<video class="fullscreen-bg__video" autoplay loop muted
  webkit-playsinline>  <source src="assets/Blurry-People.mp4"
    type='video/mp4; codecs="h.264"' >
  <source src="assets/Blurry-People.webm" type="video/webm">
</video>
```

The preceding tag is just a typical `<video>` tag in HTML5. However, there is a new attribute, called `webkit-playsinline`. This means that you want the video to play where it is on the HTML page and not open it up fullscreen with the play control. The reason is that you want this video to play in the background, while you can animate text on top of it. This is the reason you need to enable this feature by setting `AllowInlineMediaPlayback` in `config.xml`.

The second item in this template is your header and subheader, as follows:

```
<div class="center animated zoomIn">
  <h1>Beautiful App</h1>
  <h2>Fast. Easy. Cheap.</h2>
</div>
```

Note that there are `animated` and `zoomIn` classes included. These are the required classes for `animate.css` to kick in. If you run the app now, you will see the text starting to appear from a smaller size to a bigger size (that is, a zoom-in effect).

The `home.scss` file is important because it has a lot of animation logic. Let's take a look at the header text first:

```
.home {
  font-family: 'Lobster', cursive;
  color: white;
  text-shadow: 1px 0 0 gray, -1px 0 0 gray, 0 1px 0 gray,
```

```
    0 -1px 0 gray, 1px 1px gray, -1px -1px 0 gray, 1px -1px
    0 gray, -1px 1px 0 gray;
  h1 {
    font-size: 5rem;
  }
}
```

One interesting thing here is the use of the `text-shadow` attribute. This is because you want to create a thin border line around the text so that your white text can be easily seen on top of a light background.

To set the video to fullscreen, you will need it to have a negative index so that it's below the other layers. Also, the height must be 100%, as follows:

```
.fullscreen-bg {
  position: fixed;
  top: 0;
  right: 0;
  bottom: 0;
  left: 0;
  overflow: hidden;
  z-index: -100;
}

.fullscreen-bg__video {
  position: absolute;
  top: 0;
  left: 0;
  height: 100%;
}
```

Finally, in order to position the text vertically in the center, you have to create the following class:

```
.center {
  top: 50%;
  transform: translateY(-50%);
  position: absolute !important;
  text-align: center;
  width:100%;
}
```

The `center` class forces the element to have top of `50%` but then pushes the Y position `-50%` to reset the vertical pivot of the `<div>` tag in the middle area. You will rarely need to customize such classes; thus, it's good to keep the `center` class handy for future use.

Creating physics-based animation using Dynamics.js

Using physics-based animations can make your app more interactive and lively, which helps attract and retain more users. There are many methods to add physics to your component animation. For example, you could even use the CSS `animation-timing` function to add property values, such as `ease-in`, `ease-out`, or `cubic-bezier`. However, it's easier and better to use an existing JavaScript-based physic animation. `Dynamics.js` is one of those JavaScript libraries that comes with utilities and performance. Using native CSS physic features is actually not a good practice, as it comes with a frame-per-second penalty on mobile devices.

The app will show a bouncing button, which can show and hide a top quote box, as follows; it also uses physics animation:

Getting ready

This app example could work either in a browser or on a physical device. However, it's recommended that you run the app via your physical device to test for performance.

How to do it...

The following are the instructions:

1. Open a terminal window, create a new `SpinningButton` app using the `blank` template, and navigate to the `SpinningButton` folder:

```
$ ionic start SpinningButton blank
$ cd SpinningButton
```

2. Install `dynamics.js` using `npm`, as follows:

```
npm install dynamics.js --save
```

3. Open and edit the `./src/pages/home/home.html` file to replace the content with the following:

```
<ion-content class="home">
  <div class="my-card" #myCard>
    <h1>QUOTE</h1>
```

```
      <p class="body">Always remember that you are absolutely unique.
      Just like everyone else.</p>
      <p class="name">Margaret Mead</p>
    </div>
  </ion-content>
  <ion-fab center bottom>
    <button ion-fab #thisEl (click)="animateMe(thisEl)">
      <ion-icon name="mic"></ion-icon>
    </button>
  </ion-fab>
```

There is no need to have header navigation in this app because it will just be a single page.

4. Open the `home.ts` file to edit in the same folder as step 2 using the following code:

```
import { Component, ViewChild } from '@angular/core';
import { NavController } from 'ionic-angular';
import * as dynamics from 'dynamics.js';

@Component({
  selector: 'page-home',
  templateUrl: 'home.html'
})
export class HomePage {
  private isAnimating: Boolean = false;
  private isQuoteShown: Boolean = false;
  @ViewChild('myCard') myCard;
  constructor(public navCtrl: NavController) {
  }
  animateMe(el) {
    if (!this.isAnimating) {
      this.isAnimating = true;
      dynamics.animate(el._elementRef.nativeElement, {
        translateY: -50
      }, {
        type: dynamics.bounce,
        duration: 1300,
        complete: () => {
          console.log('Done animating button.');
          this.isAnimating = false;
        }
      });
      if (!this.isQuoteShown) {
        dynamics.animate(this.myCard.nativeElement, {
          translateY: 0
```

```
    }, {
        type: dynamics.spring,
        duration: 1300,
        complete: () => {
          console.log('Done animating drop down.');
          this.isAnimating = false;
        }
      });
      this.isQuoteShown = true;
    } else {
      dynamics.animate(this.myCard.nativeElement, {
        translateY: -150
      }, {
        type: dynamics.easeOut,
        duration: 900,
        friction: 50,
        complete: () => {
          console.log('Done animating drop down.');
          this.isAnimating = false;
        }
      });
      this.isQuoteShown = false;
    }
  }
}


}
```

Note that you must import the `dynamics` using ES6 import syntax.

5. Modify the `home.scss` stylesheet, as follows:

```
page-home {
    ion-content.home {
      background-color: #ecf0f1;
    }
    .my-card {
      color: white;
      transform: translate(0,-150px);
      background: #9b59b6;
      height: 150px;
      padding: 10px;
      h1 {
        font-size: 4rem;
        font-weight: 100;
        margin: 0;
      }
      p {
```

```
            color: white;
        }
        p.body {
          font-size: 16px;
          line-height: 1.5em;
          margin-bottom: 0;
          margin-top: 5px;
        }
        p.name {
          font-size: 14px;
          font-weight: bold;
          text-align: right;
          margin-top: 5px;
        }
      }
    }
  }
```

6. Navigate to your terminal, and run the app with the following command:

```
$ ionic serve
```

How it works...

The main concept behind the physics animation in this app is the `dynamics.animate` method from the `Dynamics.js` library. Let's start with the button in the template, as follows:

```
<ion-fab center bottom>
  <button ion-fab #thisEl (click)="animateMe(thisEl)">
    <ion-icon name="mic"></ion-icon>
  </button>
</ion-fab>
```

The button mentioned in the preceding code is the floating button that you can click to create a nice bouncing effect by calling the `animateMe()` method.

 To learn more about Ionic's floating button, you can refer to the Ionic documentation at
`http://ionicframework.com/docs/components/#floating-action-butto ns`.

The simple logic here is as follows:

- If the button is animated, `isAnimating` must be `True`. Once it's `True`, any additional click will not trigger the animation since we don't want the physics to kick in multiple times.
- If the top quote bar is displayed, `isQuoteShown` must be `True`. Otherwise, it will call a different animation to hide it.

You can pass many options to the `dynamics.animate` method. For example, the button will use `dynamics.bounce` as the type; thus, it will bounce up and down on each click. You can also specify the duration to be applied to the animation process itself. After the animation is done, it will trigger the callback in the `complete` function, as illustrated:

```
dynamics.animate(el._elementRef.nativeElement, {
  translateY: -50
}, {
  type: dynamics.bounce,
  duration: 1300,
  complete: () => {
    console.log('Done animating button.');
    this.isAnimating = false;
  }
});
```

An important thing to keep in mind is that `Dynamics.js` must refer to the DOM JavaScript object itself and not the DOM node or Ionic object. That's why you have to use `el._elementRef.nativeElement` to point to the native element object instead.

For the quote box, it creates a local variable, called `myCard`, in the template, as follows:

```
<div class="my-card" #myCard>
  <h1>QUOTE</h1>
  <p class="body">Always remember that you are absolutely unique.
  Just like everyone else.</p>
  <p class="name">Margaret Mead</p>
</div>
```

You must refer to this variable using the `ViewChild` decorator, as shown, so that `@Page` knows to include it as a dependency:

```
@ViewChild('myCard') myCard;
```

See also

If you are interested in learning more about native CSS physics-based animation, visit `https://developer.mozilla.org/en-US/docs/Web/CSS/animation-timing-function`.

Animating the slide component by binding a gesture to the animation state

Another way to get a *wow* experience from users is to have great-looking introduction slides. A typical app would have three to five slides to describe what the app does and how it will benefit the users. Today, many apps even add videos or interactive screens so that the users can get a *feel* for how the app may work. Such an interactive animation will require some internal development to bind touch gestures to the animation state. Animating based on a specific state is very difficult because you really have to get granular gesture data. On the other hand, it's a lot easier to just animate at the beginning or end of a state. For example, you could animate an object inside a slide when the slide completely shows up on the screen after a left swipe. However, this animation effect is not as interesting or attractive as binding the animation during the touch movement.

The app you will build in this section will have three slides that will animate when you swipe left or right:

You will see fade in and fade out animation effects between slides; the following Angular logo also moves up when you swipe left from the second slide:

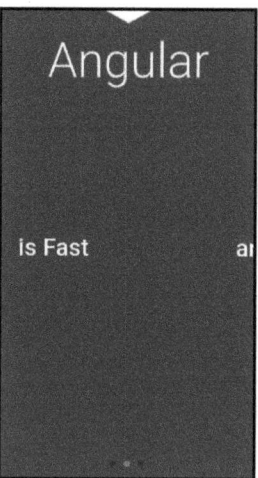

Getting ready

There is no need to test the app on a physical device because the animation is done via HTML and JavaScript. However, it's recommended that you test the app on your device to evaluate the animation performance.

How to do it...

The following are the instructions:

1. Create a new `SliderAnimation` app using the `blank` template, as follows, and go to the `SliderAnimation` folder:

```
$ ionic start SliderAnimation blank
$ cd SliderAnimation
```

2. Open the `./src/pages/home/home.html` file and modify its content using the following code:

```html
<ion-content class="home">
  <div class="slides-float">
    <div class="slide-float" #slidefloat1>
      <ion-icon name="ios-ionic"></ion-icon>
      <h1>Ionic</h1>
    </div>
    <div class="slide-float" #slidefloat2>
      <ion-icon name="logo-angular"></ion-icon>
      <h1>Angular</h1>
    </div>
    <div class="slide-float" #slidefloat3>
      <ion-icon name="logo-javascript"></ion-icon>
      <h1>Both</h1>
    </div>
  </div>
  <ion-slides #myslides pager (ionSlideDrag)="onMove()">
    <ion-slide>
      <h2>is Beautiful</h2>
    </ion-slide>
    <ion-slide>
      <h2>is Fast</h2>
    </ion-slide>
    <ion-slide>
      <h2>are Awesome</h2>
    </ion-slide>
  </ion-slides>
</ion-content>
```

The preceding template mainly uses the `<ion-slides>` tag. However, there are some layers to float on top of the `<ion-slide>` tag in order to animate them separately.

3. After this, replace the content of `./src/pages/home/home.ts` with the following code:

```typescript
import { Component, ViewChild } from '@angular/core';
import { NavController } from 'ionic-angular';

@Component({
  selector: 'page-home',
  templateUrl: 'home.html'
})
export class HomePage {
```

```
@ViewChild('myslides') myslides;
@ViewChild('slidefloat1') slidefloat1;
@ViewChild('slidefloat2') slidefloat2;
@ViewChild('slidefloat3') slidefloat3;
private rAf: any;
private bindOnProgress: boolean = false;
constructor(public navCtrl: NavController) {
  this.rAf = (function () {
    return (window as any).requestAnimationFrame || (window as
      any).webkitRequestAnimationFrame || (window as
        any).mozRequestAnimationFrame ||
    function (callback) {
      window.setTimeout(callback, 1000 / 60);
    };
  })();
}

onMove() {
  if (!this.bindOnProgress) {
    this.bindOnProgress = true;

    this.myslides.ionSlideProgress
    .subscribe(progress => {
      // (0, 1) - (0.25, 0) ==> (0-1)/(0.25-0) => -1/0.25 * x + 1
      let firstQuarter = () => {
        let slidefloat1Opacity = -1 / 0.25 * progress + 1;
        console.log('slidefloat1Opacity: ' + slidefloat1Opacity);
        this.slidefloat1.nativeElement.style.opacity =
slidefloat1Opacity;
        this.slidefloat2.nativeElement.style.opacity = 0;
      }
      // (0.25, 0) - (0.5, 1) ==> (1-0)/(0.5-0.25) => 1 / 0.25 *
x - 1 = 4
      * x - 1
      let secondQuarter = () => {
        let slidefloat2Opacity = 4 * progress - 1;
        console.log('slidefloat2Opacity: ' + slidefloat2Opacity);
        this.slidefloat2.nativeElement.style.opacity =
slidefloat2Opacity;
        this.slidefloat2.nativeElement.style.transform =
'translateY(0px)';
        this.slidefloat1.nativeElement.style.opacity = 0;
      }
      // (0.5, 0) - (0.75, -250) ==> (-250-0)/(0.75-0.5) = -250 /
0.25 =>
        -1000 * x + 500
      let thirdQuarter = () => {
        let slidefloat2transform = -1000 * progress +500;
```

```
            console.log('slidefloat2transform: ' +
slidefloat2transform);
            this.slidefloat2.nativeElement.style.transform =
'translateY(' +
        slidefloat2transform + 'px)';
            this.slidefloat3.nativeElement.style.opacity = 0;
        }
        // (0.75, 0) - (1, 1) ==> (1-0)/(1-0.75) => 1/0.25 * x -
0.75 * 4 = 4
        * x - 3
        let fourthQuarter = () => {
            let slidefloat3Opacity = 4 * progress - 3;
            console.log('slidefloat3Opacity: ' + slidefloat3Opacity);
            this.slidefloat3.nativeElement.style.opacity =
slidefloat3Opacity;
            this.slidefloat2.nativeElement.style.transform =
'translateY(-250px)';
        }

        // Animate per quarter of the total 3 slides
        if (progress <= 0.25) {
          this.rAf(firstQuarter);
        } else if ((progress > 0.25) && (progress <= 0.5)) {
          this.rAf(secondQuarter);
        } else if ((progress > 0.5) && (progress <= 0.75)) {
          this.rAf(thirdQuarter);
        } else if ((progress > 0.75) && (progress <= 1)) {
          this.rAf(fourthQuarter);
        }
      });
    }
  }

}
```

Note that the comments are used to calculate an animation formula for each object.

4. Edit `./app/pages/home/home.scss` with the following code:

```
page-home {
    .slides-float {
        .slide-float {
            top: 0;
            position: fixed;
            width: 100%;
            margin-top: 20px;
```

```
        opacity: 0;
    }
}
.home {
    background-color: DarkSlateBlue;
    h2 {
        font-size: 3rem;
    }
    ion-slide {
        color: white;
        background-color: transparent;
    }
    .slides-float {
        color: white;
        text-align: center;
        :first-child {
            opacity: 1;
        }
    }
    .slide-float {
        ion-icon {
            font-size: 150px;
        }
        h1 {
            font-weight: lighter;
            font-size: 60px;
            margin-top: 0;
        }
    }
}
```

5. Go to your Terminal, and run the app with the following command:

```
$ ionic serve
```

How it works...

The following is the general process of animation:

- Since there are three slides, the user has to swipe twice to reach the end. This means that the first swipe will be at 50% progress.
- When a user swipes left to 25%, the Ionic logo will fade out.

- When a user swipes to 50%, the Angular logo will fade in for the second slide.
- When a user swipes to 75%, the Angular logo will move up to disappear instead of fading out.
- Finally, in the last 75% to 100%, the JavaScript logo will fade in.

You probably noted that the amount of fade or movement will depend on the progress percentage. Thus, if you swipe left and right a little bit, you can see the animation responding to the gesture right away. There are two *layers* in the template. The *floating* static layer, as illustrated, must be on top and it must stay at the same position regardless of the slide that is currently shown:

```
<div class="slides-float">
  <div class="slide-float" #slidefloat1>
    <ion-icon name="ios-ionic"></ion-icon>
    <h1>Ionic</h1>
  </div>

  <div class="slide-float" #slidefloat2>
    <ion-icon name="logo-angular"></ion-icon>
    <h1>Angular</h1>
  </div>

  <div class="slide-float" #slidefloat3>
    <ion-icon name="logo-javascript"></ion-icon>
    <h1>Both</h1>
  </div>

</div>
```

The bottom layer is your typical `<ion-slides>`:

```
<ion-slides #myslides pager (ionSlideDrag)="onMove()">
  <ion-slide>
    <h2>is Beautiful</h2>
  </ion-slide>
  <ion-slide>
    <h2>is Fast</h2>
  </ion-slide>
  <ion-slide>
    <h2>are Awesome</h2>
  </ion-slide>
</ion-slides>
```

When you swipe, it's actually moving <ion-slide>. However, it also triggers the
onMove() method because you bind it with the move event. The onMove() method will
access #slidefloat1, #slidefloat2, and #slidefloat3 from the floating <div> layer.
The home.ts file is where you have to animate these individual floating slides.

There are several variables that you need to declare in the home.ts file. You will need to be
able to access the <ion-slides> object in order to call the *native* Swiper methods:

```
@ViewChild('myslides') myslides;
```

According to the Ionic documentation, the <ion-slides> object is written based on the
Swiper library; you can find more information at
http://ionicframework.com/docs/v2/api/components/slides/Slides/.

You need to bind it with the swiping event natively in order to get the correct progress data.

The following three variables are necessary to access each floating slide:

```
@ViewChild('slidefloat1') slidefloat1;
@ViewChild('slidefloat2') slidefloat2;
@ViewChild('slidefloat3') slidefloat3;
```

You need to leverage requestAnimationFrame, as follows, for the best animation
performance:

```
private rAf: any;
```

Otherwise, users will sense a *jerky* movement during a swipe because your animation is not
at 60 FPS.

Finally, you will need to bind the swipe event only once; thus, it's necessary to have a
Boolean toggle to detect the binding event:

```
private bindOnProgress: boolean = false;
```

The following code shows how to create a requestAnimationFrame object to call
whichever function is to be rendered later:

```
this.rAf = (function(){
  return  (window as any).requestAnimationFrame || (window as
  any).webkitRequestAnimationFrame || (window as
  any).mozRequestAnimationFrame ||
    function( callback ){
      window.setTimeout(callback, 1000 / 60);
    };
})();
```

The `onMove()` method is where you put all the animation logic, which must subscribe to `ionSlideProgress` Observable, as follows:

```
this.myslides.ionSlideProgress
.subscribe(progress => {
    . . .
});
```

First, let's take a look at the code at the bottom of `onMove()`, as follows:

```
if (progress <= 0.25) {
  this.rAf(firstQuarter);
} else if ((progress > 0.25) && (progress <= 0.5 )) {
  this.rAf(secondQuarter);
} else if ((progress > 0.5) && (progress <= 0.75 )) {
  this.rAf(thirdQuarter);
} else if ((progress > 0.75) && (progress <= 1 )) {
  this.rAf(fourthQuarter);
}
```

Basically, you will want to have four quarters (or segments) of animation. When you swipe from slide 1 to slide 2, it will trigger the `firstQuarter` and `secondQuarter` methods. That is, you will want to fade out the first floating slide and fade in the second floating slide at the end of the process. The concept is similar to the `thirdQuarter` and `fourthQuarter` methods. Note that you don't want to call the method directly but just pass the function reference inside `this.rAf` to have the rendering engine manage the frame rate. Otherwise, the rendered function may end up blocking other processes in the UI, which causes jerky movement.

For each of the quarters, you only have to change the `style` property, given a known **progress value**, as follows:

```
let firstQuarter = () => {
  let slidefloat1Opacity = -1/0.25 * progress + 1;
  console.log('slidefloat1Opacity: ' + slidefloat1Opacity);
  this.slidefloat1.nativeElement.style.opacity =
   slidefloat1Opacity;
  this.slidefloat2.nativeElement.style.opacity = 0;
}
```

It's important to use the arrow function here so that you can access the `this` context. You have to call `this.slidefloat2.nativeElement` to get to the `<div>` DOM object. It's really up to you to write your own `math` function to calculate the position or opacity during the slide movement with the progress value. In this example, the `slidefloat1Opacity` variable is just a linear function based on the `progress` input value.

The secondQuarter follows the same approach. However, thirdQuarter uses the transform property instead of opacity, as illustrated:

```
let thirdQuarter = () => {
  let slidefloat2transform = -1000 * progress + 500;
  console.log('slidefloat2transform: ' + slidefloat2transform);
  this.slidefloat2.nativeElement.style.transform = 'translateY(' +
   slidefloat2transform + 'px)';
  this.slidefloat3.nativeElement.style.opacity = 0;
}
```

There are many ways to make a DOM object change its position. However, it's best to leverage the transform property instead of using the left and top properties. You want to achieve the highest Frame Per Second. In the thirdQuarter method, your slidefloat2transform will be calculated, and it will update a new Y position using translateY().

Note that you must use this.bindOnProgress to disable another event binding to onProgress because, for each swipe, it will continue to add more events.

See also

- To understand more about requestAnimationFrame, you can check out the official documentation at
  https://developer.mozilla.org/en-US/docs/Web/API/window/requestAnimationFrame
- The Swiper API is located at http://idangero.us/swiper/api/
- Ionic has an official usage example at
  http://ionicframework.com/docs/components/#slides
- Ionic also provides a limited number of API for slides at
  http://ionicframework.com/docs/api/components/slides/Slides/

Adding a background CSS animation to the login page

Animation can also be completely done in CSS. In many cases, you will probably run into some interesting demos online and would like to incorporate the CSS-only code for animation. If the animation is not as critical to the user experience, you could just use to add additional effects to the app. CSS animation is great because you don't have to write JavaScript code to manage the animation and just leave the browser to process it.

In this section, you will build an app to show some floating squares in the background of your login page, as follows:

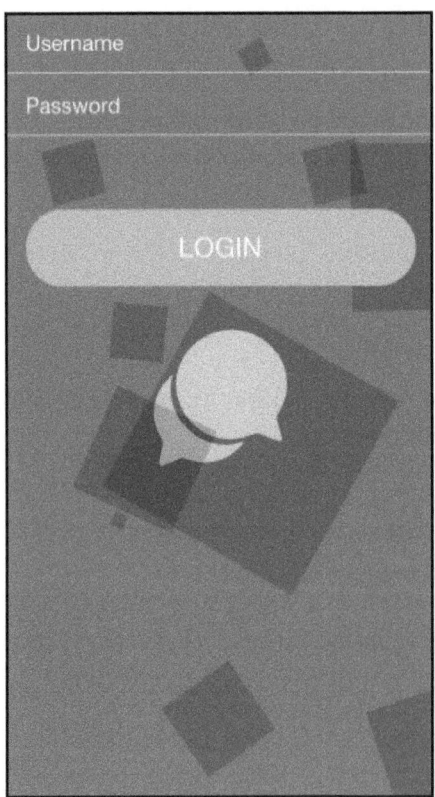

Getting ready

There is no need to test it in a physical device because CSS animation will work just fine in the Ionic app.

How to do it...

The following are the instructions:

1. Create a new `BubbleLogin` app using the `blank` template, as follows, and navigate to the `BubbleLogin` folder:

```
$ ionic start BubbleLogin blank
$ cd BubbleLogin
```

2. Open the `./src/pages/home/home.html` file and modify the content with the following code:

```
<ion-content #myContent class="home">
  <ul class="bg-bubbles">
    <li></li>
    <li></li>
    <li></li>
    <li></li>
    <li></li>
    <li></li>
    <li></li>
    <li></li>
    <li></li>
    <li></li>
  </ul>
  <ion-list>
    <ion-item>
      <ion-label>Username</ion-label>
      <ion-input type="text"></ion-input>
    </ion-item>
    <ion-item class="input-password">
      <ion-label>Password</ion-label>
      <ion-input type="password"></ion-input>
    </ion-item>
  </ion-list>
  <div padding>
    <button ion-button block round color="secondary">LOGIN</button>
  </div>
```

```
    <p class="logo">
      <ion-icon name="ios-chatbubbles"></ion-icon>
    </p>
  </ion-content>
```

The `bg-bubbles` class will convert a list of `<li>` into floating squares pieces.

3. Edit `./src/pages/home/home.scss` with the following code:

```scss
page-home {
    .home {
        background-color: SeaGreen;
        .logo {
            margin: 0;
            color: white;
            font-size: 100px;
            text-align: center;
        }
        scroll-content {
            overflow-y: hidden;
        }
        .item {
            background-color: transparent;
        }
        .item-input ion-label, .item-select ion-label, input.text-
    input {
            color: white;
        }
        ion-list > .item:first-child {
            border-top: 0;
            border-bottom: 1px solid white;
        }
        ion-list > .item:first-child .item-inner {
            margin-right: 8px;
        }
        ion-list .item-inner {
            border-bottom: 0;
        }
        .input-password {
            border-bottom: 1px solid white!important;
            item-inner {
                border-bottom: 1px solid white;
                margin-right: 8px;
            }
        }
    }
    .bg-bubbles {
        position: absolute;
```

```
top: 0;
left: 0;
width: 100%;
height: 100%;
z-index: 0;
li {
    position: absolute;
    list-style: none;
    display: block;
    width: 40px;
    height: 40px;
    background-color: black;
    opacity: 0.2;
    bottom: -160px;
    -webkit-animation: square 25s infinite;
    animation: square 25s infinite;
    -webkit-transition-timing-function: linear;
    transition-timing-function: linear;
    &:nth-child(1) {
        left: 10%;
    }
    &:nth-child(2) {
        left: 20%;
        width: 80px;
        height: 80px;
        animation-delay: 2s;
        animation-duration: 17s;
    }
    &:nth-child(3) {
        left: 25%;
        animation-delay: 4s;
    }
    &:nth-child(4) {
        left: 40%;
        width: 60px;
        height: 60px;
        animation-duration: 22s;
        background-color: black;
    }
    &:nth-child(5) {
        left: 70%;
    }
    &:nth-child(6) {
        left: 80%;
        width: 120px;
        height: 120px;
        animation-delay: 3s;
        background-color: black;
```

```
            }
            &:nth-child(7) {
                left: 32%;
                width: 160px;
                height: 160px;
                animation-delay: 7s;
            }
            &:nth-child(8) {
                left: 55%;
                width: 20px;
                height: 20px;
                animation-delay: 15s;
                animation-duration: 40s;
            }
            &:nth-child(9) {
                left: 25%;
                width: 10px;
                height: 10px;
                animation-delay: 2s;
                animation-duration: 40s;
                background-color: black;
            }
            &:nth-child(10) {
                left: 90%;
                width: 160px;
                height: 160px;
                animation-delay: 11s;
            }
        }
    }
    @-webkit-keyframes square {
        0% {
            transform: translateY(0);
        }
        100% {
            transform: translateY(-700px) rotate(600deg);
        }
    }
    @keyframes square {
        0% {
            transform: translateY(0);
        }
        100% {
            transform: translateY(-700px) rotate(600deg);
        }
    }
}
```

4. Go to your terminal, and run the app with the following command:

```
$ ionic serve
```

How it works...

Since this app does not use JavaScript for animation, you will not need to modify anything in home.ts.

The CSS will drive the animation infinitely with the following code:

```
animation: square 25s infinite;
transition-timing-function: linear;
```

You will also be using two points in the square keyframe:

```
@keyframes square {
  0%   { transform: translateY(0); }
  100% { transform: translateY(-700px) rotate(600deg); }
}
```

So, for a 0% to 100% loop, it will move 700 px vertically and rotate 600 degrees in the duration.

The reason that each square has a different size and speed is that you can customize the CSS as per the <li> tag further. Consider the following example:

```
&:nth-child(2) {
  left: 20%;
  width: 80px;
  height: 80px;
  animation-delay: 2s;
  animation-duration: 17s;
}
```

Since this animation does not generate a random number of square objects and there are a limited number of objects, you could write a customization for each <li> tag in the CSS.

Note that you have to put the animation with z-index: 0 because it will stay above other layers, such as form and button.

See also

To understand more about CSS keyframes, you can check out the Mozilla documentation at `https://developer.mozilla.org/en-US/docs/Web/CSS/@keyframes`.

6
User Authentication and Push Notifications

In this chapter, we will cover the following tasks related to authenticating users, and register and receiving push notification messages:

- Registering and authenticating users using Auth0
- Building an iOS app to receive push notifications
- Building an Android app to receive push notifications

Introduction

Tracking and engaging users are key features necessary for your app to grow. That means you should be able to register and authenticate users. Once the users start using the app, you also need to segment the users so that you can customize their interactions. Then, you can send push notifications to encourage users to revisit the app.

There are two components that you need to use for your project, as follows:

- **Auth0**: Auth0 is a cloud-based authentication service. The whole idea is that you delegate authentication of your application to Auth0. Auth0 supports many frameworks, including Ionic2+, and also supports many social providers for authentication such as Google and Facebook. On the top of that, they have excellent documentation.
- **OneSignal**: OneSignal is a service that allows us to send the push notification to both iOS and Android. As a matter of fact, it supports other platforms such as Windows, Web Push Notifications, Amazon Fire, and so on. The best part is, in general, we need different code for adding push notifications. But because of Cordova and OneSignal's abstract API, we only need to write push notification code once for both platforms.

Registering and authenticating users using Auth0

Auth0 can provide all of the user management and authentication capabilities out of the box. There are lots of providers supported by Auth0. Following are some famous providers that are supported by Auth0:

- Email/password
- Facebook
- Google
- Twitter
- Instagram
- LinkedIn
- GitHub

Depending on the app, you may not need to use all of these authentication methods. For example, it would make more sense to use a LinkedIn authentication for an app focusing on a working professional to narrow down the audiences who fit the user profile of the app.

In this chapter, we will try to simplify the authentication concept as much as possible. You will learn how to do the following things:

- Registering a new user
- Logging in and logging out a user
- Showing a user's profile information

Getting ready

You need the device to test the app because we are using Cordova plugins for authentication, which requires either device or simulator to run the app.

How to do it...

We will do it in two ways:

- Creating an app in the Auth0 dashboard
- Coding our Ionic app

Creating our app in the Auth0 dashboard

In this section, we are going to learn how we can create an app in the Auth0 dashboard. Do the following steps:

1. Go to `https://auth0.com` and create an account there.

2. After creating an account, it will open Auth0 dashboard. There is a **New Application** button. Click on it, and it will open the following dialog:

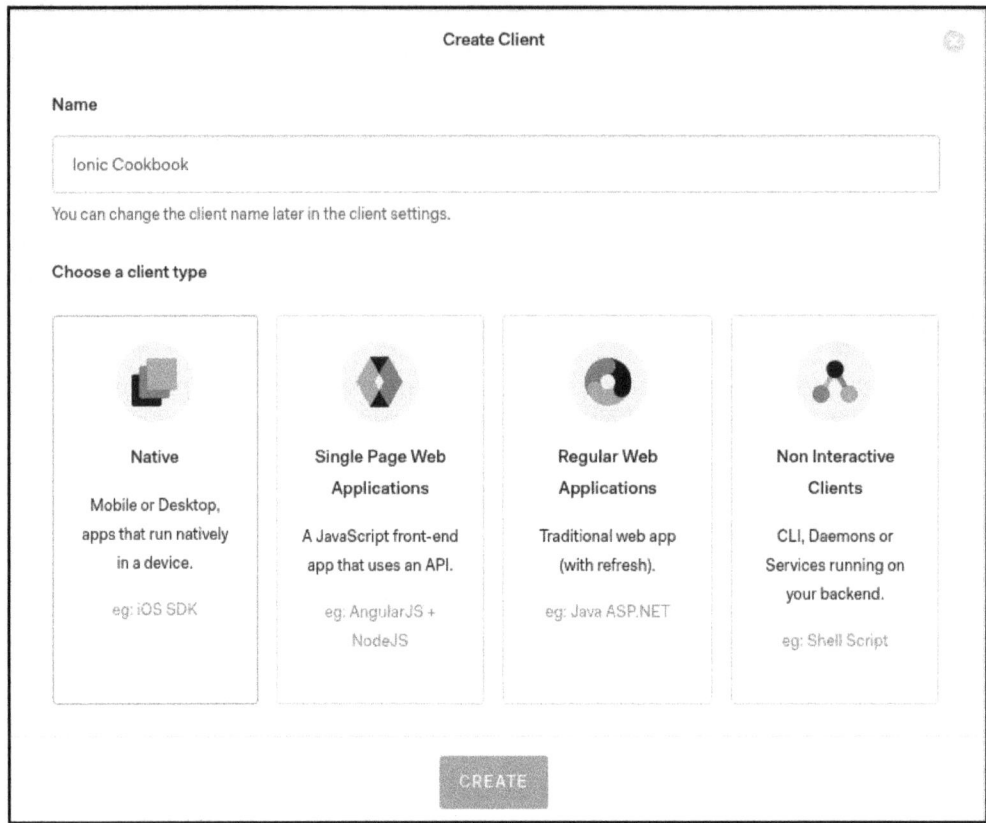

Choose a **Name** for your client and select the client type as **Native**.

3. Now, in the side menu **Dashboard**, click on **Applications** and select the Application that you created. You will see the following page:

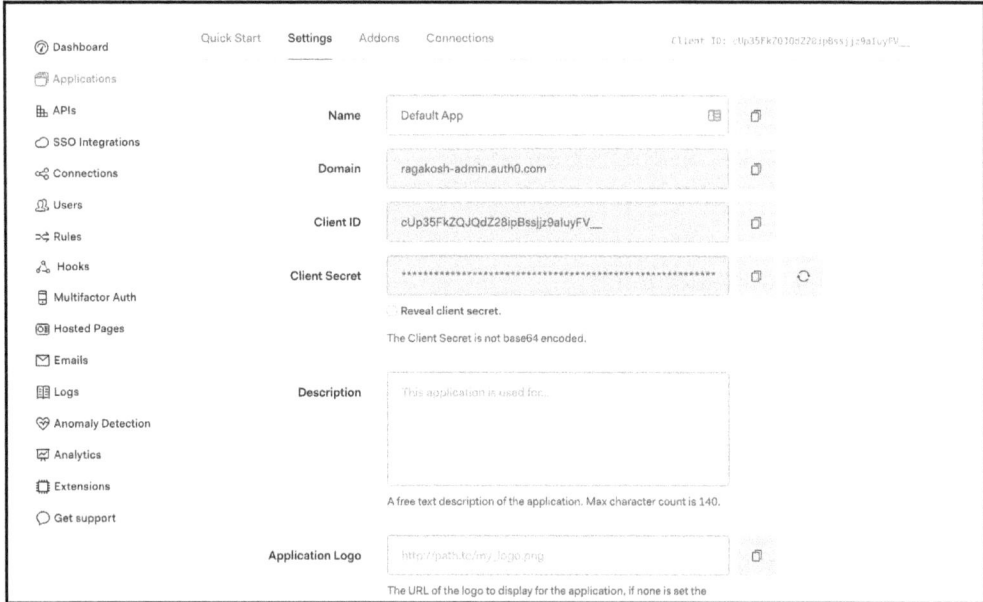

We need **Domain** and **Client ID** later in the app, so save them somewhere.

4. On the same page, in the **Allowed Callback URLs** input, add `YOUR_PACKAGE_ID://YOUR_DOMAIN/cordova/YOUR_PACKAGE_ID/callback`. Replace **YOUR_PACKAGE_ID** with the package ID of your app, and **YOUR DOMAIN** is the domain that you saved in the previous step.

5. Also, in the **Allowed Origins(CORS)** input, add `file://`.

With the latest Ionic, they are using WKWebView plugin by default, which servers the app from a local web server at `https://localhost:8080`. So you have to add it too in the Allowed Origin(CORS) section. If you are not going to use WKWebView, you don't have to add it.

6. Hit **Save Changes**.

Let's code

Now that we have already created our app in the Auth0 dashboard, it's time to write the code for it. Take the following steps:

1. Now, create a new `MySimpleAuth` app using the `blank` template, as shown in the following code, and go to the `MySimpleAuth` folder:

```
$ ionic start MySimpleAuth blank
$ cd MySimpleAuth
```

2. Install `auth0.js` and `auth0/cordova` npm packages, which are required for Auth0 authentication:

```
$ npm install auth0-js @auth0/cordova --save
```

3. We also need to install the following `Cordova` plugin:

```
$ ionic cordova plugin add cordova-plugin-safariviewcontroller
```

```
$ ionic cordova plugin add cordova-plugin-customurlscheme --variable
URL_SCHEME={YOUR_PACKAGE_ID} --variable
ANDROID_SCHEME={YOUR_PACKAGE_ID} --variable ANDROID_HOST={YOUR_DOMAIN}
--variable ANDROID_PATHPREFIX=/cordova/{YOUR_PACKAGE_ID}/callback
```

 You should change `{YOUR_PACKAGE_ID}` to your app's package ID, and `{YOUR_DOMAIN}` to your domain from Auth0 that you saved earlier in the third step.

4. You also have to add the following line to `config.xml`:

```
<preference name="AndroidLaunchMode" value="singleTask" />
```

5. Create a file at `./src/providers/auth/auth.ts` with the following code:

```
import { Injectable, NgZone } from '@angular/core';
import { Observable, Subscription } from 'rxjs';

import Auth0Cordova from '@auth0/cordova';
import Auth0 from 'auth0-js';

const auth0Config = {
  // needed for auth0
  clientID: 'sIQavE9jev8VXOTQkeb2Cn62m9s9faLN',
```

```
  // needed for auth0cordova
  clientId: 'sIQavE9jev8VXOTQkeb2Cn62m9s9faLN',
  domain: 'imtest.auth0.com',
  callbackURL: location.href,
  packageIdentifier: 'io.ionic.imtest'
};

@Injectable()
export class AuthProvider {
  auth0 = new Auth0.WebAuth(auth0Config);
  accessToken: string;
  idToken: string;
  user: any;

  constructor(public zone: NgZone) {
    this.user = this.getStorageVariable('profile');
    this.idToken = this.getStorageVariable('id_token');
  }

  private getStorageVariable(name) {
    return JSON.parse(window.localStorage.getItem(name));
  }

  private setStorageVariable(name, data) {
    window.localStorage.setItem(name, JSON.stringify(data));
  }

  private setIdToken(token) {
    this.idToken = token;
    this.setStorageVariable('id_token', token);
  }

  private setAccessToken(token) {
    this.accessToken = token;
    this.setStorageVariable('access_token', token);
  }

  public isAuthenticated() {
    const expiresAt =
JSON.parse(localStorage.getItem('expires_at'));
    return Date.now() < expiresAt;
  }

  public login() {
    const client = new Auth0Cordova(auth0Config);

    const options = {
      scope: 'openid profile offline_access'
```

```
    };

    client.authorize(options, (err, authResult) => {
      if(err) {
        throw err;
      }

      this.setIdToken(authResult.idToken);
      this.setAccessToken(authResult.accessToken);

      const expiresAt = JSON.stringify((authResult.expiresIn *
1000)
      +
      new Date().getTime());
      this.setStorageVariable('expires_at', expiresAt);

      this.auth0.client.userInfo(this.accessToken, (err, profile)=>
      {
        if(err) {
          throw err;
        }

        profile.user_metadata = profile.user_metadata || {};
        this.setStorageVariable('profile', profile);
        this.zone.run(() => {
          this.user = profile;
        });
      });
    });
  }

  public logout() {
    window.localStorage.removeItem('profile');
    window.localStorage.removeItem('access_token');
    window.localStorage.removeItem('id_token');
    window.localStorage.removeItem('expires_at');

    this.idToken = null;
    this.accessToken = null;
    this.user = null;
  }

}
```

 Make sure to use your own value for `clientID`, `domain`, and
`packageIdentifier` for `auth0Config` in `auth.ts`.

6. Open and edit `./src/app/app.module.ts` with the following code:

```
import { BrowserModule } from '@angular/platform-browser';
import { ErrorHandler, NgModule } from '@angular/core';
import { IonicApp, IonicErrorHandler, IonicModule } from 'ionic-
angular';
import { SplashScreen } from '@ionic-native/splash-screen';
import { StatusBar } from '@ionic-native/status-bar';

import { MyApp } from './app.component';
import { HomePage } from '../pages/home/home';
import { AuthProvider } from '../providers/auth/auth';

@NgModule({
  declarations: [
    MyApp,
    HomePage
  ],
  imports: [
    BrowserModule,
    IonicModule.forRoot(MyApp)
  ],
  bootstrap: [IonicApp],
  entryComponents: [
    MyApp,
    HomePage
  ],
  providers: [
    StatusBar,
    SplashScreen,
    {provide: ErrorHandler, useClass: IonicErrorHandler},
    AuthProvider
  ]
})
export class AppModule {}
```

7. Edit and replace `./src/pages/home/home.html` with the following code:

```
<ion-header>
  <ion-navbar>
    <ion-title>
      Home Page
```

```
      </ion-title>
    </ion-navbar>
  </ion-header>

  <ion-content padding>
      <div *ngIf="!auth.isAuthenticated()">
          <button ion-button block color="primary"
  (click)="auth.login()">Log In</button>
      </div>

      <div *ngIf="auth.isAuthenticated()">
        <ion-card>
          <img [src]="auth.user.picture" />
          <ion-card-content>
            <ion-card-title>{{ auth.user.name }}</ion-card-title>
          </ion-card-content>
        </ion-card>
        <button ion-button block color="primary"
        (click)="auth.logout()">Logout</button>
      </div>
  </ion-content>
```

 These are just your basic `login` and `logout` templates. It's all in a single page to keep things simple.

8. Open and edit `./src/pages/home/home.ts` with the following code:

```
import { Component } from '@angular/core';
import { NavController } from 'ionic-angular';
import { AuthProvider } from '../../providers/auth/auth';

@Component({
  selector: 'page-home',
  templateUrl: 'home.html'
})
export class HomePage {

  constructor(public navCtrl: NavController, public auth:
AuthProvider) {

  }

}
```

9. Then run this in the device using the following command in CLI:

```
$ ionic cordova run android
```

How it works

There are certain things that we need to know before digging more into code.

Auth0 uses **JWT (JSON Web Token)**, which is a compact way of sharing information between two parties via JSON. In simple terms, when the user is authenticated, Auth0 sends us JWTs, which have information about the user and also allow the user to access authenticated routes/URLs. Auth0 sends back an `access_token`, which is required for accessing authenticated routes, and it also sends us an `id_token`, which contains the user's profile information such as their username, profile picture, and so on. Both of these tokens have a short lifespan and then they expire. But along with that, Auth0 also sends us a `refresh_token`, which has a long expiry date and can be used to get a new `id_token` and `access_token`.

We configured the **Callback URL** in our app. This is the URL where Auth0 redirects the user after authentication. A callback URL includes the app's package ID, and that's why we need to mention it while installing the plugin. We also need to add `file://` in **CORS** (**Cross-Origin Resource Sharing**), because the Ionic app makes an HTTP request from `file://` origin.

 If you are using Ionic's WKWebView. It runs a local webserver inside the app. So you have to whitelist http://localhost:8080 for CORS in Auth0 Dashboard

Most of the work is in `AuthService`. AuthService allows us to log in/log out. It uses the `auth0.js` and `auth0/cordova` library for authentication. First, we are creating an `auth0Config` object. This object looks like the following:

```
const auth0Config = {
    clientID: ''
    clientId: '',
    domain: '',
    callbackURL: location.href,
    packageIdentifier: ''
};
```

- In the preceding code, you can see that `clientID` and `clientId` have the same value. It is the value that we saved earlier. The first is used by `auth0.js`, and the latter is used by `auth0/cordova`.
- The `domain` is also our **Auth0 Domain** used for authentication. We saved it earlier when we created our app on the Auth0 dashboard.
- `callbackURL` will always be `location.href`.
- `packageIdentifier` is the package ID of your app, same as in your `config.xml`.

We are then passing this config to both `Auth0.WebAuth` constructor function, and `Auth0Cordova` constructor function.

In the `login` function, we initiate authentication by calling Auth0Cordova's `authorize` function. It is important to notice that we are passing an `option` object with `scope` key into an `authorize` function as the parameter. This scope key tells Auth0 to return certain data like an email and profile after authentication is completed. We are also passing a callback function as the second parameter, which fires when authentication is completed. When authentication is initiated, Auth0Cordova opens the OS browser and redirects us to our Auth0 Domain. Here, the user can log in and register. By default, email/password authentication is configured for the app. But you can enable Google, Facebook, and GitHub authentication, and they will also appear along with email/password authentication. When the user is authenticated, the browser redirects us to our app via the **Custom URL Scheme.** Then, we store `idToken` and `accessToken` in **localstorage** and also get profile information using the `auth0.client.userInfo` function. Then later in the login method, we also save this information to **localstorage**.

In the `logout` function, we are just removing `idToken`, `accessToken`, token Expiration information, and Profile data from localstorage and also resetting the AuthService class.

In `home.html`, we show a **Log In** button when the user is not authenticated; when the user is authenticated, we show a profile picture and the username of the user, along with the **LOGOUT** button. These `login` and `logout` methods in `home.ts` call `AuthService`'s login and logout function respectively.

Here is how our app looks when the user is not authenticated:

When the user clicks on, it opens a web page for authenticating the user. It looks like the following:

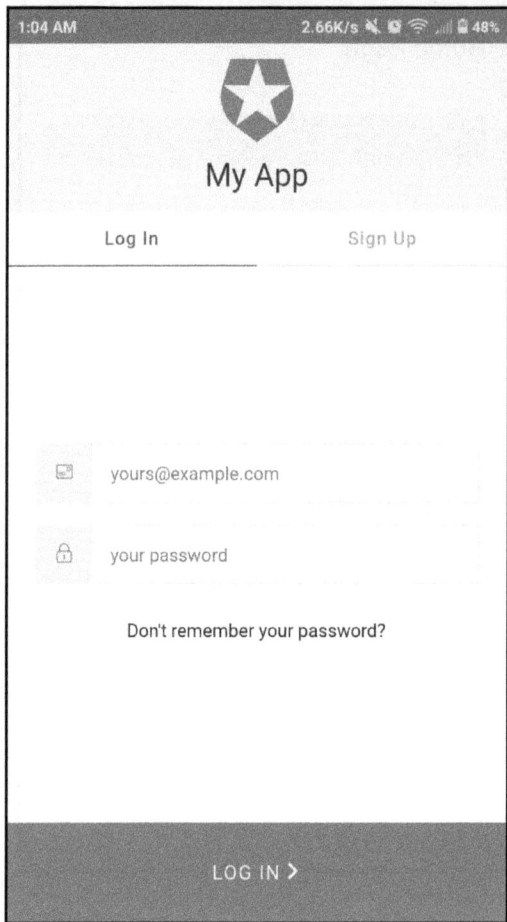

Here is how our app looks when the user is authenticated:

There's more...

You can secure your custom backend using Auth0, and access the backend inside Ionic app using the `angular2-jwt` library. Take a look at `https://github.com/auth0/angular2-jwt`.

Building an iOS app to receive push notifications

A **push notification** is an important feature to engage users frequently, especially when the users are not using the app. Many people download an app, but only open it a few times. If you send them a push notification message, it will encourage them to open the app to get involved in a new activity. Implementing push notifications is very complex if you have to build everything from scratch; however, OneSignal makes it very simple. A push notification provider is a server that can communicate with the **Apple Push Notification service** (**APNs**), or Google's **Firebase Cloud Messaging** (**FCM**). You can set up your own provider server using existing open sources, but you have to maintain this server separately and keep up with potential changes from the APN APIs.

In this section, you will learn how to do the following things:

- Set up OneSignal for iOS push notification
- Configure an iOS app, certificates (app and push), and provisioning profile
- Write code to receive push notifications

Getting ready

It's required to have a physical iOS device available in order to test for notification messages.

You must also register for the **Apple Developer Program (ADP)** in order to access `https://developer.apple.com` and `https://itunesconnect.apple.com,` because these websites will require an approved account.

In addition to that, you must have an Apple Mac and Xcode installed.

How to do it

You need the device to see the push notification. We will be doing this in multiple steps:

- Creating an Apple Signing Certificate
- Adding devices and creating a provisioning profile
- Creating push certificates for use in the OneSignal dashboard
- Configuring app in OneSignal dashboard
- Coding the application

Let's create an Apple signing certificate

Follow the instructions to create apple signging certficiates:

1. Visit the **Apple Developer** website at `https://developer.apple.com` and log in with your credentials.

2. Click on **Certificates, Identifiers & Profiles**, as illustrated in the following screenshot:

3. Select the correct device platform you are targeting. In this case, it will be **iOS, tvOS, watchOS** as shown in the following screenshot:

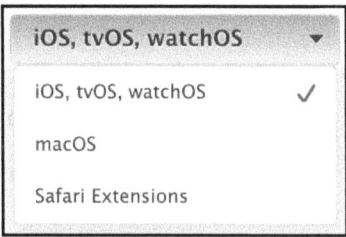

4. Navigate to **Identifiers** | **App IDs** to create an app ID, as illustrated in the following screenshot:

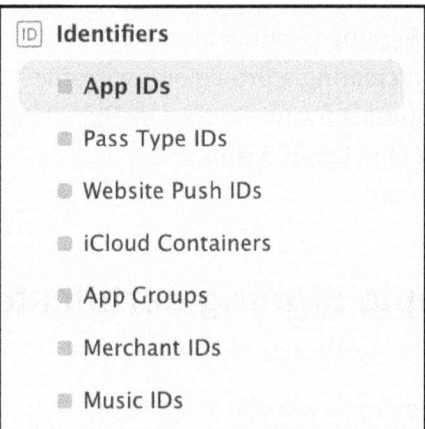

5. Click on the plus (+) button in the top-right corner of the screen, as shown in the following screenshot:

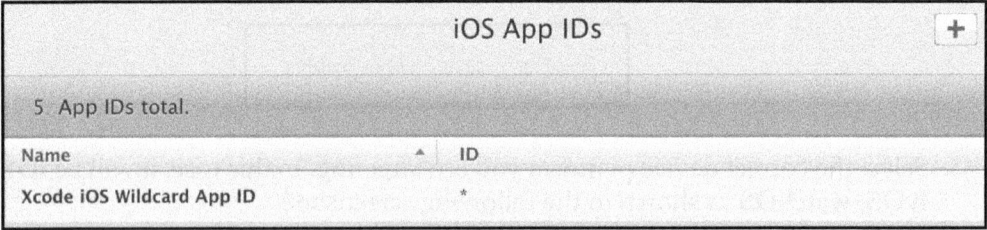

6. Fill in the form to register your app ID. The Name field could be anything. You can provide the name of your project (that is, MyiOSPush) to keep things simple, as shown:

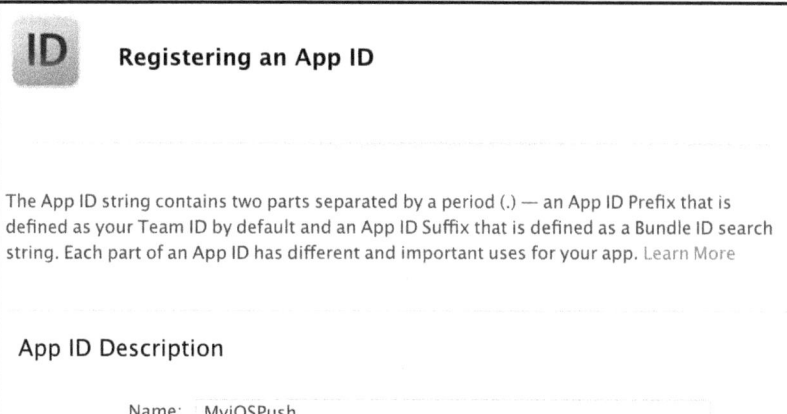

7. The important part that you need to do correctly here is the **Bundle ID**, because it must match your bundle identifier in the `./config.xml` file or Xcode, as illustrated:

App ID Suffix

● **Explicit App ID**

If you plan to incorporate app services such as Game Center, In-App Purchase, Data Protection, and iCloud, or want a provisioning profile unique to a single app, you must register an explicit App ID for your app.

To create an explicit App ID, enter a unique string in the Bundle ID field. This string should match the Bundle ID of your app.

Bundle ID: com.ionicframework.myiospush230693

We recommend using a reverse-domain name style string (i.e., com.domainname.appname). It cannot contain an asterisk (*).

○ **Wildcard App ID**

This allows you to use a single App ID to match multiple apps. To create a wildcard App ID, enter an asterisk (*) as the last digit in the Bundle ID field.

Bundle ID:

Example: com.domainname.*

8. To enable push notifications, you need to check the **Push Notifications** service on the following page:

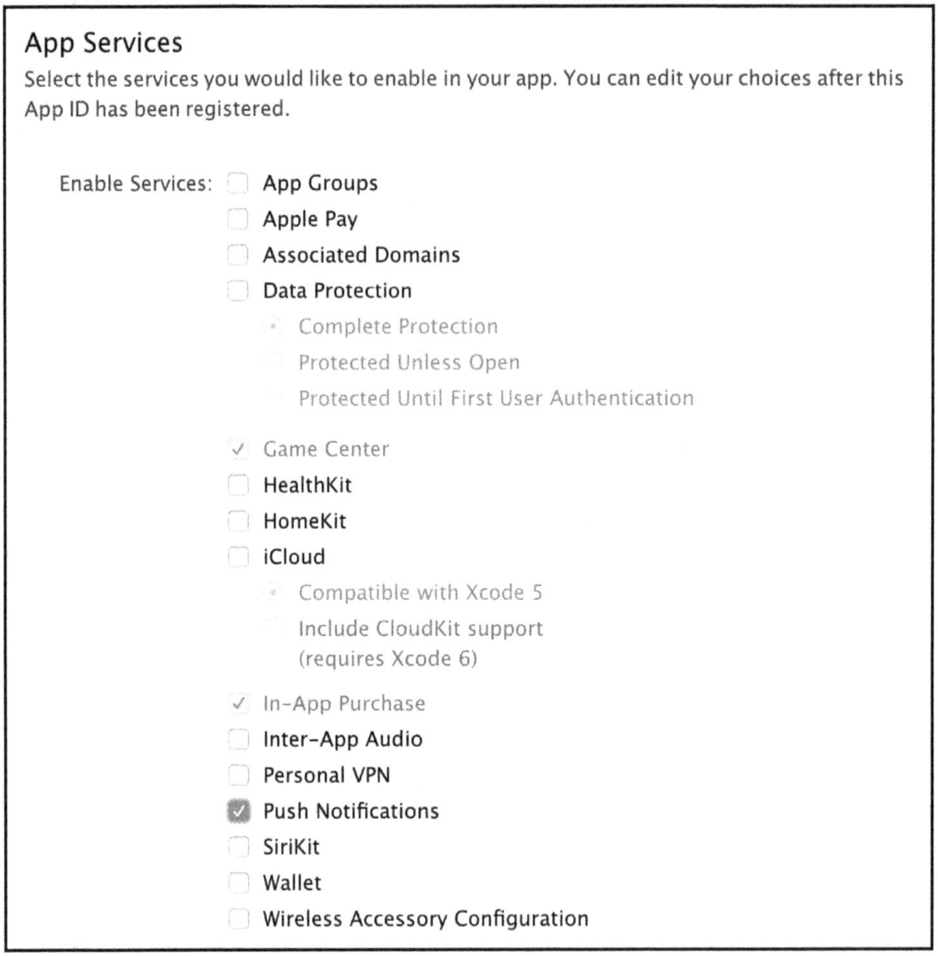

App Services

Select the services you would like to enable in your app. You can edit your choices after this App ID has been registered.

Enable Services:
- ☐ App Groups
- ☐ Apple Pay
- ☐ Associated Domains
- ☐ Data Protection
  - ◦ Complete Protection
  - Protected Unless Open
  - Protected Until First User Authentication
- ☑ Game Center
- ☐ HealthKit
- ☐ HomeKit
- ☐ iCloud
  - ◦ Compatible with Xcode 5
  - Include CloudKit support (requires Xcode 6)
- ☑ In-App Purchase
- ☐ Inter-App Audio
- ☐ Personal VPN
- ☑ Push Notifications
- ☐ SiriKit
- ☐ Wallet
- ☐ Wireless Accessory Configuration

9. Select **Register**, as shown:

10. Select **Done** to complete the step to create an app ID, as follows:

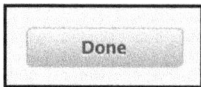

11. To start with certificate creation, you will need to generate a certificate signing request file locally on your Mac OSX using **Keychain Access**. Navigate to the **Keychain Access** in the top-left menu, and navigate to **Certificate Assistant | Request a Certificate From a Certificate Authority...**, as illustrated:

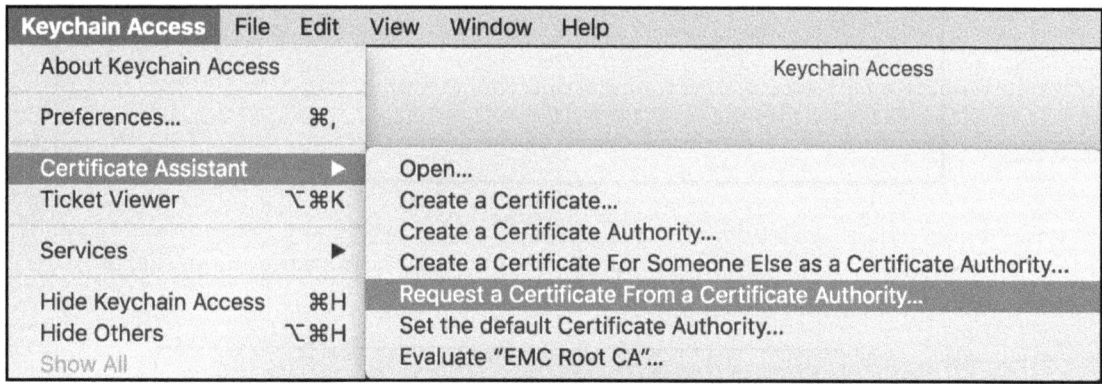

12. Enter your **User Email Address** and **Common Name**. Leave the **CA Email Address** field blank and check **Saved to disk**, as shown:

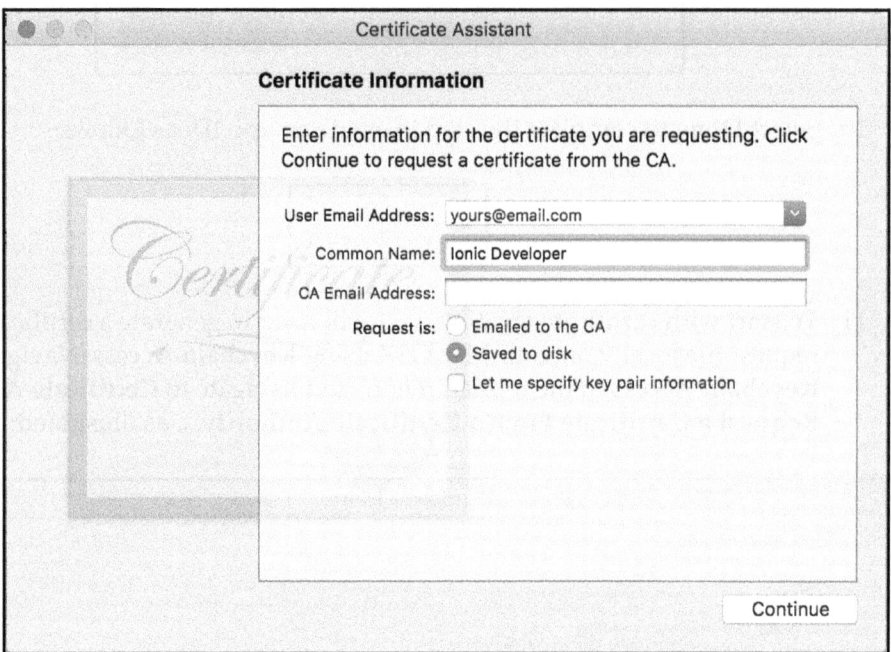

13. Save your CertificateSigningRequest.certSigningRequest file, as follows:

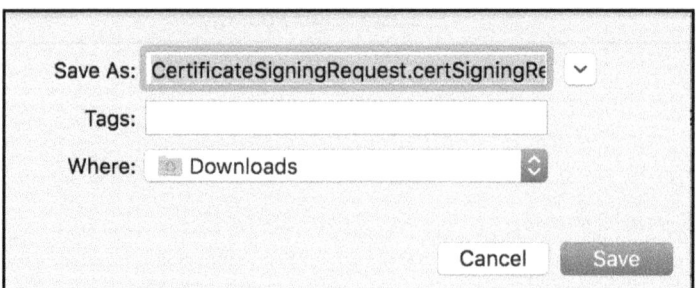

14. Navigate to the **Apple Developer** website, and navigate to **Certificates | All**, as shown:

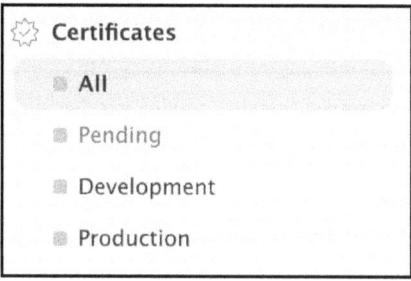

15. Click on the plus (+) button in the top-right corner to start creating a certificate, as follows:

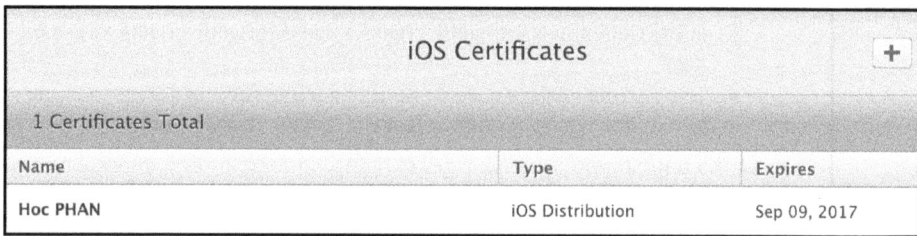

16. Now, you just have to go through the steps on the website to fill out the necessary information. In this example, you will select the **Development** version instead of **Production**, as illustrated:

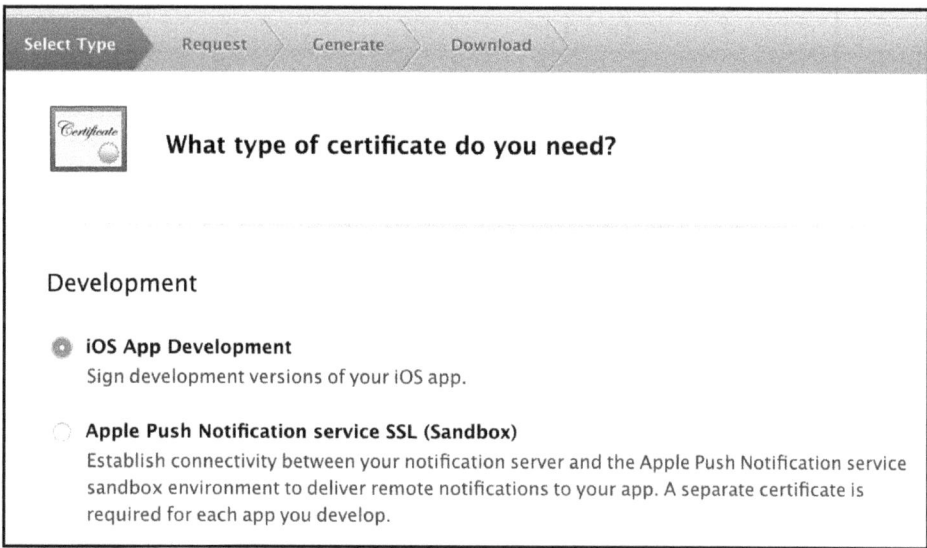

17. Click on the **Continue** button, as follows, to proceed:

To manually generate a Certificate, you need a Certificate Signing Request (CSR) file from your Mac. To create a CSR file, follow the instructions below to create one using Keychain Access.

Create a CSR file.
In the Applications folder on your Mac, open the Utilities folder and launch Keychain Access.

Within the Keychain Access drop down menu, select Keychain Access > Certificate Assistant > Request a Certificate from a Certificate Authority.

- In the Certificate Information window, enter the following information:
    - In the User Email Address field, enter your email address.
    - In the Common Name field, create a name for your private key (e.g., John Doe Dev Key).
    - The CA Email Address field should be left empty.
    - In the "Request is" group, select the "Saved to disk" option.
- Click Continue within Keychain Access to complete the CSR generating process.

Cancel	Back	**Continue**

18. Click on the **Choose File...** button, as shown in the following screenshot, to upload your signing request file that you saved earlier:

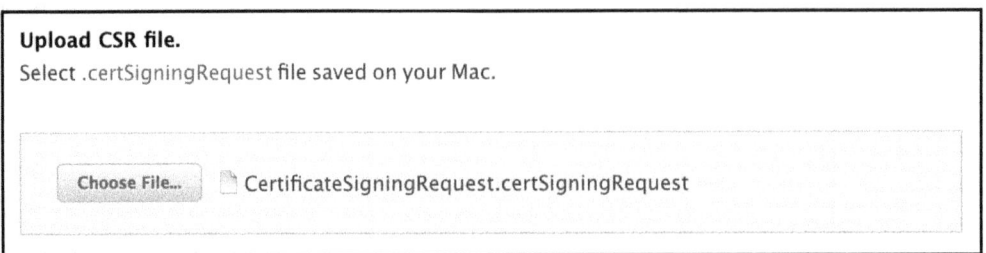

Upload CSR file.
Select .certSigningRequest file saved on your Mac.

Choose File... CertificateSigningRequest.certSigningRequest

19. Click on the **Continue** button, as illustrated, to proceed:

20. Click on the **Download** button to download your iOS Development certificate file:

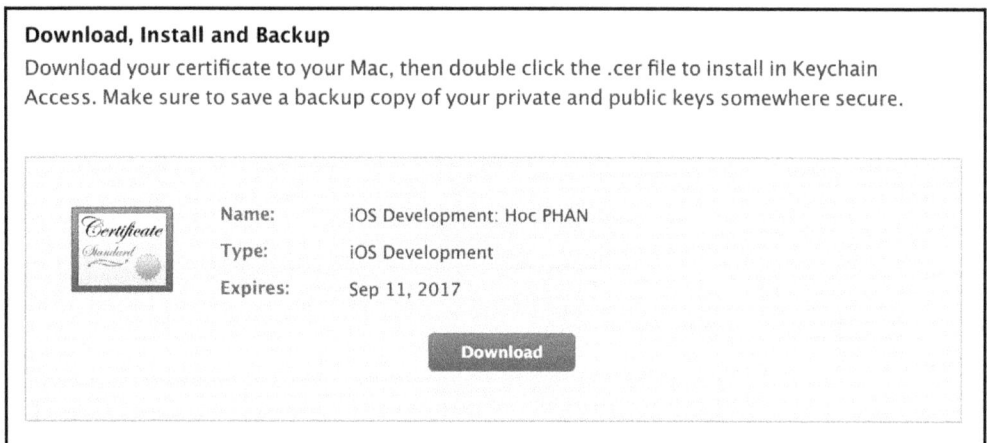

21. Click on the `.cer` file you downloaded, as shown so that it can be imported to **Keychain Access**:

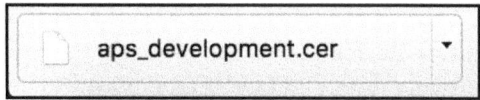

 It is very important to remember that you have to install the signing certificate on the Mac because when you will build the app, it will be used to sign the app. Just double-click the downloaded `.cer` file to install it.

Adding a device and creating the provisioning profile

1. If you need to push the app to a specific device, you must register the device. Go to **Devices | All**:

2. Click on the plus (+) button:

3. Provide the device a **UDID** and save to register the device. Observe the following screenshot:

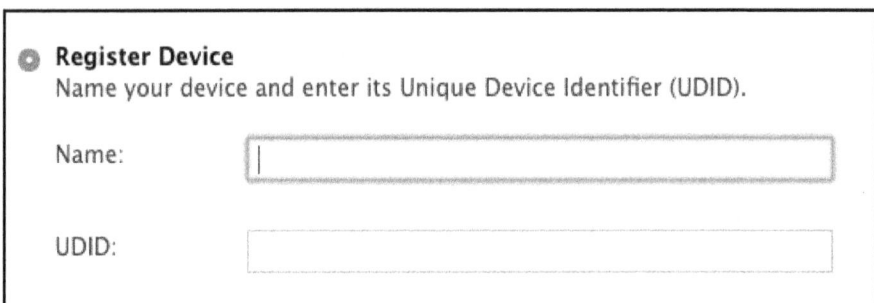

4. You'll need a provisioning profile. Navigate to **Provisioning Profiles** | **All**:

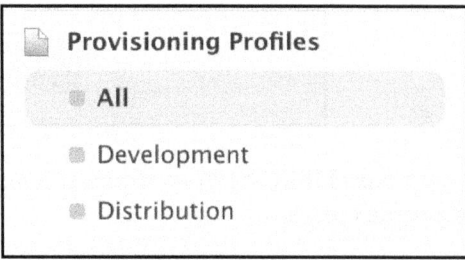

5. Click on the plus (+) button:

6. Select **iOS App Development** as your provisioning profile, since this example is for the development version only:

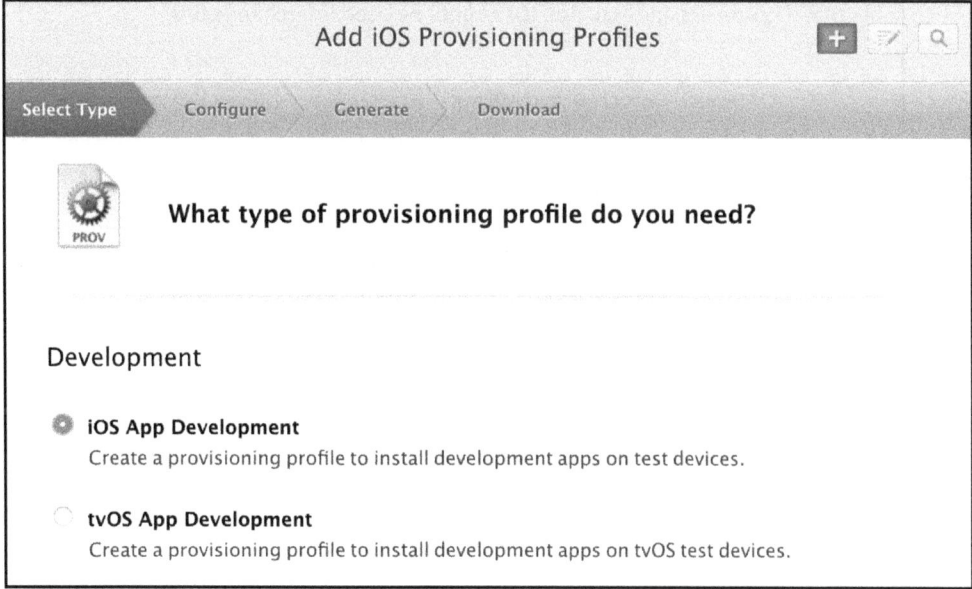

7. Click on the **Continue** button:

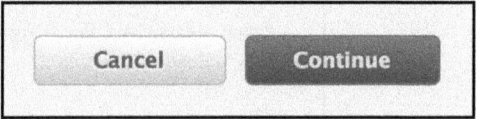

8. Select the correct **App ID** in the drop-down menu, and save to finalize your provisioning profile creation:

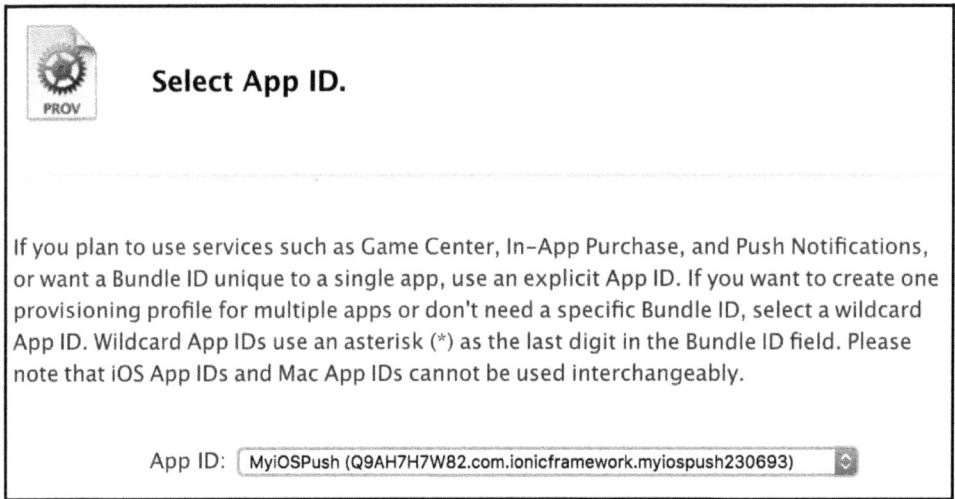

9. Click on the **Continue** button:

10. Select the iOS Development certificate you created earlier, as shown in the following screenshot:

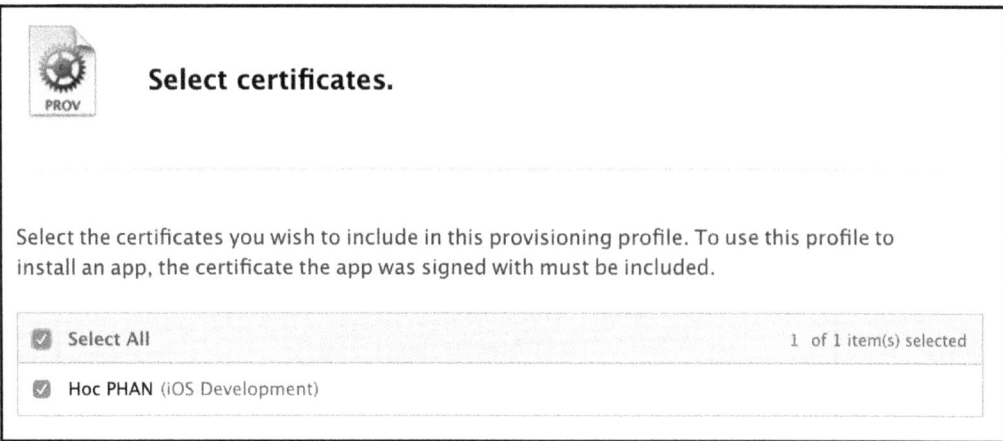

11. As illustrated, select at least one device that you want to be able to install the app for testing:

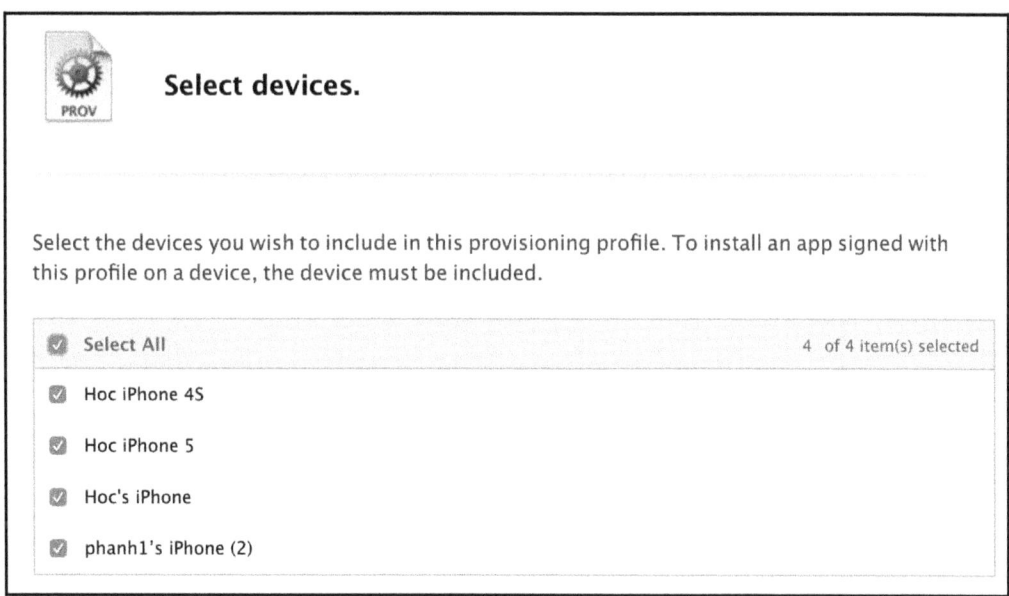

12. Provide a **Profile Name** to your provisioning profile, as shown:

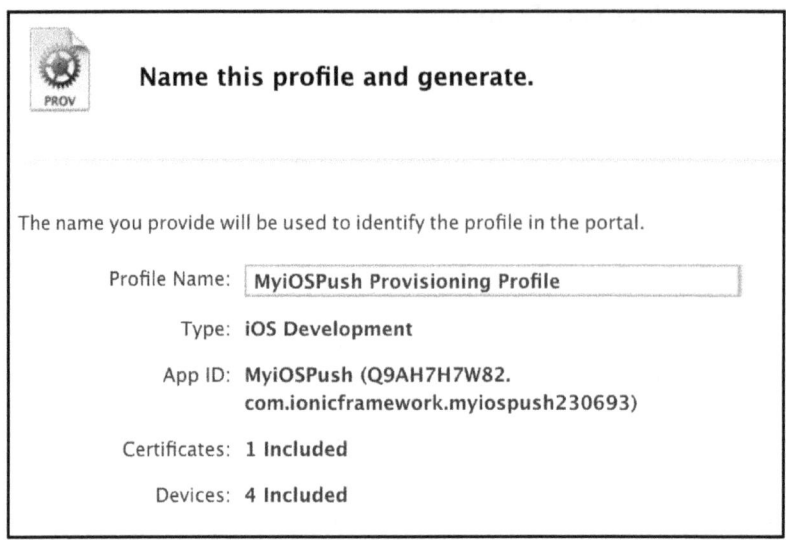

13. Click on the **Download** button to download the provisioning profile file (that is, `MyiOSPush_Provisioning_Profile.mobileprovision`):

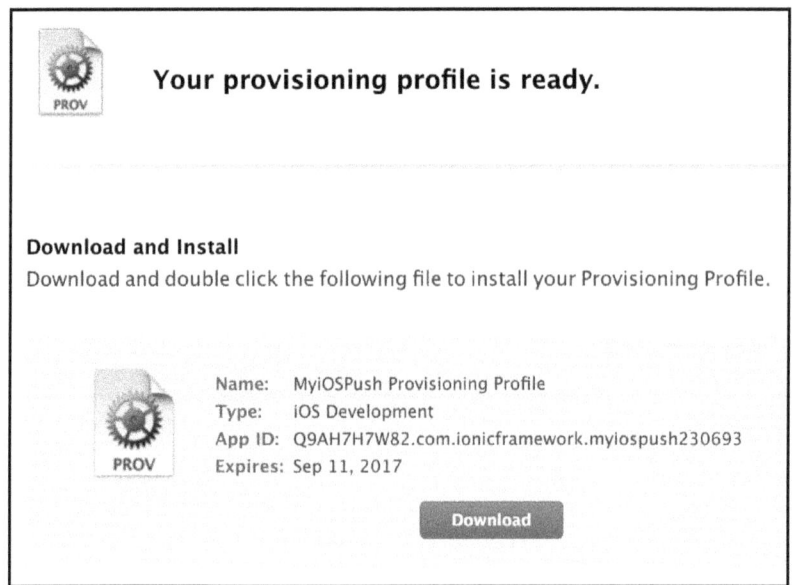

14. Click on `MyiOSPush_Provisioning_Profile.mobileprovision`, which you just downloaded, in order to import it into Xcode:

This step is very important, because if you don't import it into Xcode, your app cannot be built successfully. If your app failed to build because of an invalid provisioning profile, it's best to check the provisioning profile status in the Developer Console.

Creating a push certificate

Follow the steps to create push certificates for iOS application:

1. To enable the **Push Notification** feature, you must request a **Push Certificate**, which is different from the app certificate. Select the **App ID** that you created earlier (that is, `MyiOSPush`):

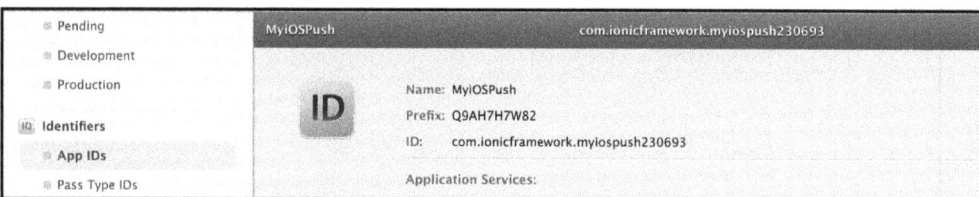

2. Click on the **Edit** button at the bottom of the page:

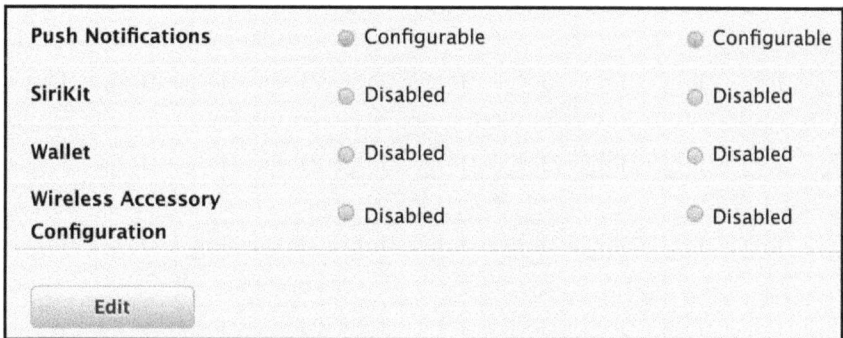

The **Push Notifications** must show the **Configurable** state. Otherwise, your app is not available for push notifications.

3. Click on the **Create Certificates...** button under the **Push Notifications** | **Development SSL Certificate** section:

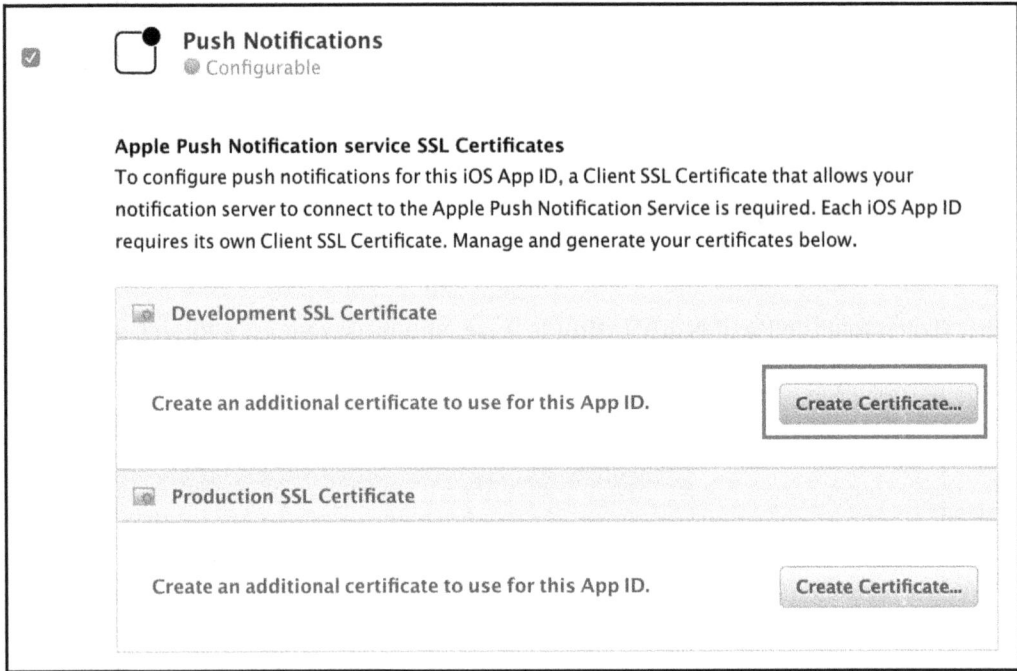

4. You will be taken to a new page to create your CSR file. Click on the **Continue** button:

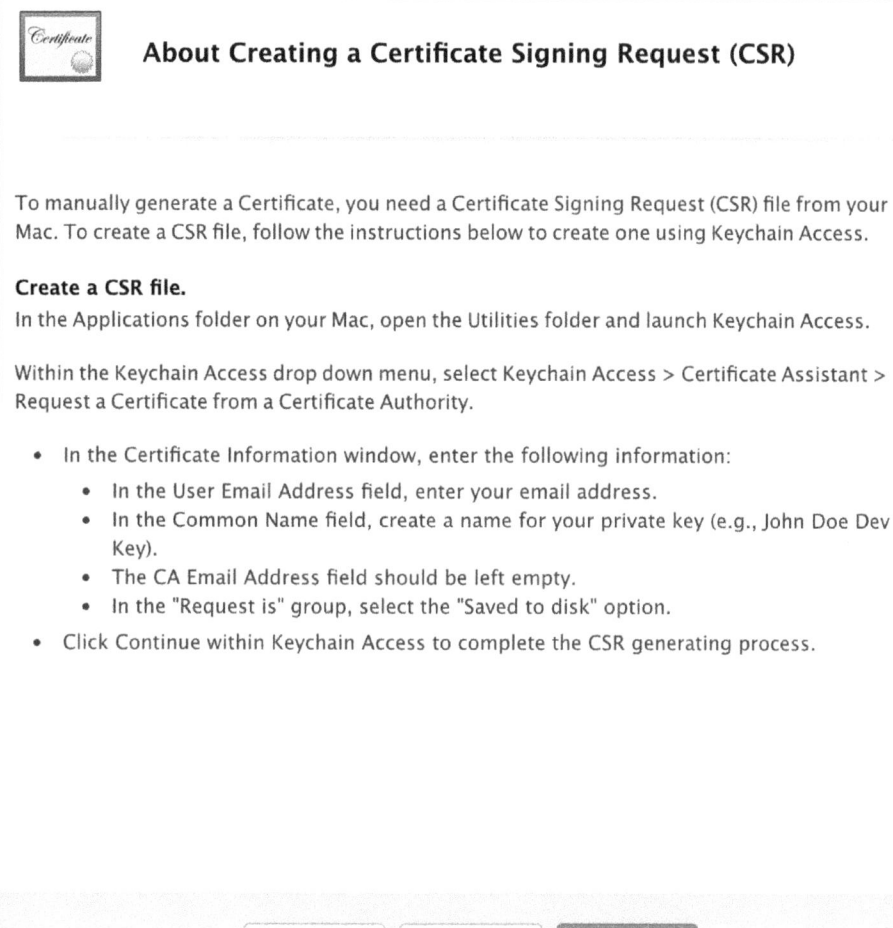

5. Click on the **Choose File...** button:

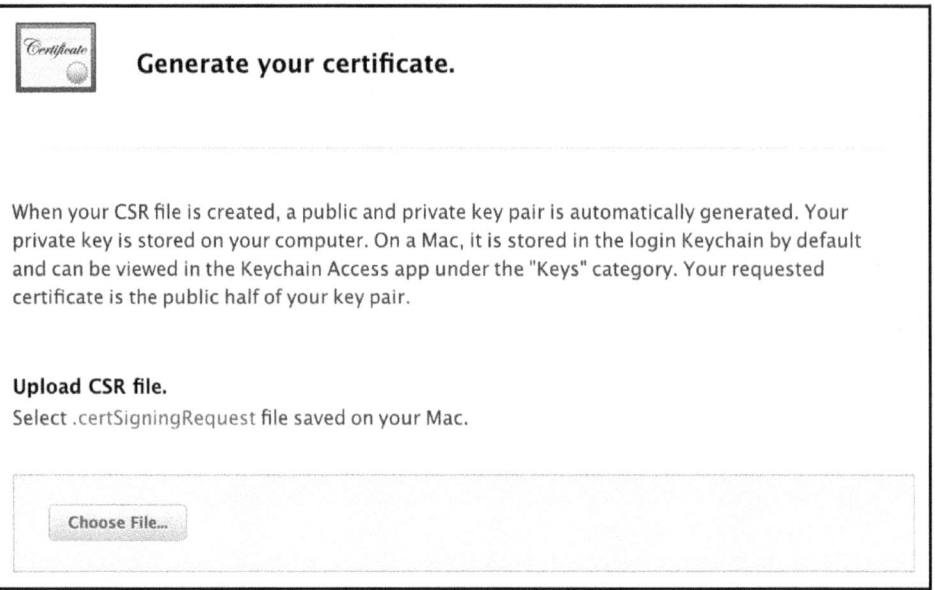

6. Locate the `CertificateSigningRequest.certSigningRequest` file that you created earlier:

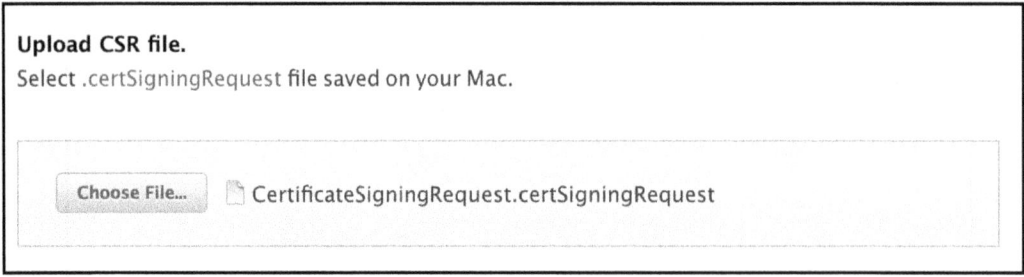

 You must upload the same `.certSigningRequest` file as you did for the app certificate. Otherwise, your app will not receive push notifications, and it's very hard to debug.

7. Click on the **Continue** button:

8. Click on the **Download** button to download the certificate file. You can name it
`aps_certificate.cer` to avoid overwriting to the earlier `.cer` file:

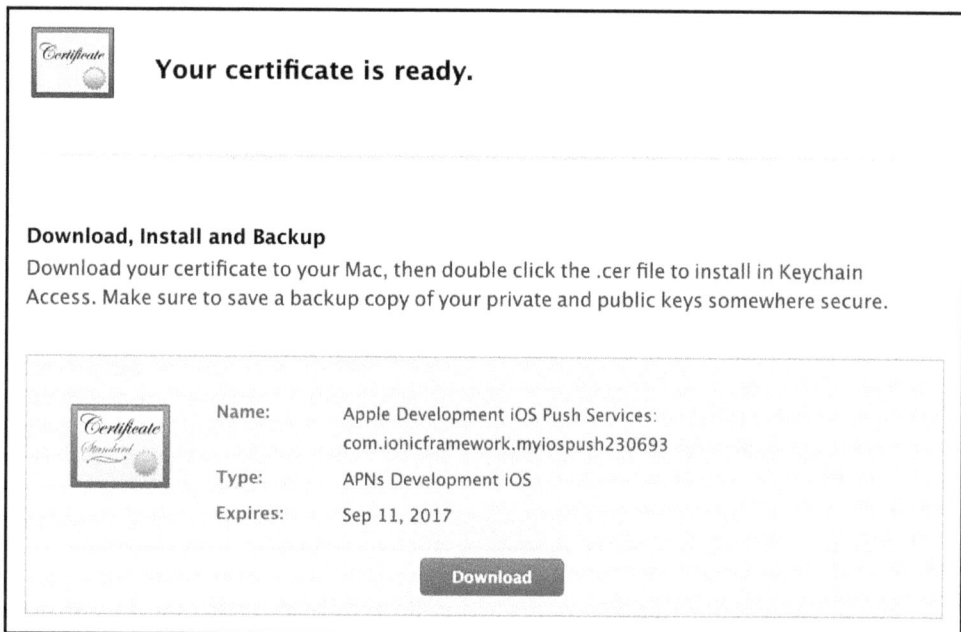

9. Once your `.cer` file is downloaded, you need to click on it to import it to
Keychain Access:

10. Locate the new push services certificate in **Keychain Access** and select it, as illustrated in the following screenshot:

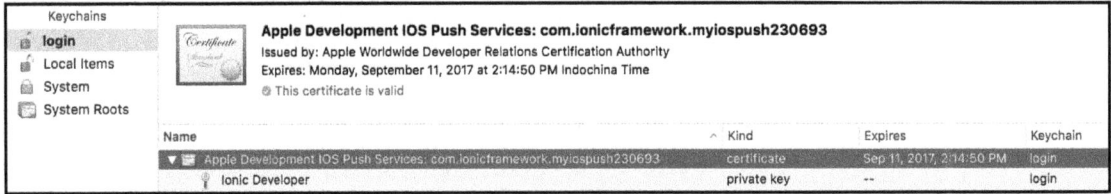

11. Right-click on the certificate and select **Export**:

12. Give it a new name to avoid overwriting it to the app certificate. This process is, basically, to convert from a `.cer` to `.p12` file for OneSignal:

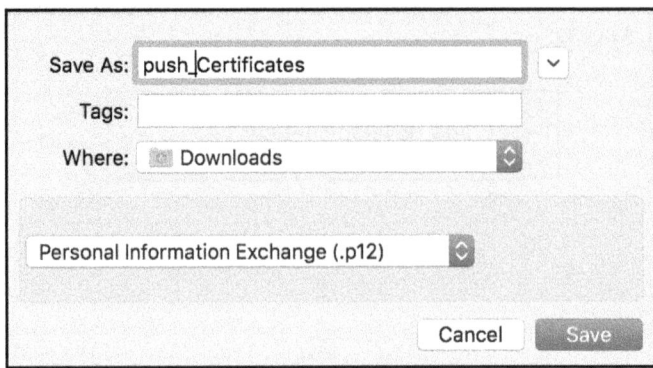

13. Provide a password for this `.p12` file to protect it:

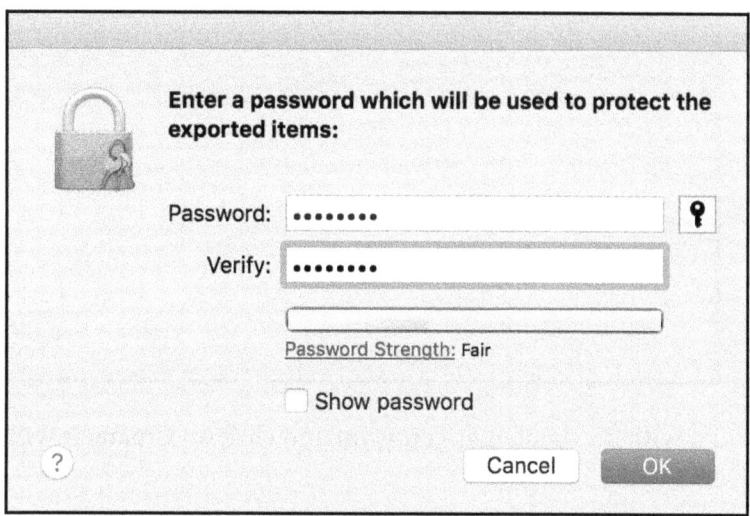

 A password for the `.p12` file is not mandatory for OneSignal, but it is in the best interest to secure it.

Now let's configure OneSignal

Follow the below steps to configure OneSignal for sending push notifications:

1. Go to `https://onesignal.com` and create an account.

2. In the dashboard, click on **Add a new app**. You will see the following dialog:

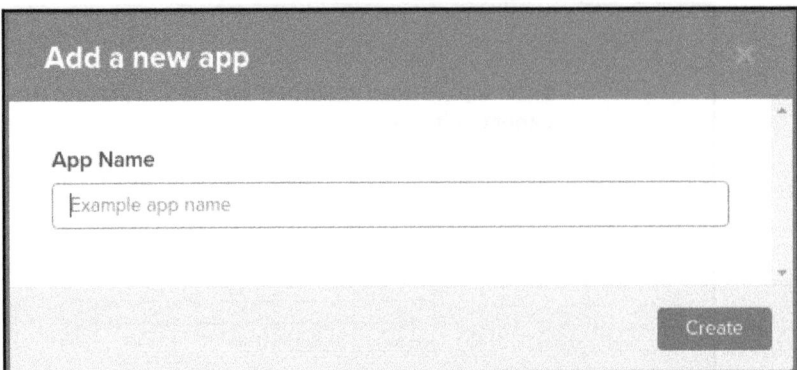

3. Fill it with the name that you want and click on **Create**. It will open the following dialog:

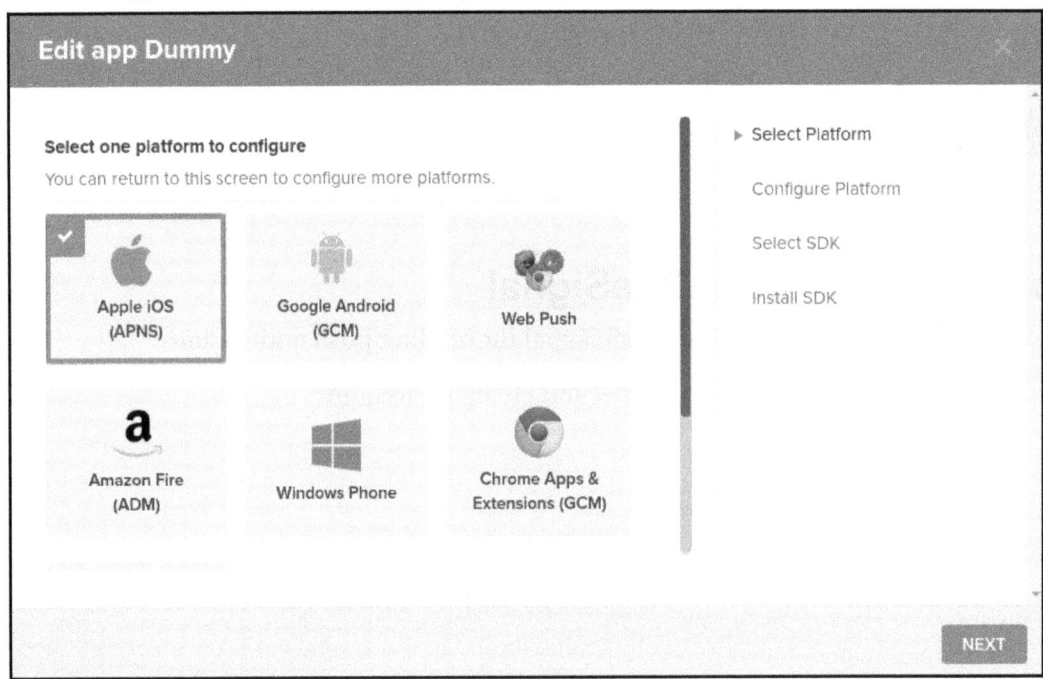

4. Select **Apple iOS** and Hit **Next**. You will see the following:

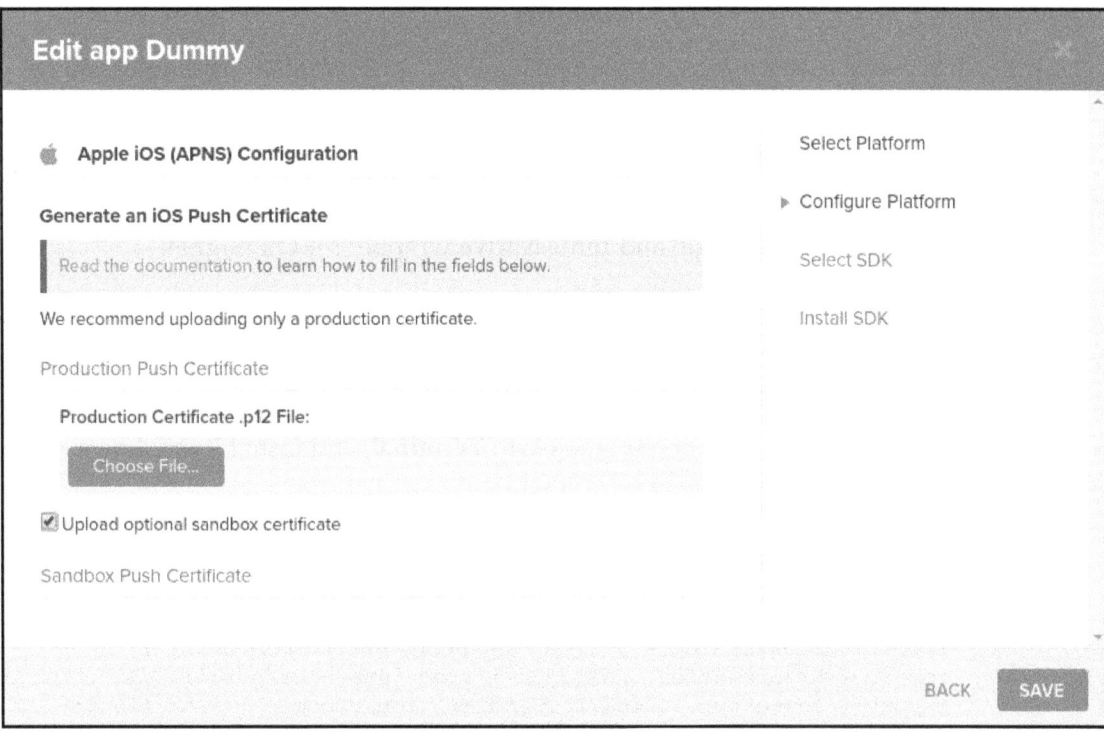

5. Select **Upload optional sandbox certificate** and upload the `.p12` file for the **push certificate** that you created earlier. Also, fill in the password for the `.p12` file. Then hit **Save**.

6. Now in the top main menu, click on **Keys & ID**. You will see **OneSignal App ID**, as shown below:

Note down the **OneSignal App ID** somewhere; we need this to configure our app.

Let's code

Follow the below steps to create the example app:

1. Now, create a new `MyiOSPush` app using the `blank` template, as shown, and go to the `MyiOSPush` folder:

```
$ ionic start MyiOSPush blank
$ cd MyiOSPush
```

2. Install the Cordova plugin and **Ionic Native** wrapper for **OneSignal**:

```
$ ionic cordova plugin add onesignal-cordova-plugin
$ npm install --save @ionic-native/onesignal
```

We need to add this `ionic-native` plugin to `app.module.ts`.

3. We also need to install `cocoapods`. Go to **Terminal**, and install it as follows:

```
sudo gem install cocoapods
pod repo update
```

4. Open and edit `./src/app/app.module.ts` with the following content:

```
import { BrowserModule } from '@angular/platform-browser';
import { ErrorHandler, NgModule } from '@angular/core';
import { IonicApp, IonicErrorHandler, IonicModule } from 'ionic-
angular';
import { SplashScreen } from '@ionic-native/splash-screen';
import { StatusBar } from '@ionic-native/status-bar';
import { OneSignal } from '@ionic-native/onesignal';

import { MyApp } from './app.component';
import { HomePage } from '../pages/home/home';

@NgModule({
  declarations: [
    MyApp,
    HomePage
  ],
  imports: [
    BrowserModule,
    IonicModule.forRoot(MyApp)
  ],
  bootstrap: [IonicApp],
  entryComponents: [
    MyApp,
```

```
      HomePage
    ],
    providers: [
      StatusBar,
      SplashScreen,
      OneSignal,
      {provide: ErrorHandler, useClass: IonicErrorHandler}
    ]
  })
  export class AppModule {}
```

5. You need to modify your home page code in order to receive notification messages. Open and edit `./src/pages/home/home.html` and paste the given code:

```html
<ion-header>
  <ion-navbar>
    <ion-title>
      Push Notification
    </ion-title>
  </ion-navbar>
</ion-header>

<ion-content padding>
  <h2 class="big-square" *ngIf="!this.messages.length">
    You have no message
  </h2>
  <h3 class="sub-title" *ngIf="!!this.messages.length">
    Your messages
  </h3>
  <ion-card *ngFor="let msg of messages">
    <ion-card-header>
      {{ msg.title }}
    </ion-card-header>
    <ion-card-content>
      {{ msg.text }}
    </ion-card-content>
  </ion-card>
</ion-content>
```

6. Replace the content of the `home.ts` file, in the same folder, with the following code:

```typescript
import { Component, ChangeDetectorRef } from '@angular/core';
import { NavController, Platform } from 'ionic-angular';
import { OneSignal } from '@ionic-native/onesignal';
```

```
@Component({
  selector: 'page-home',
  templateUrl: 'home.html'
})
export class HomePage {
  public messages = [];
  public clicked: Boolean = false;
  constructor(public navCtrl: NavController, public oneSignal:
OneSignal, platform: Platform, private changeDetector:
ChangeDetectorRef) {
    platform.ready().then(() => {
      this.oneSignalConfig();
    });
  }

  oneSignalConfig() {
  this.oneSignal.startInit("94218e7a-2307-41fa-9bc3-20783b4cde9a");
  this.oneSignal.handleNotificationReceived().subscribe((value:any)
=> {
      let msg = value.payload;
      this.messages.push({
        title: msg.title,
        text: msg.body
      });
      this.changeDetector.detectChanges();
    });
    this.oneSignal.endInit();
  }
}
```

In the `startInit` function, you have to pass your own **OneSignal App ID**, which you created earlier.

7. Replace `home.scss`, also in the `/home` folder, with the given code:

```
page-home {
    .center {
        text-align: center;
    }
    h2.big-square {
        text-align: center;
        padding: 50px;
        color: #D91E18;
        background: #F9BF3B;
    }
    h3.sub-title {
        text-align: center;
```

```
        padding: 10px;
        color: #446CB3;
        background: #E4F1FE;
    }
    ion-card ion-card-header {
        padding: 10px 16px;
        background: #F9690E;
        color: white;
    }
    ion-card ion-card-header + ion-card-content,
    ion-card .item + ion-card-content {
        padding-top: 16px;
    }
}
```

8. Connect your physical iPhone to the Mac via a USB connection.

9. Ensure that you are in the app folder, and build the app for the iOS platform, as follows:

```
$ ionic cordova run ios
```

10. The OS will prompt to allow codesign to sign using the iOS Developer certificate. You must accept this to allow access in order to build the app and upload it to your device:

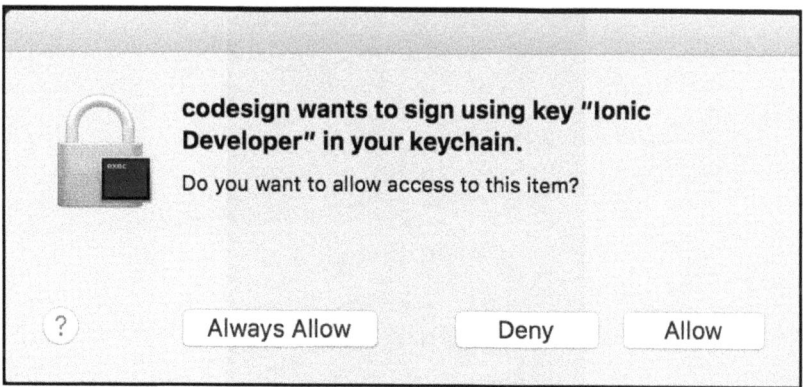

11. Verify that the app has been running successfully on the device. At this point, you have completed the push notification setup and coding. The next step is to send the push notification via the **OneSignal dashboard**. Here are the instructions:

12. After selecting your app in OneSignal, you will see following side menu:

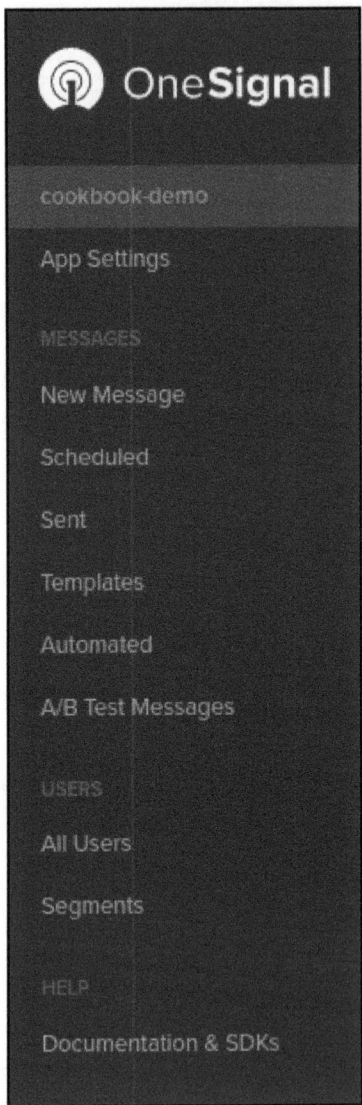

13. Click on **New Message**. You will see a screen like the following:

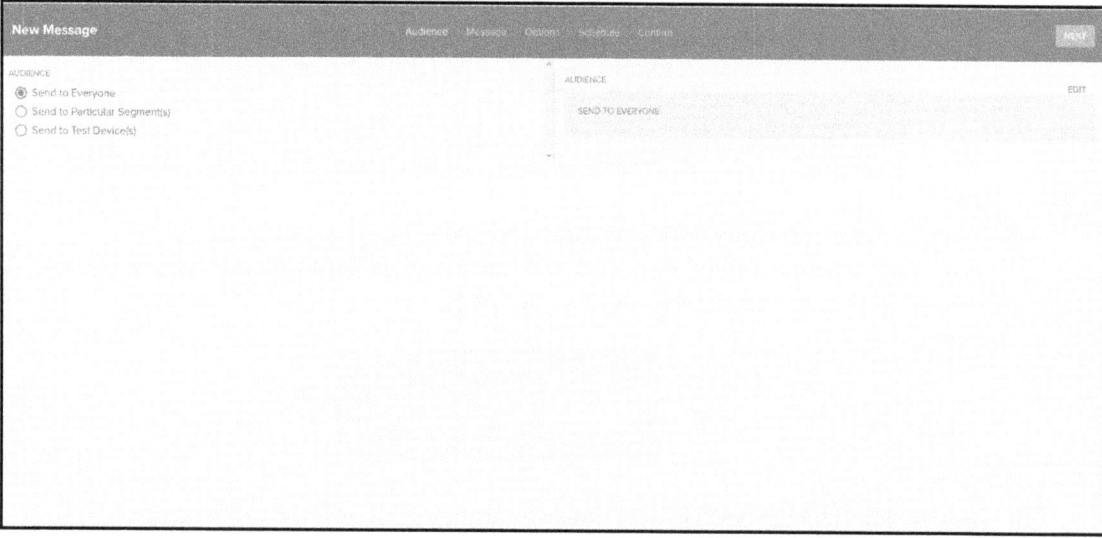

14. Select `Send to Everyone`, since at this point only you will be using the app. Then click **Next**. The following page will appear:

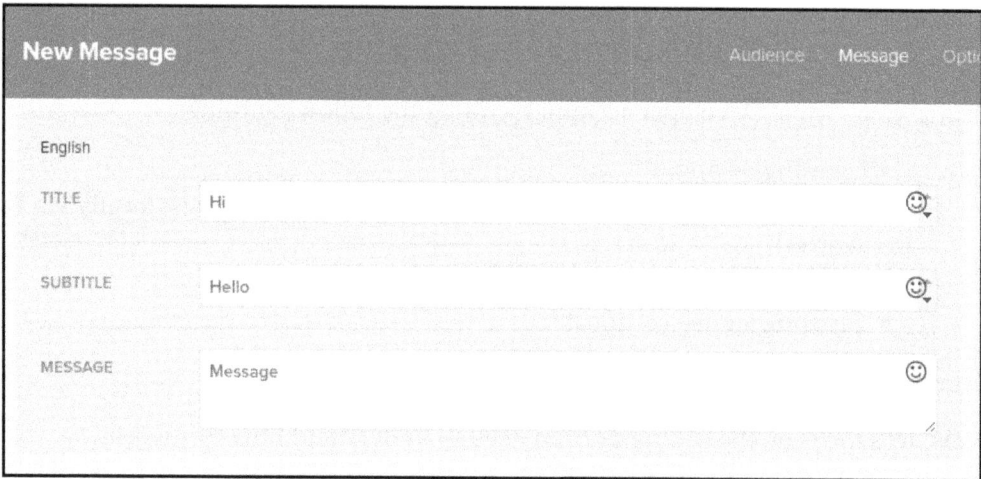

15. Type your **Title** and **Message**.

16. In the top menu, you will see the following links. At this moment, we are at **Message**:

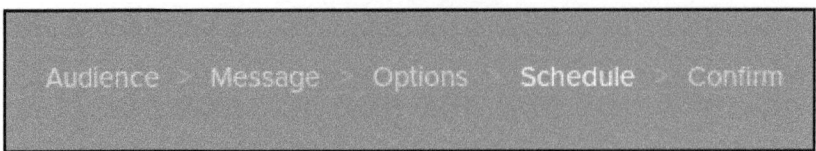

17. If you want to do some configuration and scheduling, you can do it in the following sections. Otherwise, you can jump to **Confirm** link and you will see following buttons on the top right of the page:

18. Just hit **SEND MESSAGE**, and OneSignal will deliver your push notification.

How it works

To understand how the entire process works, let's summarize what you have done, as shown in the following section:

Set up your Apple Developer account by doing the following things:

- Creating an app ID
- Creating an app certificate (after creating a signing request locally via **Keychain Access**)
- Creating a provisioning profile
- Creating a push certificate

Set up your OneSignal App

Now, let's focus on the coding portion itself to understand how this works.

Inside `NgModul`, we added an **Ionic Native** wrapper for OneSignal in the providers array.

Then, in `home.ts`, In the constructor we initialized OneSignal by calling the `oneSignalConfig()` function. In the `oneSignalConfig()` function, we called the `startInit` function, which initiated the push notification registration process. We have to pass a OneSignal App ID to this function. Then, we subscribe to the `handleNotificationReceived` observable. It is fired each time the user gets a notification. In it, we are pushing each received push notification into `this.messages` array, and then we stop the initialization process with the `endInit` function, as shown in the following code:

```
oneSignalConfig() {
    this.oneSignal.startInit("94218e7a-2307-41fa-9bc3-20783b4cde9a");
    this.oneSignal.handleNotificationReceived().subscribe((value:any) => {
      let msg = value.payload;
      this.messages.push({
        title: msg.title,
        text: msg.body
      });
      this.changeDetector.detectChanges();
    });
    this.oneSignal.endInit();
}
```

It is important to call change Detector's `detectChanges` function, otherwise, the UI will not be updated since this process is outside the scope of Angular's Change Detection.

In the `home.html` template, the messages will be displayed via the `messages` object, as shown in the following code:

```
<ion-card *ngFor="let msg of messages">
  <ion-card-header>
    {{ msg.title }}
  </ion-card-header>
  <ion-card-content>
    {{ msg.text }}
  </ion-card-content>
</ion-card>
```

Here, each `message` item has the `title` and `text` fields.

If the user doesn't open the app, you will see that the notification appears in the notification area.

This is how the app looks on an iPhone:

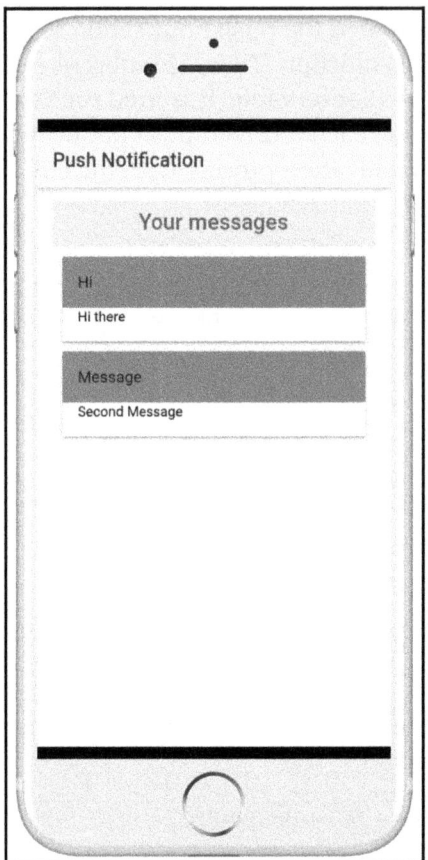

There's more...

For more information about the APNs, you can visit the official documentation at `https://developer.apple.com/library/content/documentation/NetworkingInternet/Conceptual/RemoteNotificationsPG/APNSOverview.html`

For more information about OneSignal setup, take a look at `https://onesignal.com/ionic`.

Building an Android app to receive push notifications

A push notification works in the same way as iOS for Google; however, instead of using the Apple Notification Service, you will be working through the FCM server, which is a new replacement for **Google Cloud Messaging** (**GCM**). However, OneSignal abstracts this process so that you don't have to code using a different API. You will be using the same push object as for the iOS app.

 For more information about the differences between FCM and GCM, visit the FAQs at `https://firebase.google.com/support/faq`.

In this section, you will learn how to do the following things:

- Set up OneSignal for Android push notification
- Configure the Firebase project for the push API
- Write code to receive push notifications on Android

You will be using the same code base as your iOS push notification example. The main difference is the process to set up in your Firebase and OneSignal account.

Getting ready

You can test the Android push notification using the Android emulator. So, there is no need to have a physical Android device available.

In order to gain access, you must also register for Firebase at `https://console.firebase.google.com`.

In addition to your current setup, you need to install **Android Studio**.

1. Observe the following screenshot:

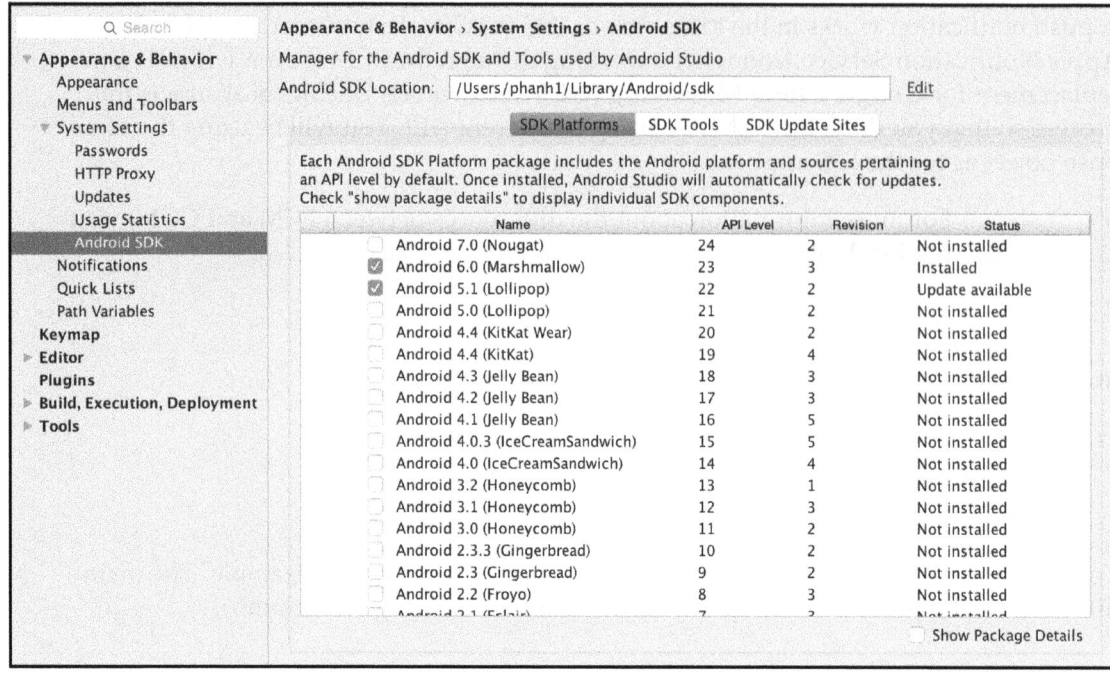

2. Android SDK Tools, Build Tools, Platform Tools and Intel **Hardware Accelerated Execution Manager (HAXM)**
   (`https://software.intel.com/en-us/android/articles/installation-instructions-for-intel-hardware-accelerated-execution-manager-windows`).Observe the following screenshot:

	Name	Version	Status
	SDK Platforms	SDK Tools	SDK Update Sites

Below are the available SDK developer tools. Once installed, Android Studio will automatically check for updates. Check "show package details" to display available versions of an SDK Tool.

	Name	Version	Status
☑	Android SDK Build Tools		Installed
☑	Android Auto API Simulators	1.0.0	Installed
☐	Android Auto Desktop Head Unit emulator	1.1	Not installed
☑	Android SDK Platform-Tools 24.0.3	24.0.3	Installed
☑	Android SDK Tools 25.2.2	25.2.2	Installed
⊟	Android Support Repository, rev 17	17.0.0	Update Available: 3...
☐	CMake 3.6.3155560	3.6.3155560	Not installed
☐	ConstraintLayout for Android 1.0.0-alpha5	1	Not installed
☐	ConstraintLayout for Android 1.0.0-alpha6	1	Not installed
☐	ConstraintLayout for Android 1.0.0-alpha7	1	Not installed
☐	ConstraintLayout for Android 1.0.0-alpha8	1	Not installed
☐	Documentation for Android SDK	1	Not installed
☐	GPU Debugging tools	1.0.3	Not installed
☑	Google Play APK Expansion Library, rev 3	3.0.0	Installed
☐	Google Play APK Expansion library	1	Not installed
☑	Google Play Billing Library, rev 5	5.0.0	Installed
☐	Google Play Licensing Library	1	Not installed
☑	Google Play Licensing Library, rev 2	2.0.0	Installed
⊟	Google Play services, rev 26	26.0.0	Update Available: 32
☑	Google Repository	32	Installed
☑	Google Web Driver, rev 2	2.0.0	Installed
☑	Intel x86 Emulator Accelerator (HAXM installer), rev 6.0.3	6.0.3	Installed
☐	LLDB 2.0	2.0.2558144	Not installed
☐	LLDB 2.1	2.1.2852477	Not installed

3. At least one **Android Virtual Device** (**AVD**) has been created (use the $ android avd command line to open AVD Manager). Observe the following screenshot:

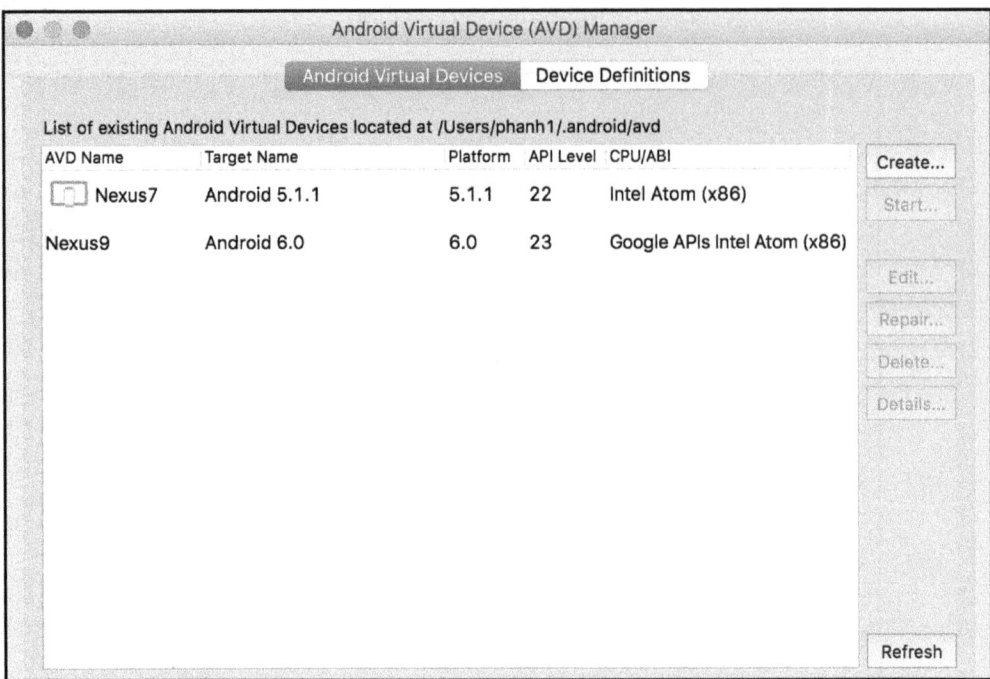

How to do it

First, we are going to configure push notifications in Firebase console and then we are going to code the example app.

Configuring Firebase for push notifications

Here are the instructions for configuring firebase console:

1. You will need a Firebase project number and a Firebase server ID in order to receive push notifications. First, let's log into the Firebase console at `https://console.firebase.google.com`.

2. Click on the **CREATE NEW PROJECT** button, and fill in a project name (that is, `MyAndroidPush`):

3. Navigate to **Grow | Notifications** in the left navigation menu:

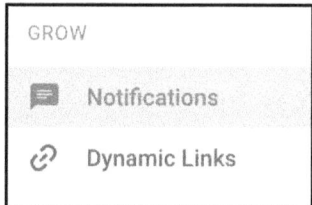

4. Select the Android icon:

 The FCM service also supports the iOS app. So, it's possible that you can use FCM for both the iOS and Android projects.

5. Provide the **Package name** in the form. You can copy and paste the **Package name** from your app project at `./config.xml`:

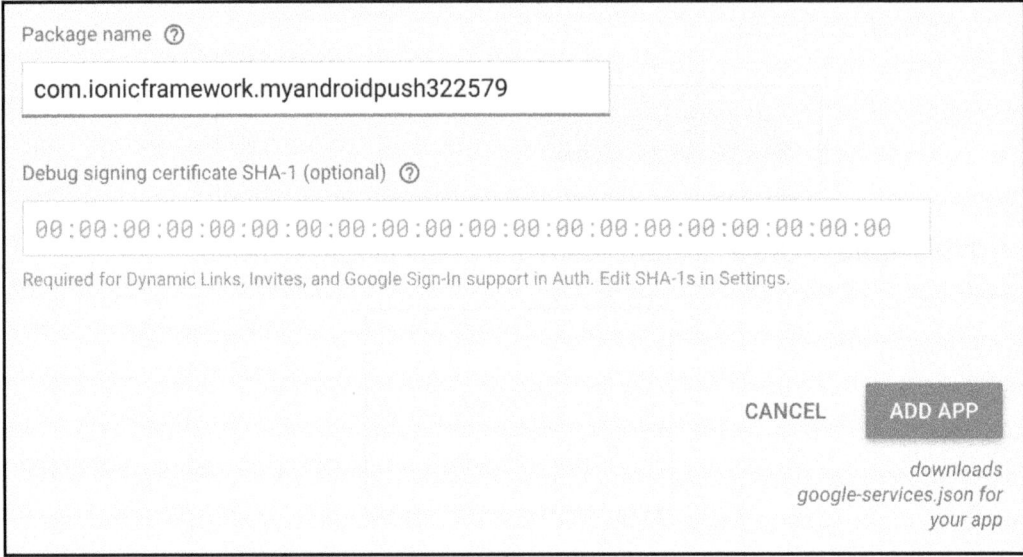

6. Select **CONTINUE**, and save the JSON file somewhere. You will not need this JSON file for the Ionic project:

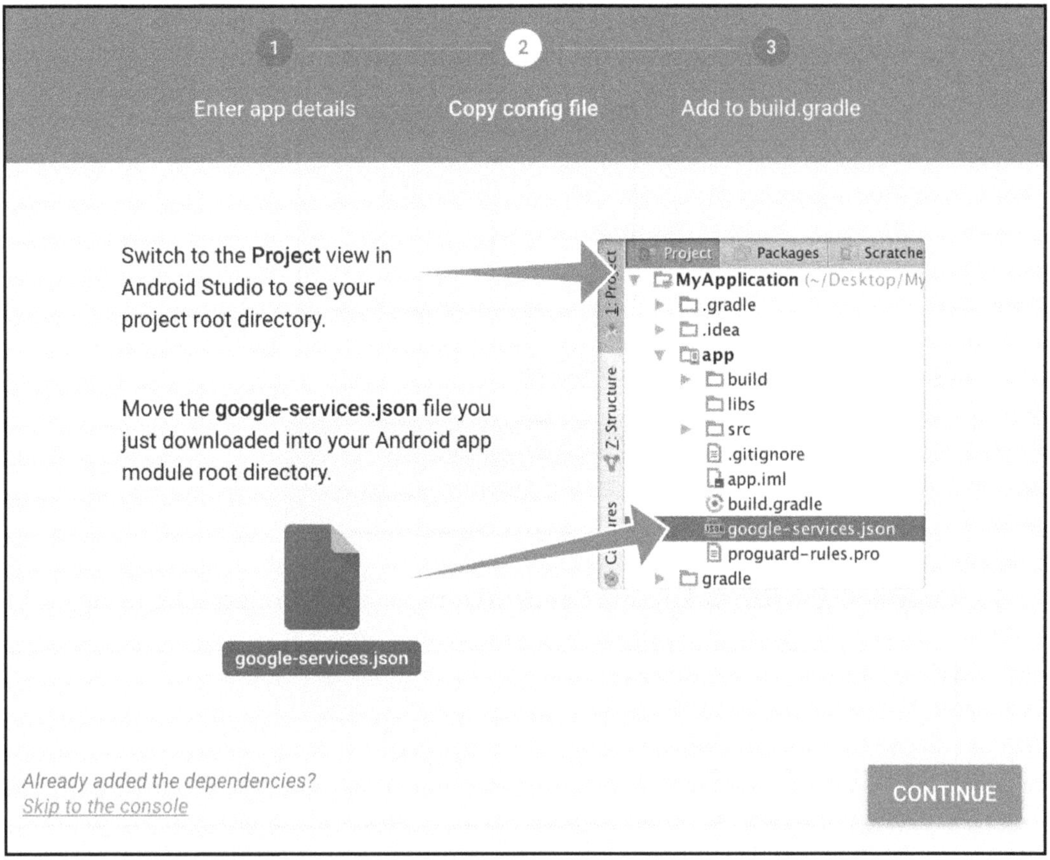
1
2
3
Enter app details
Copy config file
Add to build.gradle
Switch to the Project view in Android Studio to see your project root directory.
Move the google-services.json file you just downloaded into your Android app module root directory.
google-services.json
Project
Packages
Scratche
1: Project
Z: Structure
MyApplication (~/Desktop/My
.gradle
.idea
app
build
libs
src
.gitignore
app.iml
build.gradle
google-services.json
proguard-rules.pro
gradle
Already added the dependencies?
Skip to the console
CONTINUE

7. Click on the **FINISH** button to complete setting up of the notification service:

FINISH

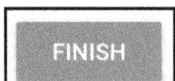

8. Now, you will need the **Server key** and **Sender ID**. Navigate to the gear icon in the top-left corner and select the **Project settings** menu item:

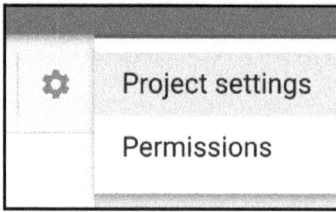

9. Select the **CLOUD MESSAGING** tab:

10. Copy both the **Server key** and **Sender ID** (the same as **Project ID** if using GCM):

Configuring OneSignal

Here are the instructions to configure OneSignal:

1. In your **OneSignal dashboard**, open your previously created app for iOS and click on **App Settings**. You will see the following page:

2. Click on the **CONFIGURE** button parallel to **Google Android Platform**. You will see the following dialog:

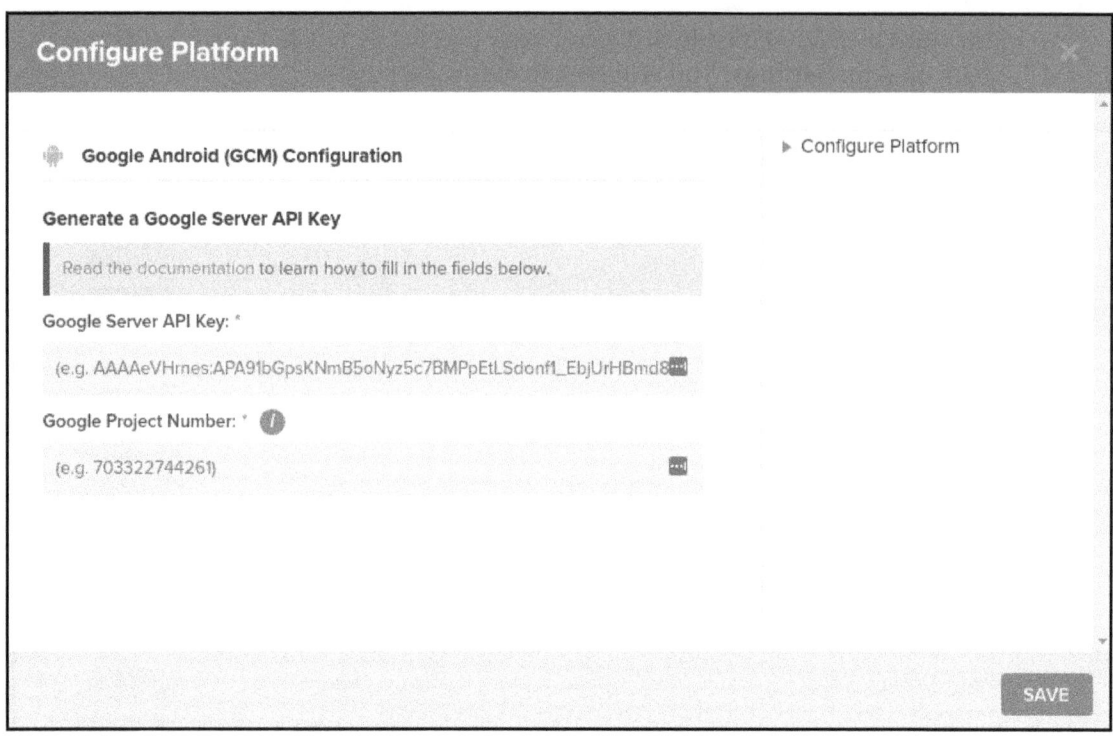

3. Enter the **Server API Key** and **Project Number** (also called a **Sender ID**) to their appropriate fields, and hit **Save**.

Let's code now

Here are the instructions for creating example app:

1. Create a new MyAndroidPush app using the blank template, as follows, and go to the MyAndroidPush folder:

```
$ ionic start MyAndroidPush blank
$ cd MyAndroidPush
```

2. Install the Cordova plugin and Ionic native wrapper for OneSignal:

```
$ ionic cordova plugin add onesignal-cordova-plugin
$ npm install --save @ionic-native/onesignal
```

3. Open and edit ./src/app/app.module.ts with the following content:

```
import { BrowserModule } from '@angular/platform-browser';
import { ErrorHandler, NgModule } from '@angular/core';
import { IonicApp, IonicErrorHandler, IonicModule } from 'ionic-angular';
import { SplashScreen } from '@ionic-native/splash-screen';
import { StatusBar } from '@ionic-native/status-bar';
import { OneSignal } from '@ionic-native/onesignal';

import { MyApp } from './app.component';
import { HomePage } from '../pages/home/home';

@NgModule({
  declarations: [
    MyApp,
    HomePage
  ],
  imports: [
    BrowserModule,
    IonicModule.forRoot(MyApp)
  ],
  bootstrap: [IonicApp],
  entryComponents: [
    MyApp,
    HomePage
  ],
  providers: [
    StatusBar,
    SplashScreen,
    OneSignal,
    {provide: ErrorHandler, useClass: IonicErrorHandler}
```

```
    ]
  })
export class AppModule {}
```

4. The code for your home page is very similar to the iOS push example. Open and edit ./src/pages/home/home.html, and paste the following code:

```
<ion-header>
  <ion-navbar>
    <ion-title>
      Push Notification
    </ion-title>
  </ion-navbar>
</ion-header>

<ion-content padding>
  <h2 class="big-square" *ngIf="!this.messages.length">
    You have no message
  </h2>
  <h3 class="sub-title" *ngIf="!!this.messages.length">
    Your messages
  </h3>
  <ion-card *ngFor="let msg of messages">
    <ion-card-header>
      {{ msg.title }}
    </ion-card-header>
    <ion-card-content>
      {{ msg.text }}
    </ion-card-content>
  </ion-card>
</ion-content>
```

5. Replace the content of the home.ts file, in the same folder, with the following code:

```
import { Component, ChangeDetectorRef } from '@angular/core';
import { NavController, Platform } from 'ionic-angular';
import { OneSignal } from '@ionic-native/onesignal';

@Component({
  selector: 'page-home',
  templateUrl: 'home.html'
})
export class HomePage {
  public messages = [];
  public clicked: Boolean = false;
  constructor(public navCtrl: NavController, public oneSignal:
```

```
OneSignal, platform: Platform, private changeDetector:
ChangeDetectorRef) {
    platform.ready().then(() => {
      this.oneSignalConfig();
    });
  }

  oneSignalConfig() {
this.oneSignal.startInit("94218e7a-2307-41fa-9bc3-20783b4cde9a",
"539293856976");
this.oneSignal.handleNotificationReceived().subscribe((value:any)
=> {
      // do something when notification is received
      let msg = value.payload;
      this.messages.push({
        title: msg.title,
        text: msg.body
      });
      this.changeDetector.detectChanges();
    });
    this.oneSignal.endInit();
  }
}
```

If you take notice, for Android, a call to `startInit` has two parameters instead of one parameter. The first parameter is **OneSignal App ID**, and the second parameter is **Google Project Number/Sender ID**.

6. Replace `home.scss`, also in the `/home` folder, with the following code:

```
page-home {
 .center {
    text-align: center;
 }
 h2.big-square {
    text-align: center;
    padding: 50px;
    color: #D91E18;
    background: #F9BF3B;
 }
 h3.sub-title {
    text-align: center;
    padding: 10px;
    color: #446CB3;
    background: #E4F1FE;
 }
 ion-card ion-card-header {
```

```
        padding: 10px 16px;
        background: #F9690E;
        color: white;
    }
    ion-card ion-card-header + ion-card-content,
    ion-card .item + ion-card-content {
        padding-top: 16px;
    }
}
```

7. Ensure that you are in the app folder and build for the Android platform, as follows:

```
$ ionic cordova run android
```

 The process of sending push notifications is exactly the same as iOS.

How it works

The process is almost the same as iOS. The reason is, OneSignal abstracts lots of things for us. The difference is that, instead of sending push notification requests to APNS, it is now sending push notification requests to Google's FCM servers. Then, it forwards the push notification to the actual device.

You will see the notification in the Android phone as follows:

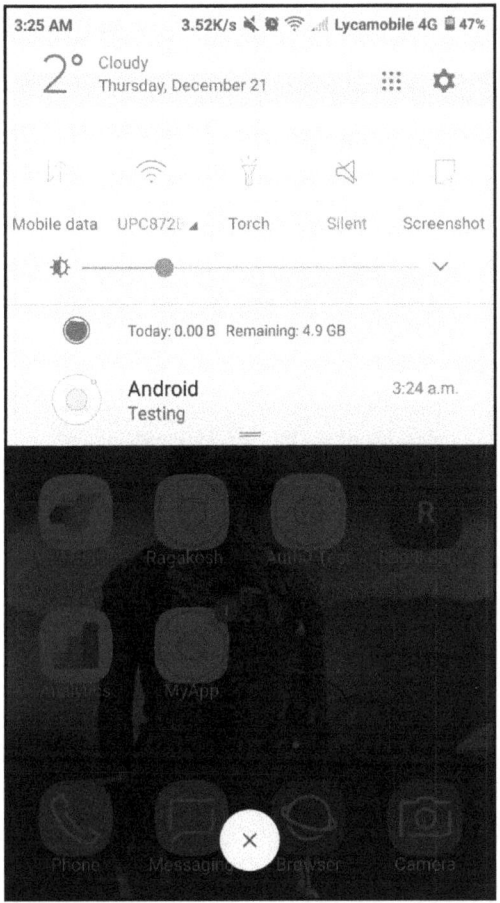

By Default, it will use app icon as a notification icon, but you can customize that for Android. Take a look at `https://documentation.onesignal.com/docs/customize-notification-icons`. On iOS, you can't customize the icon.

When you open the app, you will see notifications in the app as follows:

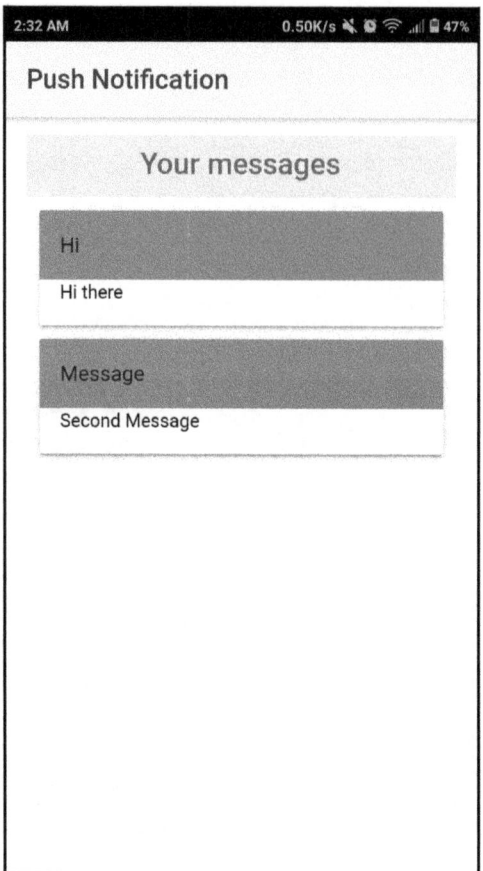

There's more...

For more information about the **Firebase Notification** service, you can visit the official documentation at `https://firebase.google.com/docs/cloud-messaging/`.

7
Supporting Device Functionalities Using Ionic Native

In this chapter, we will cover the following tasks related to native device feature support:

- Taking a photo using the camera plugin
- Sharing content using the social-sharing plugin
- Displaying a local notification using the local notification plugin
- Fingerprint authentication using the fingerprint AIO plugin.
- Creating a media player and adding a media player notification control
- Creating a taxi app using the Google Maps plugin and geocode support

Introduction

In this chapter, you will learn how to access some common features of a device, such as a camera, contact list, email, and maps. Some of these features can be written in a JavaScript-only environment, but the performance is not on a par with native support.

Cordova has a very well-supported community with many plugins. You may want to check out http://plugins.cordova.io/ to understand what is out there. Luckily, you don't need to deal with these plugins directly. You will use the Ionic Native (http://ionicframework.com/docs/v2/native/) service on top of Cordova and Angular. Keep in mind that you have to use Ionic Native instead of ngCordova for Ionic 2+ because of compatibility issues. You can only use ngCordova for Ionic 1.x.

Taking a photo using the camera plugin

In this section, you will make an app to take a picture using the device camera or load an existing picture from the device album. The picture could be either in the Base64 format or saved in a local filesystem relating to your app. The following is a screenshot of the app:

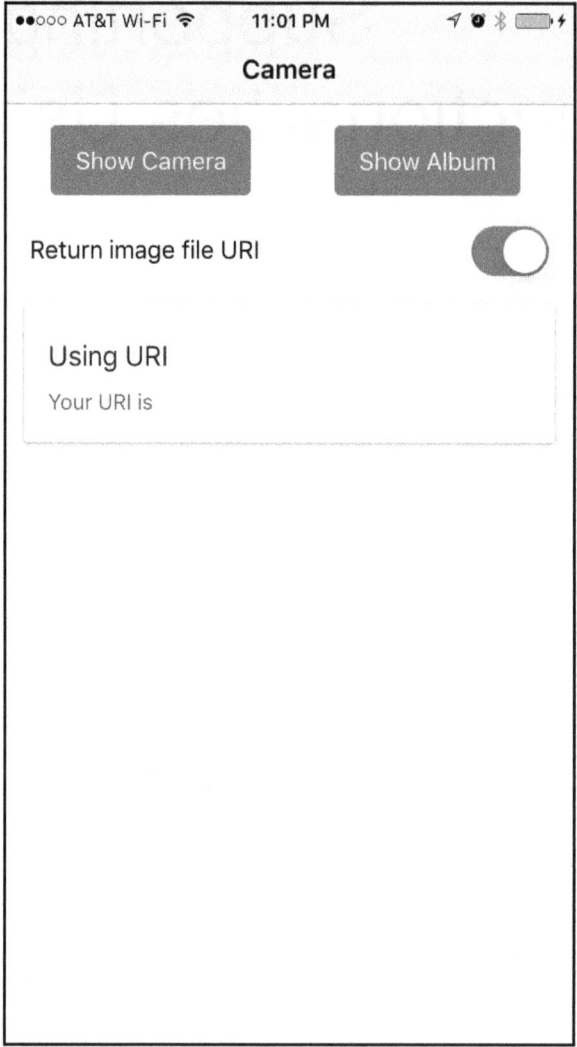

Here is the high-level process:

1. Access the Cordova camera plugin to trigger camera capture and get the image back in the Base64 or URI format
2. Parse the Base64 data or URI on an <img> DOM object
3. Display the URI if it's in the URI format
4. Capture an event of a toggle component
5. Display long data (for example, URI) using a horizontal scroll

Getting ready

You should have a physical device ready in order to test the camera capability. It's possible to just run the code via an emulator, but the filesystem support might look different across the various platforms.

How to do it...

The following are the instructions to add camera support:

1. Start a blank project (for example, MyCamera) and go to that folder:

```
$ ionic start MyCamera blank
$ cd MyCamera
```

2. Add the Cordova camera plugin and Ionic Native wrapper for the plugin using the following code:

```
$ ionic plugin add cordova-plugin-camera
$ npm install --save @ionic-native/camera
```

 You should not use the cordova add command line directly; instead use ionic cordova plugin add

You should be able to see a new folder, cordova-plugin-camera, being added to the /plugins folder.

3. Replace `./src/pages/home/home.html` with the following code:

```html
<ion-header>
  <ion-navbar>
    <ion-title>
      Camera
    </ion-title>
  </ion-navbar>
</ion-header>

<ion-content padding>
  <ion-row class="center">
    <ion-col width-50>
      <button ion-button (click)="getPicture(1)">Show Camera</
button>
    </ion-col>
    <ion-col width-50>
      <button ion-button (click)="getPicture(0)">Show Album</
button>
    </ion-col>
  </ion-row>
  <ion-item class="no-border">
    <ion-label>Return image file URI</ion-label>
    <ion-toggle energized [(ngModel)]="useURI">
    </ion-toggle>
  </ion-item>
  <ion-card>
    <img [src]="imageData" *ngIf="imageData" />
    <ion-card-content>
      <ion-card-title>
        <div *ngIf="useURI">
          Using URI
        </div>
        <div *ngIf="!useURI">
          Using Base64
        </div>
      </ion-card-title>
      <p *ngIf="useURI">
        Your URI is {{ imageData }}
      </p>
      <p *ngIf="!useURI">
        Your Base64 image has {{ (imageData + '').length }} bytes
      </p>
    </ion-card-content>
  </ion-card>
</ion-content>
```

Since you only have one page, this template will show two buttons and an area to display the image.

4. Replace ./src/pages/home/home.ts with the following code:

```
import { Component, Input } from '@angular/core';
import { NavController } from 'ionic-angular';
import { Camera } from '@ionic-native/camera';

@Component({
  selector: 'page-home',
  templateUrl: 'home.html'
})
export class HomePage {
  public imageData: string;
  @Input('useURI') useURI: Boolean = true;
  constructor(public navCtrl: NavController, public camera:Camera)
  {

  }

  getPicture(sourceType) {
    this.camera.getPicture({
      quality: 50,
      allowEdit: true,
      encodingType: this.camera.EncodingType.JPEG,
      saveToPhotoAlbum: false,
      destinationType: this.useURI ? this.camera.DestinationType.
        FILE_URI : this.camera.DestinationType.DATA_URL,
      targetWidth: 800,
      targetHeight: 800,
      sourceType: sourceType
    }).then((imageData) => {
      if (this.useURI) {
        this.imageData = imageData;
      } else {
        this.imageData = "data:image/jpeg;base64," + imageData;
      }
    }, (err) => {
      console.log(err);
    });
  }

}
```

There is only one method: getPicture(). This method will return the photo data so that the template can render.

5. Replace `.src/pages/home/home.scss` with the following code:

```scss
page-home {
    center {
        text-align: center;
    }
    .no-border .item-inner {
        border-bottom: 0;
    }
}
```

There are only a few minor changes in the styling so that you can keep them simple.

6. Replace `./src/app/app.module.ts` with the following code:

```typescript
import { BrowserModule } from '@angular/platform-browser';
import { ErrorHandler, NgModule } from '@angular/core';
import { IonicApp, IonicErrorHandler, IonicModule } from 'ionic-angular';
import { SplashScreen } from '@ionic-native/splash-screen';
import { StatusBar } from '@ionic-native/status-bar';
import { Camera } from '@ionic-native/camera';

import { MyApp } from './app.component';
import { HomePage } from '../pages/home/home';

@NgModule({
  declarations: [
    MyApp,
    HomePage
  ],
  imports: [
    BrowserModule,
    IonicModule.forRoot(MyApp)
  ],
  bootstrap: [IonicApp],
  entryComponents: [
    MyApp,
    HomePage
  ],
  providers: [
    StatusBar,
    SplashScreen,
    Camera,
    {provide: ErrorHandler, useClass: IonicErrorHandler}
  ]
```

```
})
export class AppModule {}
```

7. Connect your device to your computer.
8. Go to the Terminal and execute the following command line for iOS:

```
$ ionic cordova run ios
```

If you are not able to push the app to your physical device using the preceding command line, you can use `ionic cordova run ios --device` to specify the CLI to use the physical device instead of a simulator.

If you want to run the app on your Android device, use the following code:

```
$ ionic cordova run android
```

When you run the app and take a picture, you should see the app, as shown in the following screenshot:

How it works...

`Camera.getPicture()` is just an abstraction of `navigator.camera.getPicture()` from the Cordova camera plugin. If you are already familiar with Cordova or ngCordova from Ionic 1, this should be very familiar. Let's start with the template. You have the following two buttons, which trigger the same, `getPicture()`, method:

```
<button ion-buton (click)="getPicture(1)">Show Camera</button>
<button ion-buton (click)="getPicture(1)">Show Camera</button>
```

These are just different ways to access photos: either from the camera itself or from the existing photos in the phone's album. For the photo to render, you need to pass the photo data into the `src` attribute, as follows:

```
<img [src]="imageData" *ngIf="imageData" />
```

Note that you only want to show this `<img>` tag when `imageData` exists with some data. The `imageData` variable could be Base64 or an internal URL of the photo. To specify this option, there is a toggle button, as shown here:

```
<ion-toggle energized [(ngModel)]="useURI"></ion-toggle>
```

You will use the `useURI` variable inside the class, as illustrated, to determine which format to return the photo data in:

```
@Input('useURI') useURI: Boolean = true;
```

Both `useURI` and `sourceType` will be used in the `getPicture()` function, as follows:

```
Camera.getPicture({
    quality: 50,
    allowEdit: true,
    encodingType: Camera.EncodingType.JPEG,
    saveToPhotoAlbum: false,
    destinationType: this.useURI ? Camera.DestinationType.FILE_URI
      : Camera.DestinationType.DATA_URL,
    targetWidth: 800,
    targetHeight: 800,
    sourceType: sourceType
}).then((imageData) => {
    if (this.useURI) {
      this.imageData = imageData;
    } else {
      this.imageData = "data:image/jpeg;base64," + imageData;
    }
}, (err) => {
```

```
        console.log(err);
    });
```

It's important to adjust the quality, `targetWidth`, and `targetHeight` to low so that the photo is not too big, which could crash the device, especially when it doesn't have enough memory. When you return the Base64 data, it must be prefixed with the string `data:image/jpeg;base64`.

It is also important to note that inside `app.module.ts`, we are adding the `Camera` plugin to the NgModule's provider's array. This is very important because it allows us to use the plugin via Angular's Dependency Injection system. We have to do this for each plugin throughout this chapter.

One item that isn't discussed here is the ability to post image data to the server. The common scenario is to upload the file from the filesystem. It's not a good idea to send data as Base64 because of the data size, which is double the original binary size.

There's more...

It is possible to create Instagram-like filter effects using just JavaScript. You can leverage an existing library, such as `Filterous` (`https://github.com/girliemac/Filterous`), to modify the image canvas directly.

There is an Instagram plugin (`https://github.com/vstirbu/InstagramPlugin`) for Cordova on GitHub. You could write some extra code to pass the image to Instagram. The user must have Instagram installed on the phone first, though. This idea is nice when you plan to do some cool image processing (for example, adding funny text) before letting Instagram perform the photo filter operation.

You could even add the Cordova's social network plugin and post the resulting images to Twitter or Facebook.

Sharing content using the social sharing plugin

If you develop an app with shareable content, you might want to utilize the native device feature to share via the device's authorized social media accounts. There are several benefits to using this approach. First, users don't need to open a separate browser to log in to their social media account each time they want to share. Second, all the information can be filled out programmatically, such as title, body, link, or image. Finally, since this is a native feature of the device, the menu selection allows users to see multiple accounts, which they are already familiar with, to choose from. The social sharing plugin can greatly enhance the user experience.

This is the app that you will build:

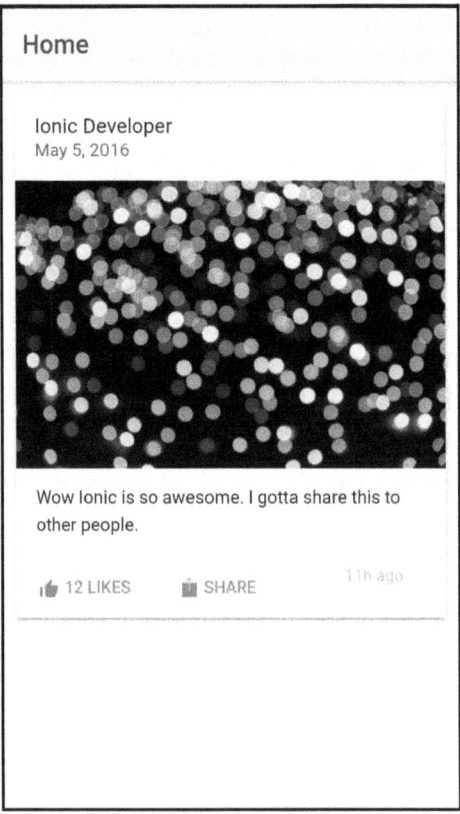

When the user clicks on the **SHARE** button, the app will show the following native button menu for social media account selection:

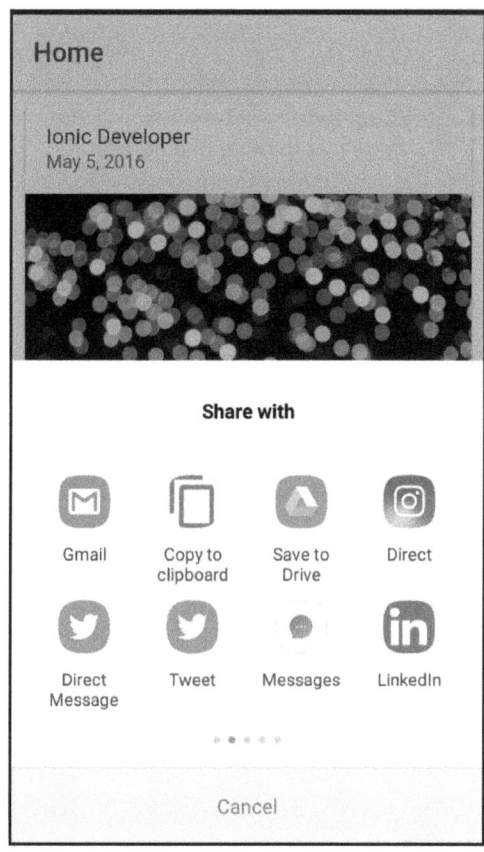

If the user selects Twitter, a popup will show up with all the information prefilled, as illustrated in the following screenshot:

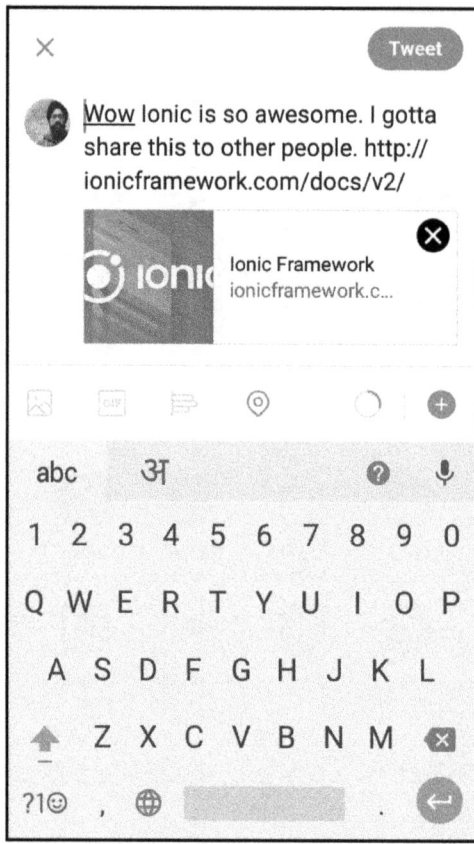

After posting on Twitter, the user goes right back to the app without ever leaving it.

Getting ready

You should have a physical device or simulator ready in order to test the social sharing capability.

How to do it...

The following are the instructions:

1. Start a blank project (for example, `LinkSocialShare`), as follows, and go to that folder:

```
$ ionic start LinkSocialShare blank
$ cd LinkSocialShare
```

2. Add the social sharing plugin and Ionic Native wrapper for the plugin with the following command line:

```
$ ionic plugin add cordova-plugin-x-socialsharing
$ npm install --save @ionic-native/social-sharing
```

3. Open `./src/pages/home/home.html` and replace its contents with the following code:

```
<ion-header>
  <ion-navbar>
    <ion-title>
      Home
    </ion-title>
  </ion-navbar>
</ion-header>

<ion-content>
  <ion-card>
    <ion-item>
      <h2 #messageSubject>Ionic Developer</h2>
      <p>May 5, 2016</p>
    </ion-item>
    <img
src="https://source.unsplash.com/category/technology/600x390">
    <ion-card-content>
      <p #messageBody>Wow Ionic is so awesome. I gotta share this
to other people.</p>
    </ion-card-content>
    <ion-row>
      <ion-col>
        <button ion-button color="primary" clear small icon-left>
          <ion-icon name="thumbs-up"></ion-icon>
          <div>12 Likes</div>
        </button>
      </ion-col>
      <ion-col>
```

```
            <button ion-button color="primary" clear small icon-left
            (click)="sendShare(messageBody.innerText,
    messageSubject.innerText,'http://ionicframework.com/docs/v2/')">
                <ion-icon name="ios-share"></ion-icon>
                <div>Share</div>
            </button>
        </ion-col>
        <ion-col center text-center>
            <ion-note>
                11h ago
            </ion-note>
        </ion-col>
    </ion-row>
  </ion-card>
</ion-content>
```

This is a very simple page with the card element. The **Like** button is there just for cosmetic reasons without code implementation. However, all the JavaScript logic will focus on the
SHARE button.

4. Open `./src/pages/home/home.ts`, as shown here:

```
import { Component } from '@angular/core';
import { NavController } from 'ionic-angular';
import { SocialSharing } from '@ionic-native/social-sharing';
@Component({
  selector: 'page-home',
  templateUrl: 'home.html'
})
export class HomePage {

  constructor(public navCtrl: NavController, public socialSharing:
SocialSharing) {

  }

  sendShare(message, subject, url) {
    this.socialSharing.share(message, subject, null, url);
  }

}
```

5. Replace `./src/app/app.module.ts` with the following code:

```
import { BrowserModule } from '@angular/platform-browser';
import { ErrorHandler, NgModule } from '@angular/core';
```

```
import { IonicApp, IonicErrorHandler, IonicModule } from 'ionic-
angular';
import { SplashScreen } from '@ionic-native/splash-screen';
import { StatusBar } from '@ionic-native/status-bar';
import { SocialSharing } from '@ionic-native/social-sharing';
import { MyApp } from './app.component';
import { HomePage } from '../pages/home/home';

@NgModule({
  declarations: [
    MyApp,
    HomePage
  ],
  imports: [
    BrowserModule,
    IonicModule.forRoot(MyApp)
  ],
  bootstrap: [IonicApp],
  entryComponents: [
    MyApp,
    HomePage
  ],
  providers: [
    StatusBar,
    SplashScreen,
    SocialSharing,
    {provide: ErrorHandler, useClass: IonicErrorHandler}
  ]
})
export class AppModule {}
```

6. Go to the Terminal and execute either of the following command lines:

```
$ ionic run ios
$ ionic run android
```

How it works...

You can start looking at the template because that is where the social media content is extracted from. The subject value is from the `#messageSubject` local variable, as illustrated:

```
<ion-item>
  <h2 #messageSubject>Ionic Developer</h2>
  <p>May 5, 2016</p>
</ion-item>
```

In the preceding case, the subject is `Ionic Developer` because you will access `messageSubject.innerText` later on. `messageSubject` is just referencing your H2 DOM node.

Similarly, the body is from `#messageBody`, as shown here:

```
<ion-card-content>
  <p #messageBody>Wow Ionic 2 is so awesome. I gotta share this to other
people.</p>
</ion-card-content>
```

When the user clicks on the **SHARE** button, it will trigger the `sendShare()` method, as follows:

```
<button ion-button color="primary" clear small icon-left
        (click)="sendShare(messageBody.innerText,
         messageSubject.innerText,
         'http://ionicframework.com/docs/v2/')">
```

Let's take a look at your `home.ts` to understand how `sendShare()` works.

First, you need to import the `SocialSharing` module from Ionic Native, as illustrated:

```
import { SocialSharing } from '@ionic-native/social-sharing';
```

To share your content and trigger the social media menu, the logic, as shown, is very simple:

```
sendShare(message, subject, url) {
  SocialSharing.share(message, subject, null, url);
}
```

If you want to share a file, you can replace the third parameter (where it is `null`) with the URL to the user's local filesystem. This is useful when you want people to send a PDF or JPG via email or post it on Facebook.

There's more...

To see the latest update of the social sharing plugin, you can visit the documentation page at `http://ionicframework.com/docs/v2/native/social-sharing/`.

Displaying a local notification using the local notification plugin

When you are developing mobile applications, your app might want to notify the user about something. If the information is coming from the backend, we use push notifications. But, if the information is generated by the app, locally on the device, we can use a local notification for that.

This recipe is intended to help you understand how local notifications work.

When you open the app, you will see the following page.

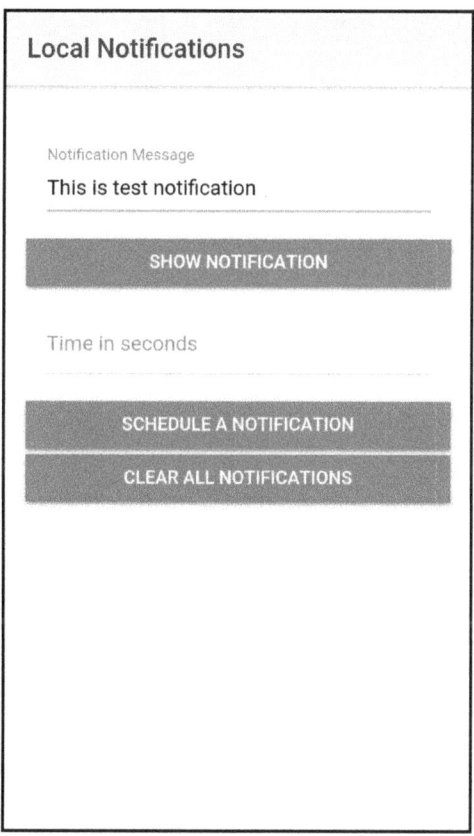

You can input anything in the input box and then click on **SHOW NOTIFICATION**. You can also schedule a notification to show later. This is what a notification looks like in the notification area:

Getting ready

You should have a physical device ready in order to test local notifications.

How to do it...

Here are the instructions:

1. Create a blank Ionic app (for example, `Notifications`) and `cd` to that folder, as shown here:

```
$ ionic start Notifications blank
$ cd Notifications
```

2. Install the local notification plugin and Ionic native wrapper for the plugin using the following command:

```
$ ionic cordova plugin add cordova-plugin-local-notification
$ npm install --save @ionic-native/local-notifications
```

3. Open `./src/pages/home/home.html` and replace with the following code:

```
<ion-header>
  <ion-navbar>
    <ion-title>
      Local Notifications
    </ion-title>
  </ion-navbar>
</ion-header>

<ion-content padding>
  <ion-item padding>
    <ion-label color="primary" stacked>Notification Message</ion-
```

```
label>
    <ion-input placeholder="Enter Notification Text here"
[(ngModel)]="message"></ion-input>
  </ion-item>
  <button full ion-button color="primary"
(click)="showNotification('now')">Show Notification</button>
  <ion-item padding>
    <ion-label>Time in seconds</ion-label>
    <ion-datetime displayFormat="ss Second" placeholder=""
[(ngModel)]="time"></ion-datetime>
  </ion-item>
  <button full ion-button color="primary"
(click)="showNotification('future')">Schedule a
Notification</button>
  <button full ion-button color="primary"
(click)="clearNotifications()">Clear all Notifications</button>
</ion-content>
```

4. Open `./src/pages/home/home.ts` and replace with the following code:

```
import { Component } from '@angular/core';
import { NavController } from 'ionic-angular';
import { LocalNotifications } from '@ionic-native/local-
notifications';

@Component({
  selector: 'page-home',
  templateUrl: 'home.html'
})
export class HomePage {
  notifications:Array<any> = [];
  id: number = 1;
  message:string;
  time:number;
  constructor(public navCtrl: NavController,
    private localNotifications: LocalNotifications) {
  }

  showNotification(type) {
    if(type === 'now') {
      this.localNotifications.schedule({
        id: this.id,
        text: this.message,
      });
    } else {
      this.localNotifications.schedule({
        id: this.id,
        text: this.message,
```

```
        at: new Date(new Date().getTime() + this.time * 100),
      });
    }
    this.id++;
  }

  clearNotifications() {
    this.localNotifications.clearAll();
  }

}
```

5. Replace `./src/app/app.module.ts` with the following code:

```
import { BrowserModule } from '@angular/platform-browser';
import { ErrorHandler, NgModule } from '@angular/core';
import { IonicApp, IonicErrorHandler, IonicModule } from 'ionic-
angular';
import { SplashScreen } from '@ionic-native/splash-screen';
import { StatusBar } from '@ionic-native/status-bar';
import { LocalNotifications } from '@ionic-native/local-
notifications';

import { MyApp } from './app.component';
import { HomePage } from '../pages/home/home';

@NgModule({
  declarations: [
    MyApp,
    HomePage
  ],
  imports: [
    BrowserModule,
    IonicModule.forRoot(MyApp)
  ],
  bootstrap: [IonicApp],
  entryComponents: [
    MyApp,
    HomePage
  ],
  providers: [
    StatusBar,
    SplashScreen,
    LocalNotifications,
    {provide: ErrorHandler, useClass: IonicErrorHandler}
  ]
})
export class AppModule {}
```

6. Run the app in the Terminal using the following command line:

```
$ ionic run ios
$ ionic run android
```

How it works...

First, let's take a look at the template `home.html`:

```
<ion-content padding>
  <ion-item padding>
    <ion-label color="primary" stacked>Notification Message</ion-label>
    <ion-input placeholder="Enter Notification Text here"
[(ngModel)]="message"></ion-input>
  </ion-item>
  <button full ion-button color="primary"
(click)="showNotification('now')">Show Notification</button>
  <ion-item padding>
    <ion-label>Time in seconds</ion-label>
    <ion-datetime displayFormat="ss Second" placeholder=""
[(ngModel)]="time"></ion-datetime>
  </ion-item>
  <button full ion-button color="primary"
(click)="showNotification('future')">Schedule a Notification</button>
  <button full ion-button color="primary"
(click)="clearNotifications()">Clear all Notifications</button>
</ion-content>
```

We have an input field where we add text for notifications. Then we have a button to show notifications immediately. Then we have an `ion-datetime` input, which is used to specify the time in seconds. It will be used to schedule a notification for the future, using the **Schedule a Notification** button. Finally, we have a **Clear all Notifications** button to clear notifications in the device's notification area.

In your `home.ts`, you must import the `LocalNotifications` module first, as shown here:

```
import { LocalNotifications } from '@ionic-native/local-notifications';
```

When someone clicks on the **Show Notification** or **Schedule a Notification** buttons, it fires the **Show Notification** button. Here is the `showNotification` method:

```
showNotification(type) {
    if(type === 'now') {
      this.localNotifications.schedule({
        id: this.id,
```

```
        text: this.message,
      });
    } else {
      this.localNotifications.schedule({
        id: this.id,
        text: this.message,
        at: new Date(new Date().getTime() + this.time * 100),
      });
    }
    this.id++;
  }
```

The `showNotifications` method takes an argument `type`. `type` is used to determine if we want to show a notification immediately or at some time in the future. if `type` is equal to now, we show it immediately; otherwise, we schedule the notification to show up later on. For showing notifications, we use the plugin's `schedule` method. We have to specify the `id`, `text`, and `at` values. The `at` value is used to schedule a notification for showing in the future.

The `clearNotifications` method clears all the notifications.

There's more...

Take a look at the GitHub page of the local notification plugin for more information, at `https://github.com/katzer/cordova-plugin-local-notifications`.

Fingerprint authentication using the fingerprint AIO plugin

Gone are the days when you wanted to just use a password authentication system. Authentication is becoming stronger and more intuitive. Most iOS devices these days have a fingerprint sensor and this trend is now starting to prevail in Android devices too. Users can secure their devices using a fingerprint password. Luckily, for developers like us, we can use the same technology to secure content inside our application, which the user can access after authentication.

In this recipe, we are creating an unlock secret app. It is basically a joke app. The home page looks like the following.

When the user clicks on the **Reveal Secret** button, it shows the **Fingerprint Authentication** dialog:

And when the user authenticates, we show a joke on the screen. It is as simple as that:

Getting ready

You should have a physical device with a fingerprint sensor in order to test this application.

How to do it...

Here are the instructions:

1. Create a blank Ionic app (for example, `FingerAuth`) and `cd` to that folder, as shown here:

```
$ ionic start FingerAuth blank
$ cd FingerAuth
```

2. Install the fingerprint `aio` plugin and the Ionic Native wrapper, using the following command:

```
$ ionic cordova plugin add cordova-plugin-fingerprint-aio
$ npm install --save @ionic-native/fingerprint-aio
```

3. Open `./src/pages/home/home.html` and replace with the following code:

```html
<ion-content padding>
  <h1 padding>Secrets</h1>
  <p *ngIf="!isAvailable">This Device doesn't have Fingerprint
Sensor</p>
  <p *ngIf="isAvailable && quote">{{quote.joke}}</p>
  <button id="reveal-button" color="primary" *ngIf="!!isAvailable"
ion-button round (click)="authenticate()">Reveal a Secret</button>
</ion-content>
```

4. Open `./src/pages/home/home.ts` and replace with the following code:

```typescript
import { Component } from '@angular/core';
import { NavController, Platform } from 'ionic-angular';
import { HttpClient } from '@angular/common/http';
import { FingerprintAIO } from '@ionic-native/fingerprint-aio';

@Component({
  selector: 'page-home',
  templateUrl: 'home.html'
})
export class HomePage {
  quote:any = {};
  isAvailable: Boolean;
  constructor(public navCtrl: NavController,
    private faio: FingerprintAIO,
    private http: HttpClient,
    private platform: Platform) {

  }
```

```
ionViewDidLoad() {
  this.checkAvailablity();
}

checkAvailablity() {
  this.platform.ready()
  .then(()=> {
    this.faio.isAvailable().then((value)=> {
      console.log(value);
      this.isAvailable = true
    }).catch(() => {
      this.isAvailable = false;
    });
  });
}

authenticate() {
  this.faio.show({
    clientId: 'Ionic Fingerprint Auth',
    clientSecret: 'password', //Only necessary for Android
    localizedFallbackTitle: 'Use Pin', //Only for iOS
    localizedReason: 'Please authenticate' //Only for iOS
  })
  .then((result: any) => {
    this.reveal();
  });
}

reveal() {
  const url = "http://api.icndb.com/jokes/random/";
  this.http.get(url)
  .subscribe((data:any) => {
    this.quote = data.value;
  });
}

}
```

5. Replace `./src/pages/home/home.scss` with the following code:

```
page-home {
    ion-content {
        .scroll-content {
            text-align:center;
            background-color: black;
            color:white;
            #reveal-button {
                height:200px;
```

```
                        width:200px;
                        border-radius:100%;
                  }
              }
          }
      }
```

6. Replace `./src/app/app.module.ts` with the following code:

```
import { BrowserModule } from '@angular/platform-browser';
import { ErrorHandler, NgModule } from '@angular/core';
import { IonicApp, IonicErrorHandler, IonicModule } from 'ionic-
angular';
import { SplashScreen } from '@ionic-native/splash-screen';
import { StatusBar } from '@ionic-native/status-bar';
import { HttpClientModule } from '@angular/common/http';
import { FingerprintAIO } from '@ionic-native/fingerprint-aio';

import { MyApp } from './app.component';
import { HomePage } from '../pages/home/home';

@NgModule({
  declarations: [
    MyApp,
    HomePage
  ],
  imports: [
    BrowserModule,
    HttpClientModule,
    IonicModule.forRoot(MyApp)
  ],
  bootstrap: [IonicApp],
  entryComponents: [
    MyApp,
    HomePage
  ],
  providers: [
    StatusBar,
    SplashScreen,
    FingerprintAIO,
    {provide: ErrorHandler, useClass: IonicErrorHandler}
  ]
})
export class AppModule {}
```

7. Run the app in the Terminal, using the following command line:

```
$ ionic cordova run ios
$ ionic cordova run android
```

How it works...

First, let's take a look at the template home.html:

```
<ion-content padding>
  <h1 padding>Secrets</h1>
  <p *ngIf="!isAvailable">This Device doesn't have Fingerprint Sensor</p>
  <p *ngIf="isAvailable && quote">{{quote.joke}}</p>
  <button id="reveal-button" color="primary" *ngIf="!!isAvailable" ion-
button round (click)="authenticate()">Reveal a Secret</button>
</ion-content>
```

If the device doesn't have a fingerprint sensor, we display a notice on the screen saying that **This Device doesn't have Fingerprint Sensor**. Otherwise, we show a **Reveal a Secret** Button. When the user clicks on it, it opens a **Fingerprint Authentication** dialog.

In your home.ts, you must import the FingerprintAIO module first, as shown here:

```
import { FingerprintAIO } from '@ionic-native/fingerprint-aio';
```

When the page is loaded, we check the availability of the sensor in ionViewDidLoad hook via the plugin's isAvailable method. It returns a promise. If it is resolved, it means the sensor is available. The authenticate method is fired when the user clicks on the **Reveal a secret** button in the UI.

Here is the authenticate() method:

```
authenticate() {
  this.faio.show({
    clientId: 'Ionic Fingerprint Auth',
    clientSecret: 'password', //Only necessary for Android
    localizedFallbackTitle: 'Use Pin', //Only for iOS
    localizedReason: 'Please authenticate' //Only for iOS
  })
  .then((result: any) => {
    this.reveal();
  });
}
```

Inside this method, we call the plugin's show method, which returns a promise. If the promise is resolved, it means the user is authenticated and we reveal the joke. Otherwise, we do nothing.

There's more...

You can read more about the fingerprint AIO plugin at `https://github.com/NiklasMerz/cordova-plugin-fingerprint-aio`.

Creating a media player with the Media Player notification control

Media Player is an important app in a user's phone. Almost every media app has a control in the notification area nowadays. In this recipe, we are going to create a very simple media player with **Play** and **Pause** buttons and we will add Media Player controls in the notification area.

This is what the home page of our app will look like:

And this is what the notification area will look like:

When the user clicks on the **Play** button inside the app, it shows controls in the notification area. When the user clicks on the **Pause** button inside the app, it updates the music controls too. This also works the other way around. You can play and pause the media from Music Control in the notification area.

Getting ready

You should have a physical device ready in order to test this app, since it uses the Cordova plugin.

How to do it...

Here are the instructions:

1. Create a blank Ionic app (for example, `MediaPlayer`) and `cd` to that folder, as shown here:

```
$ ionic start MediaPlayer blank
$ cd MediaPlayer
```

2. Install the Music Control plugin and it's Ionic Native wrapper using the following command:

```
$ ionic cordova plugin add cordova-plugin-music-controls
$ npm install --save @ionic-native/music-controls
```

3. Open `./src/pages/home/home.html` and replace with the following code:

```
<ion-header>
  <ion-navbar>
    <ion-title>
      Music Player
    </ion-title>
  </ion-navbar>
</ion-header>
```

```
<ion-content padding>
    <ion-item>
      <ion-thumbnail item-left>
        <img src="{{track.art}}">
      </ion-thumbnail>
      <div item-content style="width:100%">
        <p><strong>{{track.title}}</strong> o
        <em>{{track.artist}}</em></p>
      </div>
    </ion-item>

    <ion-row id="music-controls">
      <ion-col (click)="play()"><ion-icon name="play"></ion-
icon></ion-col>
      <ion-col (click)="pause()"><ion-icon name="pause"></ion-
icon></ion-col>
    </ion-row>
</ion-content>
```

4. Open `./src/pages/home/home.ts` and replace with the following code:

```
import { Component } from '@angular/core';
import { NavController } from 'ionic-angular';
import { MusicControls } from '@ionic-native/music-controls';
import { AudioProvider} from '../../services/audio-service';

@Component({
  selector: 'page-home',
  templateUrl: 'home.html'
})
export class HomePage {
  track = {
    src:
'https://ia801609.us.archive.org/16/items/nusratcollection_20170414
_0953/Man%20Atkiya%20Beparwah%20De%20Naal%20Nusrat%20Fateh%20Ali%20
Khan.mp3',
    artist: 'Nusrat Fateh Ali Khan',
    title: 'Man Atkiya Beparwah De Naal',
    art:
'https://ia801307.us.archive.org/31/items/mbid-42764450-04e5-459e-b
022-00847fc8fb94/mbid-42764450-04e5-459e-
b022-00847fc8fb94-12391862253_thumb250.jpg',
    preload: 'metadata' // tell the plugin to preload metadata such
as duration for this track, set to 'none' to turn off
  };

  constructor(public navCtrl: NavController, public
musicControls:MusicControls,
```

```
      public audioProvider: AudioProvider) {}

      play() {
        this.audioProvider.play(this.track.src);
        this.createControls();
      }

      pause() {
        this.audioProvider.pause();
        this.musicControls.updateIsPlaying(false);
      }

      createControls() {
        this.musicControls.create({
          track : this.track.title,
          artist : this.track.artist,
          cover : this.track.art,
          isPlaying : true,
          hasPrev : false,
          hasNext : false,
          dismissable : true,
        });

        this.musicControls.subscribe().subscribe(action => {
          const message = JSON.parse(action).message;
          switch(message) {
            case 'music-controls-play':
              this.play();
            break;

            case 'music-controls-pause':
              this.pause();
            break;
          }
        });

        this.musicControls.listen();
      }
    }
```

5. Replace `./src/pages/home/home.scss` with the following code:

```
page-home {
    #music-controls {
        text-align:center;
        font-size: 2.5rem;
    }
}
```

6. Create a file at `./src/services/audio-service.ts` and add the following content:

```
import { Injectable } from '@angular/core';

@Injectable()
export class AudioProvider {
    track:any;
    isPaused: Boolean = false;
    url;
    play(url) {
        if(this.url !== url) {
            this.url = url;
            this.track = new Audio(url);
            this.track.load();
        }
        this.track.play();
    }
    pause() {
        this.track.pause();
        this.isPaused = true;
    }
}
}
```

7. Replace `./src/app/app.module.ts` with the following code:

```
import { BrowserModule } from '@angular/platform-browser';
import { ErrorHandler, NgModule } from '@angular/core';
import { IonicApp, IonicErrorHandler, IonicModule } from 'ionic-angular';
import { SplashScreen } from '@ionic-native/splash-screen';
import { StatusBar } from '@ionic-native/status-bar';
import { MusicControls } from '@ionic-native/music-controls';

import { MyApp } from './app.component';
import { HomePage } from '../pages/home/home';
import { AudioProvider} from '../services/audio-service';

@NgModule({
  declarations: [
    MyApp,
    HomePage
  ],
  imports: [
    BrowserModule,
    IonicModule.forRoot(MyApp)
  ],
```

```
    bootstrap: [IonicApp],
    entryComponents: [
      MyApp,
      HomePage
    ],
    providers: [
      StatusBar,
      SplashScreen,
      MusicControls,
      AudioProvider,
      {provide: ErrorHandler, useClass: IonicErrorHandler}
    ]
  })
  export class AppModule {}
```

8. Run the app in the Terminal using the following command line:

```
$ ionic cordova run ios
$ ionic cordova run android
```

How it works...

First, let's take a look at the template `home.html`:

```
<ion-content padding>
    <ion-item>
      <ion-thumbnail item-left>
        <img src="{{track.art}}">
      </ion-thumbnail>
      <div item-content style="width:100%">
        <p><strong>{{track.title}}</strong> ○ <em>{{track.artist}}</em>
      </p>
      </div>
    </ion-item>

    <ion-row id="music-controls">
      <ion-col (click)="play()"><ion-icon name="play"></ion-icon></ion-col>
      <ion-col (click)="pause()"><ion-icon name="pause"></ion-icon></ion-col>
    </ion-row>
</ion-content>
```

It is very simple. We are showing the track's thumbnail and track title along with the track artist in `ion-item`. Then we have the `play` and `pause` buttons, shown inside `ion-row`.

At `home.ts`, we have a list of audio tracks for our media player. For the sake of simplicity, I just added a single track, so that we don't add too much extra functionality and we remain focused on the plugin part. Then we have the `play` and `pause` methods. These methods are linked to the `play` and `pause` buttons in the UI and they are fired when the user clicks on them.

Inside the `play` button, we fire AudioProvider's `play` method with the track's source `url` and also call the `createControls` method. This `createControls` method creates **Music Control** in the notification area of the device.

Inside the `pause` button, we fire AudioProvider's `pause` method and also update Music Control by telling it that we have paused the audio and it changes the UI accordingly.

In the `createControls()` method:

```
createControls() {
  this.musicControls.create({
    track : this.track.title,
    artist : this.track.artist,
    cover : this.track.art,
    isPlaying : true,
    hasPrev : false,
    hasNext : false,
    dismissable : true,
  });

  this.musicControls.subscribe().subscribe(action => {
    const message = JSON.parse(action).message;
    switch(message) {
      case 'music-controls-play':
        this.play();
      break;

      case 'music-controls-pause':
        this.pause();
      break;
    }
  });

  this.musicControls.listen();
}
```

Also, take a look at our miniature `AudioProvider`:

```
export class AudioProvider {
  track:any;
```

```
isPaused: Boolean = false;
url;
play(url) {
    if(this.url !== url) {
        this.url = url;
        this.track = new Audio(url);
        this.track.load();
    }
    this.track.play();
    this.isPaused = false;
}
pause() {
    this.track.pause();
    this.isPaused = true;
}

}
```

In the `play` method, we get `url` as an argument. if the new `url` is different to the previous one, we make the `Audio` object using the url and load the media and then we play the media and set `this.isPaused` to `true`.

In the `pause` method, we pause the track and set the `this.isPaused` Boolean to `true`, which is by default set to `false`.

There's more...

For the sake of simplicity, we used only the play and pause buttons. But it is easy to implement forthcoming and previous features in the notification area as well as the app. Take a look at the GitHub page of the plugin at `https://github.com/homerours/cordova-music-controls-plugin`.

Creating a taxi app using the Google Maps plugin and geocode support

Today, many mobile apps utilize different mapping features, such as showing the current location, creating routes, and providing suggestive business searches. This section will show you how to use Ionic Native's Google Maps plugin to provide mapping support.

You will create a taxi app that can do the following things:

- Display Google Maps in fullscreen
- Add a button overlay on top of the map
- Detect the current device location
- Add a marker with any text

This is the screenshot of the taxi app:

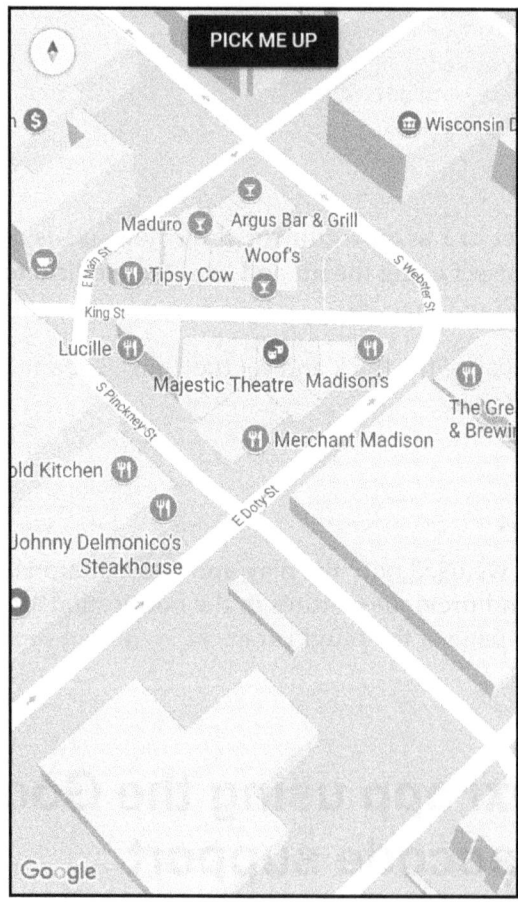

When users click on the **PICK ME UP** button, it will go to the current device location and show longitude and latitude information:

It is possible to use the HTML5 and JavaScript version of geolocation and maps instead of the Cordova plugin's. However, you will see a negative impact on performance. It's very obvious that if you use the SDK, map rendering and optimization tends to be faster. In addition, HTML5 geolocation sometimes has some strange bugs that require the user to accept permission twice-once for the app and once for the inside browser object.

Getting ready

The Google Maps plugin requires a Google Maps API key for your project. You need a Google account and login to get started:

1. Navigate to the Google APIs Console at `https://console.developers.google.com/cloud-resource-manager`.

2. Create a project if you don't have one yet. Just fill in the required fields:

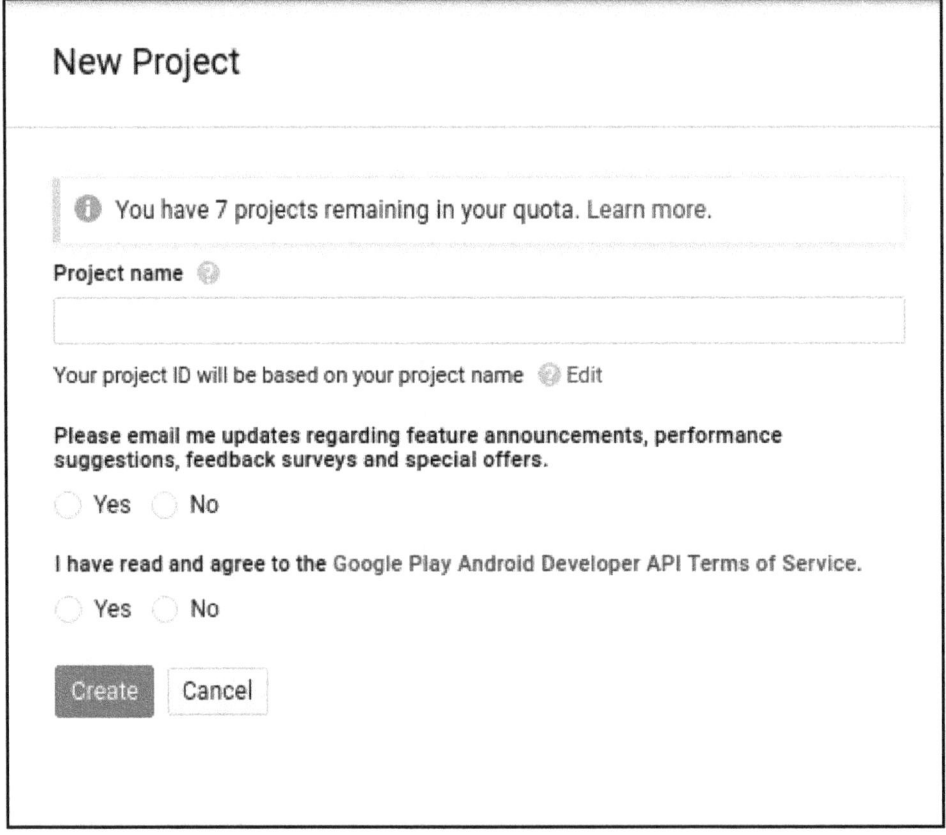

3. You need to enable the **Google Maps SDK for iOS**, the **Google Maps Android API**, or both. It depends on how many platforms you plan to support. Let's select **Google Maps SDK for iOS** for this example:

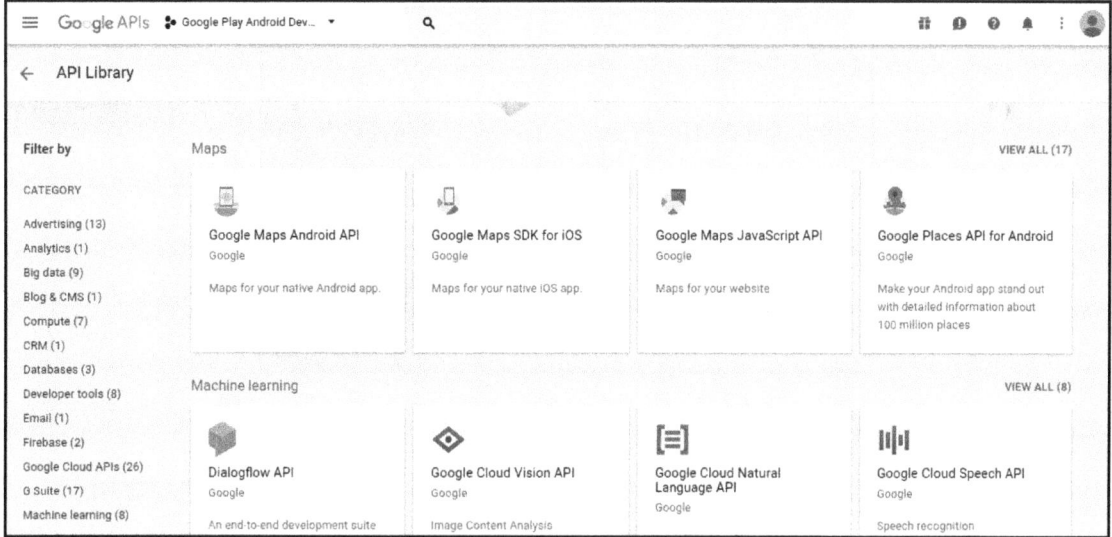

4. Click on the **Enable** button:

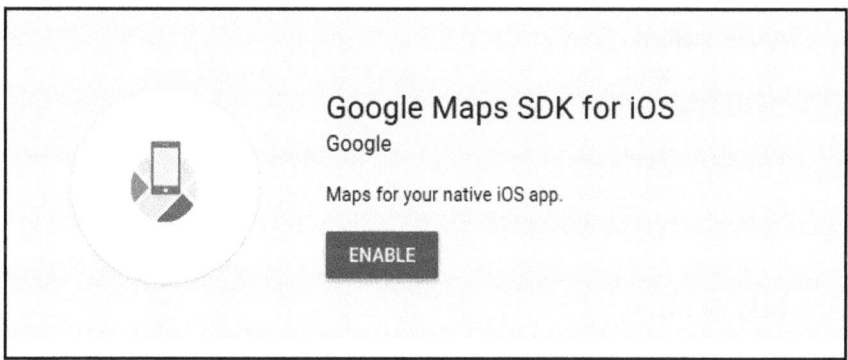

5. Go to **Credentials** to create your own key:

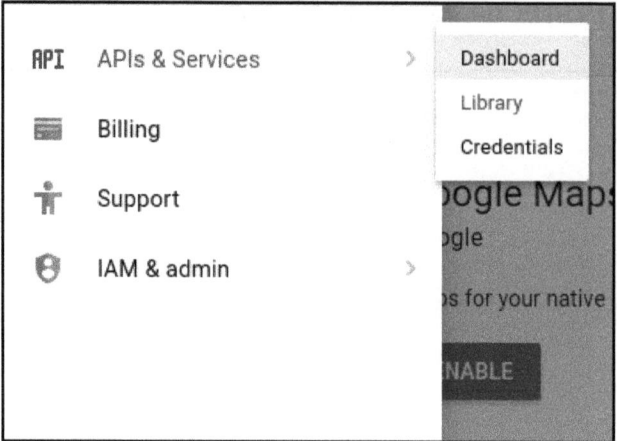

6. Click on the **Create credential | API key** option:

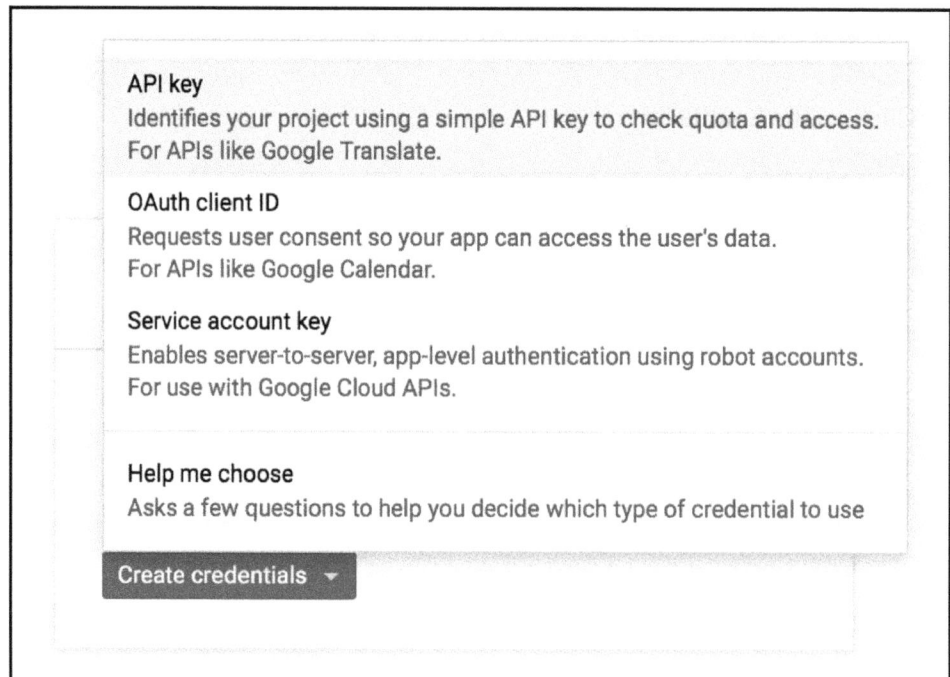

7. Select the **RESTRICT KEY** option. In the following example, you will select the **iOS apps** radio button:

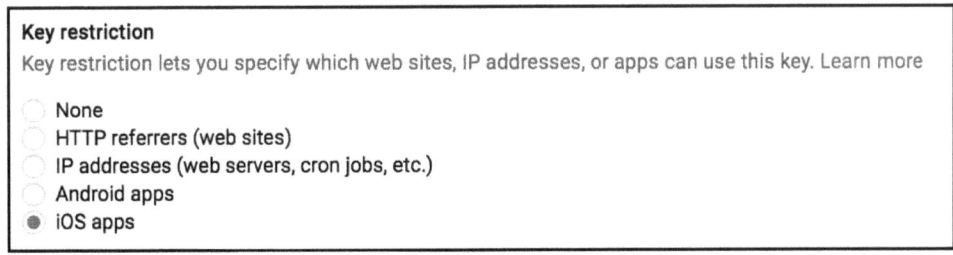

8. Fill in your app's Bundle ID. You might not know exactly what it is yet because Ionic will create a random ID. So just put in `com.ionicframework.starter` and change that later:

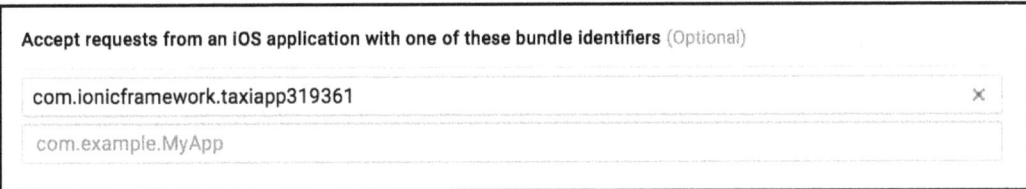

9. Click on the **Save** button.
10. Now you should see the key for the iOS applications section as follows:

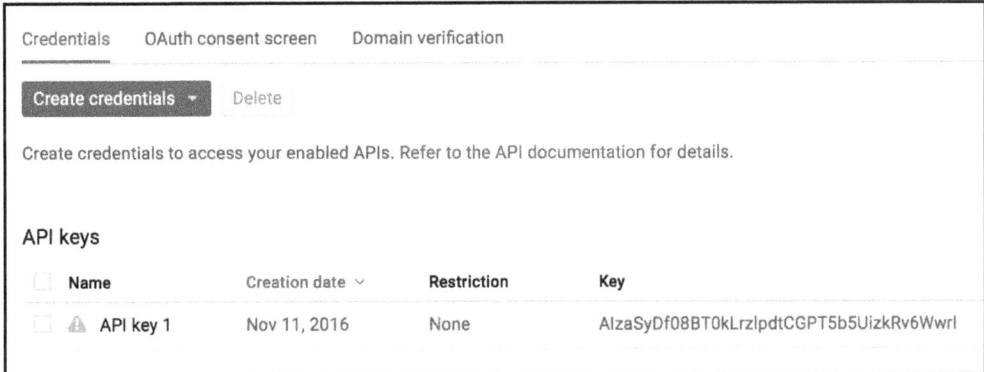

11. Copy the API key so that you can use it to add the Cordova Google Maps plugin.

How to do it...

Let's start an Ionic project from scratch and add Google Maps features, as follows:

1. Create a blank Ionic project, as shown, and go to that folder:

```
$ ionic start TaxiApp blank
$ cd TaxiApp
```

2. Replace the iOS platform with version 3.9.0 with the following command lines:

```
$ ionic platform remove ios
$ ionic platform add ios@3.9.0
$ ionic platform add android
```

You have to pick `ios@3.9.0` specifically because the current version of the Cordova Google Maps plugin only works with this version. Otherwise, your build will fail. You should experiment with the newest version if possible.

3. Install the Google Maps plugin with your copied key replacing `YOUR_IOS_API_KEY_IS_HERE`, as follows:

```
$ cordova plugin add cordova-plugin-googlemaps --variable
API_KEY_FOR_IOS="YOUR_IOS_API_KEY_IS_HERE"`
```

If you do this for both iOS and Android, use the following command line:

```
$ cordova plugin add cordova-plugin-googlemaps --variable
API_KEY_FOR_ANDROID="key" --variable API_KEY_FOR_IOS="key"
```

You have to use the Cordova CLI here because using the Ionic CLI to add Google Maps with the API Key will not work

4. Open `./src/pages/home/home.html` to modify your template, as shown here:

```
<ion-content [ngClass]="{'no-scroll': mapRendered}">
  <div id="map">
    <button ion-button color="dark" (click)="getMyLocation()">PICK
ME UP</button>
  </div>
</ion-content>
```

The main element here is your `div` with the `map` ID because that is where you have to inject the Google Maps object.

5. Edit your `./src/pages/home/home.ts` in the same folder:

```
import { Component } from '@angular/core';
import { NavController, Platform } from 'ionic-angular';
import {
  GoogleMaps, GoogleMap, GoogleMapsEvent, GoogleMapOptions,
  CameraPosition, LatLng, MarkerOptions, Marker
} from '@ionic-native/google-maps';
@Component({
  selector: 'page-home',
  templateUrl: 'home.html'
})
export class HomePage {
  public map: GoogleMap;
  public mapRendered: Boolean = false;

  constructor(public navCtrl: NavController, public platform:
Platform) {
    this.platform.ready().then(() => {
      this.showMap();
    });
  }


  showMap() {
    let mapOptions: GoogleMapOptions = {
      camera: {
        target: {
          lat: 43.0741904,
          lng: -89.3809802
        },
        zoom: 18,
        tilt: 30
      }
    };

    this.map = GoogleMaps.create('map', mapOptions);
    this.map.one(GoogleMapsEvent.MAP_READY)
    .then(() => {
      console.log('Map is ready!');
      this.mapRendered = true;
    });
  }
```

```
getMyLocation() {
  this.map.getMyLocation().then((location) => {
    var msg = ["I am here:\n",
      "latitude:" + location.latLng.lat,
      "longitude:" + location.latLng.lng].join("\n");
    let position = {
      target: location.latLng,
      zoom: 15
    };
    this.map.moveCamera(position);
    let markerOptions: MarkerOptions = {
      'position': location.latLng,
      'title': msg
    };
    this.map.addMarker(markerOptions).then((marker:Marker) => {
      marker.showInfoWindow();
    });
  });
}
```

6. Make some minor adjustments to the style sheet so that the map can take over the full screen. Edit `./src/pages/home/home.scss`, as illustrated here:

```
ion-app._gmaps_cdv_ .nav-decor{
    background-color: transparent !important;
}

page-home {
    text-align: center;
    #map {
        height: 100%;
        z-index: 9999;
    }
    .no-scroll {
        .scroll-content {
            overflow-y: hidden;
        }
    }
}
```

7. Go to the Terminal and then run the application:

```
$ ionic cordova run ios
$ ionic cordova run android
```

You can use either one of the preceding command lines, depending on the platform.

How it works...

The core of this app is mainly in the JavaScript code-home.ts. In order to use the plugin object, you should declare it on top, as shown here:

```
import {
    GoogleMaps,GoogleMap,GoogleMapsEvent,GoogleMapOptions,
    CameraPosition,LatLng,MarkerOptions,Marker
} from '@ionic-native/google-maps';
```

While it might seem that there are a lot of moving parts, the basic flow is very simple, as listed here:

1. Whenever Ionic and Cordova are ready, trigger platform.ready().then to initialize the map by calling showMap() in the constructor of the HomePage.
2. When a user clicks on the button, the app will call getMyLocation to get the location data.
3. The data will be used to create the marker and move the map's camera to center on that location.

It's important to know that GoogleMaps.create does take some time to process, and it will trigger a *ready* event once it has successfully created the map. That's why you need to add an event listener for GoogleMapsEvent.MAP_READY. This example does not do anything right after the map is ready, but later, you could add more processing functions, such as jumping to the current location automatically or adding more markers on top of the map.

When the user clicks on the PICK ME UP button, it will trigger the getMyLocation() method. The location object returned will contain the latitude (location.latLng.lat) and longitude (location.latLng.lng). To move the camera anywhere, just call map.moveCamera by passing the location coordinate (location.latLng). To add a marker, call map.addMarker with the position and title as HTML.

There's more...

The Cordova Google Maps plugin has many more features, such as the following:

- Showing an InfoWindow
- Adding a marker with multiple lines
- Modifying icons
- Text styling

- Base64-encoded icons
- Clicking on a marker
- Clicking on an InfoWindow
- Creating a draggable marker
- Dragging events
- Creating a flat marker

Since you cannot pop up a `div` on top of native Google Maps, the marker features are very handy. Some additional scenarios are as follows:

- **Touch a marker and go to a page**: You just need to listen to the `GoogleMapsEvent.MARKER_CLICK` event and do whatever is needed in the callback function.
- **Show an avatar/profile image as a marker**: The `addMarker` takes the Base64 image string. Thus, you can pass something like this in the argument title-`canvas.toDataURL()`.

Note that Google has a quota on free API usage. For example, you cannot exceed one request per second per user, and you can only have a couple of thousand requests per day. This quota changes all the time, but it's important to know about it. In any case, if you have problems with your key, you have to go back to the **Credentials** page and regenerate the key. In order to change the key manually in your app, you have to edit `/plugins/ios.json`. Look for the following two places:

```
"*-Info.plist": {
  "parents": {
    "Google Maps API Key": [
      {
        "xml": "<string>YOUR_IOS_API_KEY_IS_HERE</string>",
        "count": 1
      }
    ]
  }
}
```

Along with the following code:

```
"plugin.google.maps": {
  "API_KEY_FOR_IOS": "YOUR_IOS_API_KEY_IS_HERE",
  "PACKAGE_NAME": "com.ionicframework.starter"
}
```

You just need to edit the `YOUR_IOS_API_KEY_IS_HERE` line and replace it with your new key.

There are a lot of ways to work with Google Maps. You can visit the GitHub page of the Google Maps plugin to learn more, at `https://github.com/mapsplugin/cordova-plugin-googlemaps`.

8
Theming the App

In this chapter, we will cover the following tasks related to app theme customization:

- Viewing and debugging themes for a specific platform
- Customizing themes based on the platform

Introduction

Although Ionic has its own out-of-the-box default themes, you might want to customize your app's look and feel even further. There are several methods, as follows:

- Changing the style sheet within the Sass file
- Detecting platform-specific types (iOS, Android, Windows) in JavaScript and applying custom classes or AngularJS conditions

Either of the preceding two methods should work, but it's highly recommended to apply customization in a Sass file before the app is built, in order to achieve maximum rendering performance.

Viewing and debugging themes for a specific platform

One of the biggest challenges in developing an app is ensuring that it has the desired look and feel for each platform. Specifically, you want to write the code and theme once and have it just work. Another challenge is figuring out the workflow on a daily basis, from writing code and previewing it in the browser to deploying to a device for testing purposes. You want to minimize a lot of unnecessary steps. It's certainly difficult if you have to rebuild the app and test it independently for each mobile platform.

Ionic CLI provides seamless integration to improve your workflow to ensure that you can *catch* all the issues for each platform ahead of time. You can quickly view the app on various platforms in the same browser window. This feature is powerful because now you can make a side-by-side comparison for each screen with specific interaction. If you want to debug JavaScript code, you employ the same web developer tool that you have been using in the browser. This capability will save you a lot of time instead of waiting to push the app to a physical device, which could take minutes if your app is getting larger.

In this example, you will learn how to modify a theme quickly using Sass variables. Then, you will run the app and inspect different platforms for UI consistency.

Getting ready

There is no need to test the theme on a physical device because Ionic can render iOS, Android, and Windows phone in the browser.

How to do it...

Here are the instructions:

1. Create a new app using the `tutorial` template, as shown, and go to the folder:

```
$ ionic start ThemeApp tutorial
$ cd ThemeApp
```

 In Ionic 1, you need to set up Sass dependencies because Ionic uses a number of external libraries for this. However, Ionic has no such requirements because all the dependencies are added when you create the project.

2. Open the .../src/theme/variable.scss file, and replace the $colors variable with the following commands:

```
$colors: (
  primary:    #2C3E50, // #387ef5,
  clear:      white,
  secondary:  #446CB3, // #32db64,
  danger:     #96281B, // #f53d3d,
  light:      #BDC3C7, // #f4f4f4,
  dark:       #6C7A89, // #222,
  favorite:   #16A085 // #69BB7B
);
```

 The default color codes can be commented out, as shown in the preceding code.

3. Open app.html and add the clear attribute to the following code block:

```
<ion-toolbar clear>
  <ion-title>Pages</ion-title>
</ion-toolbar>
```

4. Open the ./src/pages/hello-ionic/hello-ionic.html file and replace the contents with the given code:

```
<ion-header>
  <ion-navbar color="primary">
    <button ion-button menuToggle>
      <ion-icon name="menu"></ion-icon>
    </button>
    <ion-title>Hello Ionic</ion-title>
  </ion-navbar>
</ion-header>


<ion-content padding class="getting-started">

  <h3>Welcome to your first Ionic app!</h3>

  <p>
    This starter project is our way of helping you get a functional
app running in record time.
  </p>
  <p>
    Follow along on the tutorial section of the Ionic docs!
```

```
    </p>
    <p>
        <button ion-button color="secondary" menuToggle>Toggle
Menu</button>
    </p>

</ion-content>
```

5. Test run the app in the browser, and you should be able to see a screen, as follows:

$ ionic serve -l

The -l (lima) command means to render the app for all three platforms.

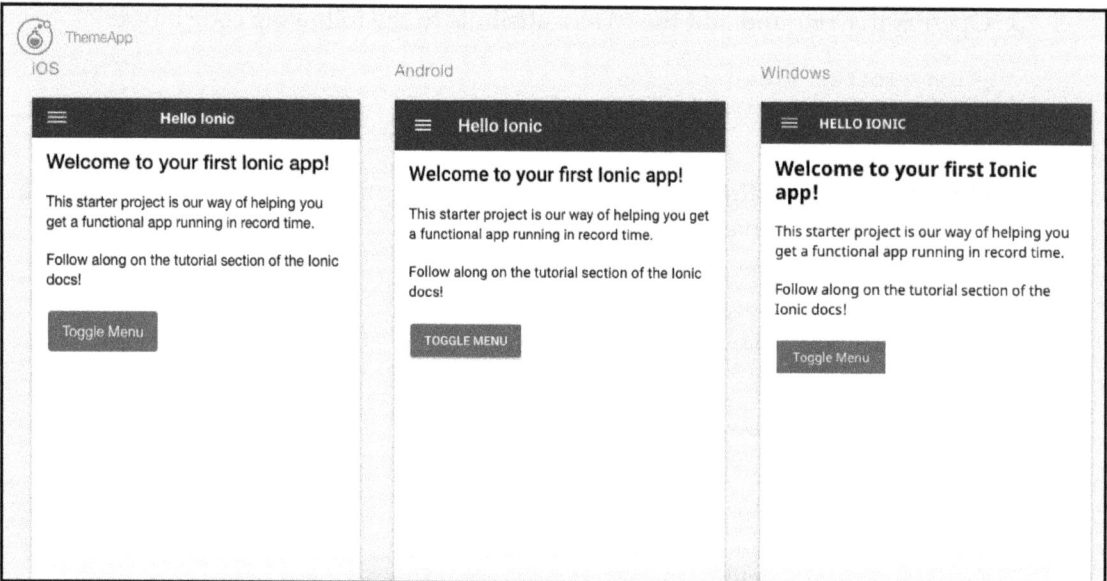

How it works...

Ionic has made it very easy to develop and test themes for different platforms. Your typical flow is to modify the theme variable in `variables.scss` first. You should not modify any `.css` files directly. Also, the Ionic project now makes it safe so that you can't accidentally edit the wrong core theme files, because those core files are no longer in the app folder location.

To update the default color, you just have to modify the color code in `variables.scss`. You can even add more color names, such as `clear: white`, and Ionic will automatically take care of the rest. That means the `clear` keyword is available as a value-to-color attribute on any Ionic element that accepts the color attribute. A few examples are as follows:

```
<ion-navbar color="primary">
<button ion-button color="secondary" menuToggle>
<ion-toolbar color="clear">
```

The Ionic CLI is a very useful tool for debugging your theme in different platforms. To get help on how to use the Ionic CLI, you can type the following command line in the console:

```
$ ionic -h
```

This will list all the options available for you to choose from. Under the `serve` option, you should familiarize yourself with some of the important features, which are as follows:

Parameters	Description
`--consolelogs|-c`	Prints app console logs to Ionic CLI
`--serverlogs|-s`	Prints dev server logs to Ionic CLI
`--browser|-w`	Specifies the browser to use (Safari, Firefox, and Chrome)
`--browseroption|-o`	Specifies a path to open to (`/#/tab/dash`)
`--lab|-l`	Tests your apps on multiple screen sizes and platform types

There's more...

You can get more color palettes by visiting Matheus Cruz Rocha's cloned repository at `https://github.com/innovieco/ionic-flat-colors`.

Customizing themes based on the platform

Each mobile platform vendor has its own design guideline. This section will go over an example of a typical workflow to develop, view, debug, and address the app theme differently for iOS, Android, and Windows phone. In traditional development (using either the native language or other hybrid app solutions), you have to keep separate repositories for each platform in order to customize the theme. This could be very inefficient in the long run.

Ionic has many built-in features to support theme changes based on the detected platform. It makes it very convenient by separating Sass variables for each platform. This will eliminate a lot of unnecessary customizations. As a developer, you'd rather focus on the app experience than spend time managing the platform.

The example in this section covers two possible customizations using Sass and JavaScript. The following screenshot shows an iOS, Android, and Windows app with a different title bar color and text:

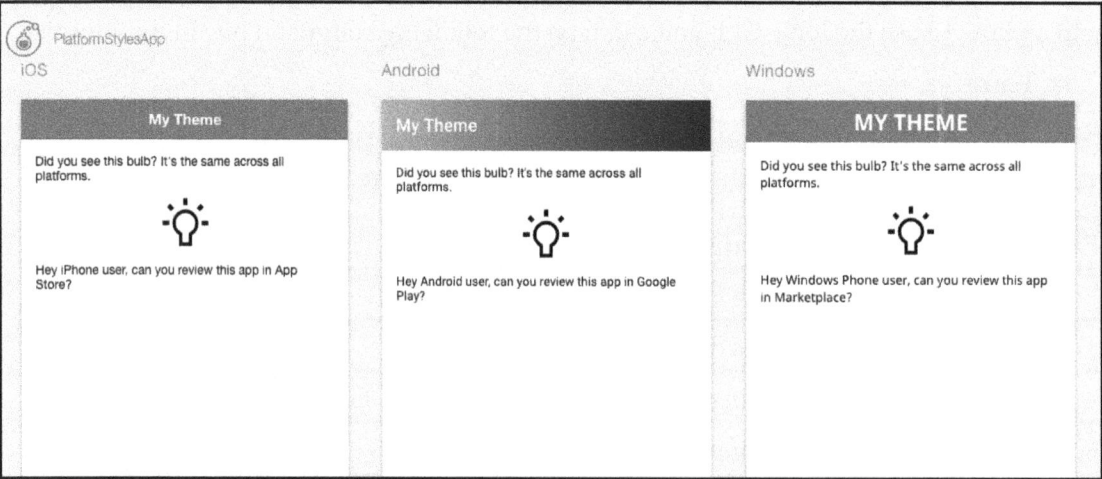

Getting ready

There is no need to test themes on a physical device because Ionic can render all three platforms in the browser.

How to do it...

Here are the instructions:

1. Create a new app using the `blank` template and go into the project folder:

```
$ ionic start PlatformStylesApp blank
$ cd PlatformStylesApp
```

2. Open the `./src/app/app.module.ts` file and replace the entire body with the following:

```
import { NgModule } from '@angular/core';
import { IonicApp, IonicModule } from 'ionic-angular';
import { MyApp } from './app.component';
import { HomePage } from '../pages/home/home';

@NgModule({
  declarations: [
    MyApp,
    HomePage
  ],
  imports: [
    IonicModule.forRoot(MyApp, {
      backButtonText: 'Go Back',
      iconMode: 'md',
      modalEnter: 'modal-slide-in',
      modalLeave: 'modal-slide-out',
      tabbarPlacement: 'bottom',
      pageTransition: 'ios',
    })
  ],
  bootstrap: [IonicApp],
  entryComponents: [
    MyApp,
    HomePage
  ],
  providers: []
})
export class AppModule {}
```

This example expands the use of Ionic Bootstrap, which will be discussed now.

3. Open `./src/pages/home/home.ts` and replace the code with the following:

```
import { Component } from '@angular/core';
import { Platform } from 'ionic-angular';
```

```
import { NavController } from 'ionic-angular';
@Component({
  selector: 'page-home',
  templateUrl: 'home.html'
})
export class HomePage {
  platform: any;
  isIOS: Boolean;
  isAndroid: Boolean;
  isWP: Boolean;
  constructor(private navController: NavController, platform:
    Platform) {
    this.platform = platform;
    this.isIOS = this.platform.is('ios');
    this.isAndroid = this.platform.is('android');
    this.isWP = this.platform.is('windows');
    console.log(this.platform);
  }
}
```

4. Open the `./src/pages/home/home.html` file and change the template to:

```
<ion-header>
  <ion-navbar primary [ngClass]="{'large-center-title': isWP}">
    <ion-title>
      My Theme
    </ion-title>
  </ion-navbar>
</ion-header>
<ion-content padding>
  Did you see this bulb? It's the same across all platforms.
  <p class="center">
    <ion-icon class="large-icon" name="bulb"></ion-icon>
  </p>
  <p *ngIf="isIOS">
    Hey iPhone user, can you review this app in App Store?
  </p>
  <p *ngIf="isAndroid">
    Hey Android user, can you review this app in Google Play?
  </p>
  <p *ngIf="isWP">
    Hey Windows Phone user, can you review this app in Marketplace?
  </p>
</ion-content>
```

This is the only template for the app, but its UI will look different depending on the detected platform.

5. Replace `./src/pages/home/home.scss` with the following style sheet:

```
page-home {
    .large-icon {
        font-size: 60px;
    }
    .center {
        text-align: center;
    }
    .header .toolbar[primary] .toolbar-background {
        background: #1A2980;
        background: -webkit-linear-gradient(right, #1A2980,
        #26D0CE);
        background: -o-linear-gradient(right, #1A2980, #26D0CE);
        background: linear-gradient(to left, #1A2980, #26D0CE);
    }
    .large-center-title {
        text-align: center;
        .toolbar-title {
            font-size: 25px;
        }
    }
}
```

There is no need to change the global variables. Thus, you only modify the styles for one page. The purpose is to demonstrate the ability to customize for each platform.

6. Test-run the app in the browser using the following command:

```
$ ionic serve -l
```

How it works...

Ionic automatically created platform-specific parent classes and put them at the `<body>` tag. The iOS app will include the `.ios` class. The Android app will have the `.md` class. So, for style sheet customization, you can leverage those existing classes to change the look and feel of your app.

Ionic documentation has a list of all platform modes and configuration properties at `http://ionicframework.com/docs/v2/theming/platform-specific-styles/`.

Platform	Mode	Details
iPhone/iPad/iPad	ios	The iOS style is used across all Apple products
Android	md	md means **Material Design** as this is the default design for Android devices
Windows Phone	wp	Viewing on any Windows device inside Cordova or Electron uses the Windows styles
Core	md	Material Design is the default for all others

First, let's take a look at the Ionic Bootstrap class from Ionic Angular. You declared this in the `app.module.ts` file:

```
IonicModule.forRoot(MyApp, {
    backButtonText: 'Go Back',
    iconMode: 'md',
    modalEnter: 'modal-slide-in',
    modalLeave: 'modal-slide-out',
    tabbarPlacement: 'bottom',
    pageTransition: 'ios',
})
```

This statement basically instructs the app to bootstrap with the `MyApp` object. The second parameter is where you can inject your customized configuration properties. There is a list of all config properties at `http://ionicframework.com/docs/v2/api/config/Config/`.

One main thing to point out here is `iconMode`. Icons are very different for each platform in Ionic. The entire Ionicons set is now separated by the platform name. There are three platforms according to Ionic's documentation page, at `http://ionicframework.com/docs/v2/ionicons/`.

You can even search for the icon name using the **Search Ionicons** buttons, as follows:

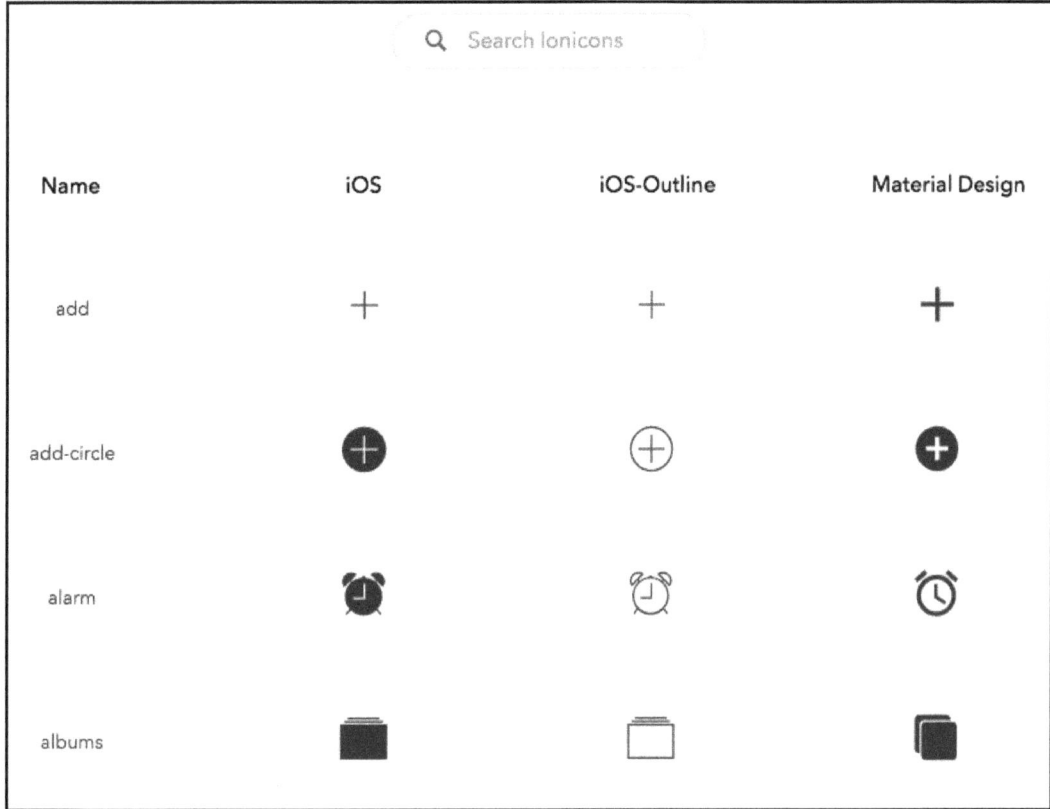

Note that you don't need to worry about which icon to pick for which platform. Even though in this example, the code forces you to choose the iOS icon for all three platforms, you could just use the icon name and let Ionic decide which icon to use:

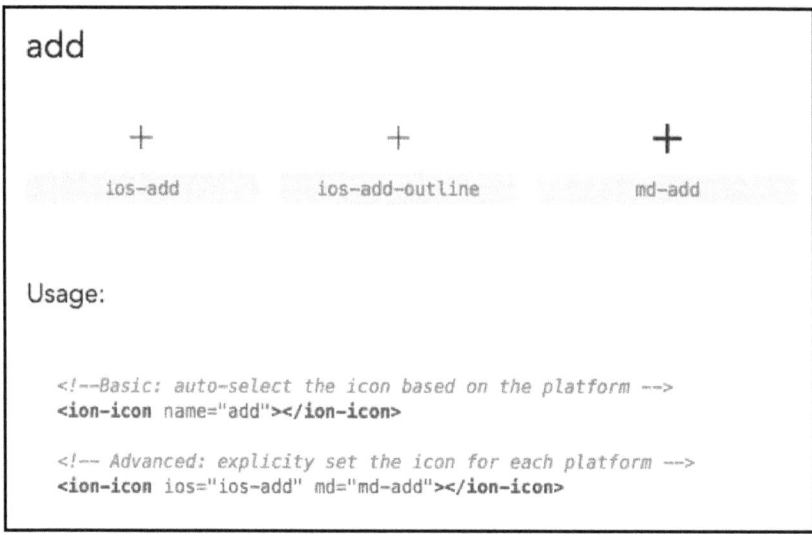

For example, when you state the icon name as "add", Ionic will use "md-add" if the user is using Android, as follows:

```
<ion-icon name="add">
</ion-icon>
```

There are several ways to theme your app based on the platform. First, you could add variables to detect the current platform, as in the HomePage class, as illustrated:

```
export class HomePage {
  platform: any;
  isIOS: Boolean;
  isAndroid: Boolean;
  isWP: Boolean;
  constructor(private navController: NavController, platform: Platform) {
    this.platform = platform;
    this.isIOS = this.platform.is('ios');
    this.isAndroid = this.platform.is('android');
    this.isWP = this.platform.is('windows');
    console.log(this.platform);
  }
}
```

`this.platform = platform` is what Ionic provides. If you open up the browser console while running the app, you can inspect the `platform` object:

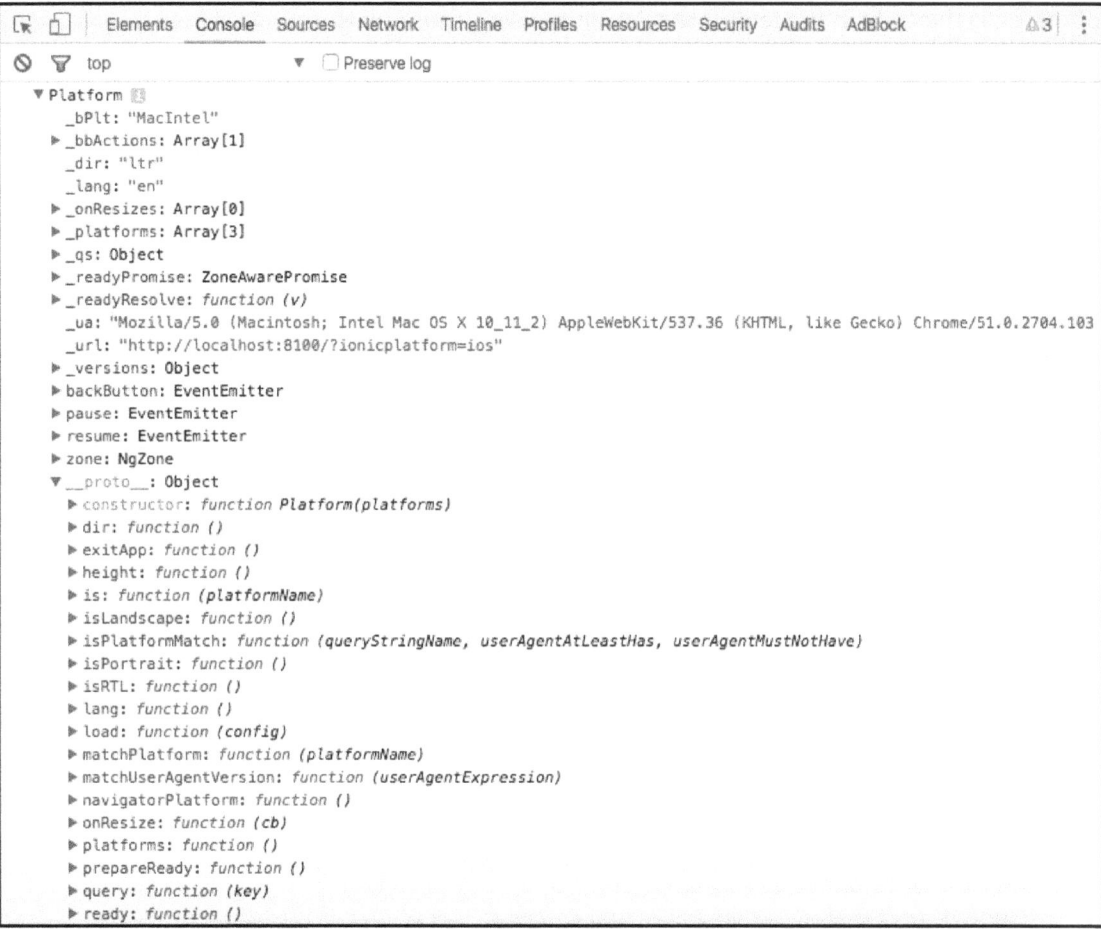

This `platform` object has a rich amount of information. This is similar to `ionic.platform` in Ionic 1. However, it has been restructured significantly.

By making the platform variables available to the view, you can use it to hide or show a specific DOM using `ngIf`. It's recommended to use `ngIf` instead of `ngShow`, because `ngShow` may show and hide the element right away, creating a *flickering* effect. The following is the code in the template relating to using those platform variables:

```
<p *ngIf="isIOS">
  Hey iPhone user, can you review this app in App Store?
</p>
<p *ngIf="isAndroid">
  Hey Android user, can you review this app in Google Play?
</p>
<p *ngIf="isWP">
  Hey Windows Phone user, can you review this app in Marketplace?
</p>
```

Finally, you could change the theme using platform classes directly. Consider the following example:

```
.header-md .toolbar[primary] .toolbar-background {
  background: #1A2980;
  background: -webkit-linear-gradient(right, #1A2980, #26D0CE);
  background: -o-linear-gradient(right, #1A2980, #26D0CE);
  background: linear-gradient(to left, #1A2980, #26D0CE);
}
```

This means that, whenever it's a material design mode (`.md` class), you will override the classes with your own styles. The preceding example shows an interesting CSS gradient, which works very nicely in mobile devices.

There's more...

Further device information is available from the `Platform` class. You can even detect iPad devices at `http://ionicframework.com/docs/v2/api/platform/Platform/`.

Advanced Topics 9

In this chapter, we will cover some advanced topics, as follows:

- Lazy loading pages in Ionic
- Internationalization (i18n) using `ngx-translate`
- Creating documentation for Ionic apps

Introduction

In this chapter, we will work on some advanced topics related to Ionic apps, such as lazy loading pages for performance, deep linking Ionic pages, and adding a multiple languages feature and creating documentation for Ionic apps.

Lazy loading in Ionic

Web applications have become bigger and more complex day by day. We have a web version of Photoshop now, and there are even more complex applications that exist on the web. The web was not conceived for these kinds of applications. If your application is very big, and you are loading your whole application at the first load, chances are that your application has bad performance. What if you can load only that part of JavaScript that is required for that particular page/view? This is where lazy loading comes in. Lazy loading is the process of loading only part of an application that a user wants to see. You can lazy load not only JavaScript but also CSS.

In Angular, you can do lazy loading using router configuration. However, Ionic doesn't have Angular router or router config. In this recipe, you will learn how to do lazy loading in Ionic.

Getting ready

You can test your app in the browser because lazy loading is not dependent on the device.

How to do it...

The following are the instructions for lazy loading:

1. Create a new app LazyLoading using the blank template and navigate to the Lazy Loading folder, as follows:

```
$ ionic start LazyLoading blank
$ cd LazyLoading
```

2. Create a new file named home.module.ts inside the /src/pages/home folder, and add the following content to it:

```
import { NgModule } from "@angular/core";
import { IonicPageModule } from "ionic-angular";
import { HomePage } from "./home";
@NgModule({
 declarations: [HomePage],
 imports: [IonicPageModule.forChild(HomePage)]
})
export class HomePageModule {}
```

3. Add the IonicPage decorator to the HomePage's Component, as follows:

```
import { Component } from "@angular/core";
import { NavController, IonicPage } from "ionic-angular";

@IonicPage()
@Component({
  selector: "page-home",
  templateUrl: "home.html"
})
export class HomePage {
  constructor(public navCtrl: NavController) {}
}
```

4. Create a `/src/pages/second/second.ts` file and add the following content:

```
import { Component } from "@angular/core";
import { IonicPage, NavController, NavParams } from "ionic-
angular";

@IonicPage()
@Component({
  selector: "page-second",
  templateUrl: "second.html"
})
export class SecondPage {
  constructor(public navCtrl: NavController, public navParams:
NavParams) {}
}
```

5. Create a `/src/pages/second/second.html` file with the following content:

```
<ion-header>
  <ion-navbar>
    <ion-title>Second</ion-title>
  </ion-navbar>
</ion-header>

<ion-content padding>
</ion-content>
```

6. Create the `/src/pages/second/second.module.ts` file with the following content:

```
import { NgModule } from '@angular/core';
import { IonicPageModule } from 'ionic-angular';
import { SecondPage } from './second';

@NgModule({
  declarations: [
    SecondPage,
  ],
  imports: [
    IonicPageModule.forChild(SecondPage),
  ],
})
export class SecondPageModule {}
```

7. Open `/src/app/app.component.ts` and update the value of `rootPage`, as follows:

```
rootPage: any = "HomePage";
```

8. Open `/src/app/app.module.ts` and update it as follows:

```
import { BrowserModule } from "@angular/platform-browser";
import { ErrorHandler, NgModule } from "@angular/core";
import { IonicApp, IonicErrorHandler, IonicModule } from "ionic-
angular";
import { SplashScreen } from "@ionic-native/splash-screen";
import { StatusBar } from "@ionic-native/status-bar";

import { MyApp } from "./app.component";

@NgModule({
  declarations: [MyApp],
  imports: [BrowserModule, IonicModule.forRoot(MyApp)],
  bootstrap: [IonicApp],
  entryComponents: [MyApp],
  providers: [
    StatusBar,
    SplashScreen,
    { provide: ErrorHandler, useClass: IonicErrorHandler }
  ]
})
export class AppModule {}
```

9. Now, run the app using the following command:

```
$ ionic serve
```

How it works...

The idea of lazy loading is the same as any other type of technology. However, the implementation of Ionic is very different, even if you compare it with Angular's lazy loading.

First, you need to create a feature module for the Ionic Page that you want to lazy load. In our case, we created `home.module.ts`. It looks as follows:

```
import { NgModule } from "@angular/core";
import { IonicPageModule } from "ionic-angular";
import { HomePage } from "./home";
```

```
@NgModule({
  declarations: [HomePage],
  imports: [IonicPageModule.forChild(HomePage)]
})
export class HomePageModule {}
```

It's a feature module where a declarations array has `HomePage`, and we use the `IonicPageModule.forChild` method in the imports array with `HomePage` as an input to it so that we can access `Ionic` inside HomePage.

Secondly, we need to decorate our `HomePage` class using the `IonicPage` decorator in `home.ts`, as follows:

```
...
import { IonicPage } from 'ionic-angular';

@IonicPage()
@Component({..})
export class HomePage {}
```

Finally, we need to substitute `HomePage` to `'HomePage'` (in quotes) to make lazy loading possible. For example, whenever we want to push `HomePage` to navigation stack, we would call the `push` function, as follows:

`navCtrl.push('HomePage');` instead of:`navCtrl.push(HomePage);`

Also, we need to remove any import of the page that we are lazily loading. Owing to this, we had to remove reference to `HomePage` from `app.module.ts`.

There's more...

When you configure lazy loading for Ionic application, you are also adding one more feature, that is, access to pages using URL. Along with deep linking Cordova plugin and this feature, you can easily implement deep linking for Ionic applications—think of this as an exercise.

You can find the link to deep linking plugin at `https://github.com/BranchMetrics/cordova-ionic-phonegap-branch-deep-linking`.

See also

Check out more on lazy loading in this blog post at `https://webpack.js.org/guides/lazy-loading/`.

Internationalization (i18n) using ngx-translate

Having English as the primary language for your application is good. However, chances are that there are people who don't know English who may use your application. It's good to have multiple languages for using application. This is called as internationalization of application. In this part, we will use the `ngx-translate` library of Angular to implement the multiple language features in the Ionic application.

This is what the app looks like:

Getting ready

You can run this application inside the browser.

How to do it...

The following are the instructions to do it:

1. Create a new `TranslateApp` using the `blank` template and navigate inside the folder, as follows:

```
$ ionic start TranslateApp blank
$ cd TranslateApp
```

2. Install `ngx-translate/core` and `ngx-translate/http-loader`, as follows:

```
npm install @ngx-translate/core @ngx-translate/http-loader --save
```

3. Create the `en.json` file inside the `/src/assets/i18n` folder and add the following content:

```
{
   "Hello": "Hello",
   "Good Morning": "Good Morning"
}
```

4. Create the `de.json` file inside the `/src/assets/i18n` folder and add the following content:

```
{
   "Hello": "Hallo",
   "Good Morning": "Guten Morgen"
}
```

5. Open `/src/pages/home/home.html` and update it as follows:

```
<ion-header>
  <ion-navbar>
    <ion-title>
       Ionic Language
    </ion-title>
  </ion-navbar>
</ion-header>

<ion-content padding>
```

```
<ion-item>
  {{'Hello' | translate }}, {{ 'Good Morning' | translate }}
</ion-item>
<ion-item>
  <ion-label>Language</ion-label>
  <ion-select [(ngModel)]="language" (ionChange)="setLang()">
    <ion-option value="en">English</ion-option>
    <ion-option value="de">Deutsch</ion-option>
  </ion-select>
</ion-item>
</ion-content>
```

6. Open /src/pages/home/home.ts and update it as follows:

```
import { Component } from "@angular/core";
import { NavController } from "ionic-angular";
import { TranslateService } from "@ngx-translate/core";

@Component({
  selector: "page-home",
  templateUrl: "home.html"
})
export class HomePage {
  language: string = "en";
  constructor(
    public navCtrl: NavController,
    private translate: TranslateService
  ) {
    translate.setDefaultLang("en");
    translate.use("en");
  }

  setLang() {
    console.log(this.language);
    this.translate.use(this.language);
  }
}
```

7. Open app.module.ts inside the /src/app folder and update it as follows:

```
import { BrowserModule } from "@angular/platform-browser";
import { ErrorHandler, NgModule } from "@angular/core";
import { IonicApp, IonicErrorHandler, IonicModule } from "ionic-
angular";
import { SplashScreen } from "@ionic-native/splash-screen";
import { StatusBar } from "@ionic-native/status-bar";

import { MyApp } from "./app.component";
```

```
import { HomePage } from "../pages/home/home";

import { TranslateModule, TranslateLoader } from "@ngx-
translate/core";
import { TranslateHttpLoader } from "@ngx-translate/http-loader";
import { HttpClientModule, HttpClient } from
"@angular/common/http";

export function HttpLoaderFactory(http: HttpClient) {
  return new TranslateHttpLoader(http);
}

@NgModule({
  declarations: [MyApp, HomePage],
  imports: [
    BrowserModule,
    HttpClientModule,
    TranslateModule.forRoot({
      loader: {
        provide: TranslateLoader,
        useFactory: HttpLoaderFactory,
        deps: [HttpClient]
      }
    }),
    IonicModule.forRoot(MyApp)
  ],
  bootstrap: [IonicApp],
  entryComponents: [MyApp, HomePage],
  providers: [
    StatusBar,
    SplashScreen,
    { provide: ErrorHandler, useClass: IonicErrorHandler }
  ]
})
export class AppModule {}
```

8. Run the app, as follows:

$ ionic serve

How it works...

In this example, we are using `ngx-translate` for internationalization. It's a fairly simple process. The basic idea is that we have a JSON file for each of the languages that we want to support in our app. For example, `en.json` for English and `de.json` for German. In the JSON file, we have keys and values. Values are translated texted that we want to show in our app, and keys are something that we are going to put inside the app.

It's also important that we need to have the same keys for multiple languages and different values based on the translation. Take a look at the following two JSON files:

`en.json`:

```
{
  "Hello": "Hello",
  "Good Morning": "Good Morning"
}
```

`de.json`:

```
{
  "Hello": "Hallo",
  "Good Morning": "Guten Morgen"
}
```

Both files have two key-value pairs, keys are same but the values are different.

Now, in our templates, we use those two keys:

```
{{'Hello' | translate }}, {{ 'Good Morning' | translate }}
```

We use Angular interpolation and add the key with quotes here along with the `translate` pipe, which comes from the `ngx-translate` library. Basically, it transforms the `key` into the correct `value` based on the selected language.

To change the language, we use `TranslateService` from `ngx-translate`. It has the `setDefault` method to set the default language, and the `use` method to switch language. So, in our `home.html`, when a user switches the language using `ion-select`, we call our `setLang` function, which under the hood calls the TranslateService's `use` method with the appropriate language code, such as *en* or *de*.

Finally, we also need to configure `ngx-translate` in `app.module.ts`. We need to import `TranslateModule.forRoot()` in the root `NgModule` of the application. We also have to configure the loader for `TranslateModule`. Here, we are using `TranslateHttpLoader` to load translations from `/assets/i18n/[lang].json` were lang code is alphabetic language code such `en` for English.

It's also important to note that in order to use **AOT (Ahead of Time)** compilation, we will need to use factory function, as follows:

```
export function HttpLoaderFactory(http: HttpClient) {
  return new TranslateHttpLoader(http);
}
```

So, the configuration looks as follows:

```
TranslateModule.forRoot({
    loader: {
      provide: TranslateLoader,
      useFactory: HttpLoaderFactory,
      deps: [HttpClient]
    }
})
```

See also

Check out the documentation for `ngx-translate`, at `https://github.com/ngx-translate/core`.

Creating documentation for Ionic app

So far, we have added things and features which are targeted at the user of the application. In this recipe, we will add the ability to generate documentation from source code using TSDocs, Gulp, and Ionic CLI Hooks. Documentation is a very important aspect of the developer experience. I personally believe that it should be part of Ionic by default.

This is how the documentation will look like:

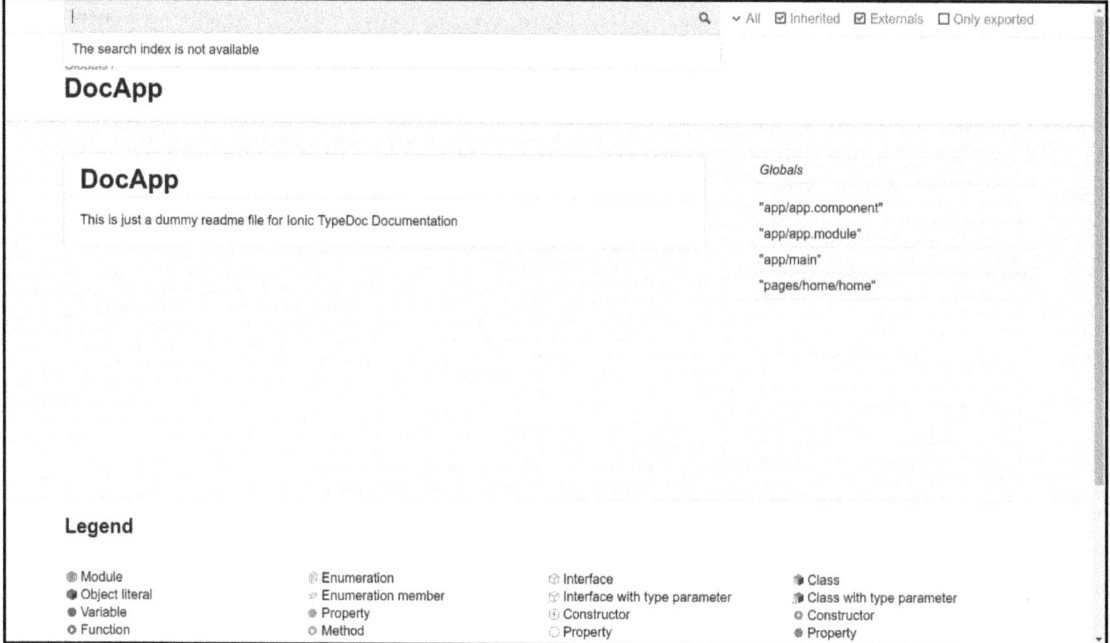

Getting ready

You can run this inside the browser.

How to do it...

The following are the instructions to create the example app:

1. Create a new `DocApp` using a `blank` template and navigate inside the folder, as follows:

```
$ ionic start DocApp blank
$ cd DocApp
```

2. Install the following `npm` dev dependencies for using `typedoc`:

```
$ npm install --save-dev gulp gulp-connect gulp-typedoc typedoc
```

3. Create `gulpfile.js` in the `root` directory of the app and add the following content:

```
var gulp = require("gulp");
var connect = require("gulp-connect");
var typedoc = require("gulp-typedoc");
var config = {
  root: "docs/"
};

gulp.task("typedoc", function() {
  return gulp.src(["src/**/*.ts"]).pipe(
    typedoc({
      module: "commonjs",
      target: "es6",
      experimentalDecorators: true,
      out: config.root,
      name: "DocApp",
      readme: "./README.md"
    })
  );
});

gulp.task("serve:docs", ["typedoc"], function() {
  connect.server({
    root: config.root,
    livereload: true
  });
});
```

4. Open `/src/pages/home/home.ts` and update it as follows:

```
import { Component } from "@angular/core";
import { NavController } from "ionic-angular";

@Component({
  selector: "page-home",
  templateUrl: "home.html"
})
export class HomePage {
  constructor(public navCtrl: NavController) {}

  /**
    * Following is the way you write documentation
    *
    * @param username Username of the user
    * @returns It returns a string value
```

```
    */
    dummyFunction(username: string) {
      return username;
    }
  }
```

5. Run the app, as follows:

```
$ gulp serve:docs
```

How it works...

We are using `TypeDoc`, which is a documentation generator for a TypeScript application. It uses TSDoc comments, which are very similar to the popular JSDoc. All of the magic work is done in `gulpfile.js`.

First, we have a typedoc task. Basically, it takes all TypeScript src files using `gulp.src(["src/**/*.ts"])` and pipe it to typedoc. Then, typedoc generates the documentation based on the class's structure and TSDoc comments in the file. You can learn about the configuration about TypeDoc from their website at `http://typedoc.org`. Basically, here we are configuring site title, the location of docs, and the bunch of other things.

If you take a look inside `home.ts`, we have `dummyFunction`, which looks as follows:

```
/**
 * Following is the way you write documentation
 *
 * @param username Username of the user
 * @returns It returns a string value
 */
dummyFunction(username: string) {
  return username;
}
```

The comments before the function are the TSDoc comments. They have a specific structure that we need to learn and with the help of these comments we can generate meaningful documentation.

Finally, we run a gulp task, `gulp serve:docs`, in the terminal, which generate and serves the docs using a web server in the browser.

See also

- You can also make it work along with Ionic CLI, as generating docs while serving the app using Ionic serve. Take a look at Ionic CLI Hooks at `https://ionicframework.com/docs/cli/configuring.html#hooks`.
- Learn more on TSDoc at `https://github.com/Microsoft/tsdoc`.

10
Publishing the App for Different Platforms

In this chapter, we will cover the following tasks related to publishing and future-proofing an app:

- Adding versioning to future-proof the app
- Building and publishing an app for iOS
- Building and publishing an app for Android

Introduction

In the past, it was very cumbersome to build and successfully publish an app. However, there is much documentation and many unofficial instructions on the internet today that can pretty much address any problem that you may run into. In addition, Ionic also comes with its own CLI to assist in this process. This chapter will guide you through the app building and publishing steps at a high level. You will learn how to do the following things:

- Add versioning to future-proof the app
- Publish your app to App Store or Google Play

The purpose of this chapter is to provide ideas on what to look for and some *gotchas*. Apple and Google constantly update their platforms and processes; so, the steps may not look exactly the same over time.

Adding versioning to future-proof the app

It's typical that you don't think about keeping track of the app version for a particular user. However, as the app grows in regard to the number of users and releases, you will soon face the problem of update issues and incompatibilities. For example, a user may run an old version of your app but all your backend APIs now expect new parameters from a newer app version. Therefore, you may want to think about a strategy to detect the app version locally in order to notify the users of an update requirement. This is also helpful if your backend processes differently for a specific app version.

The app which you are going to build is very simple. It will detect the current version and store the information in a service. This is a screenshot of the app:

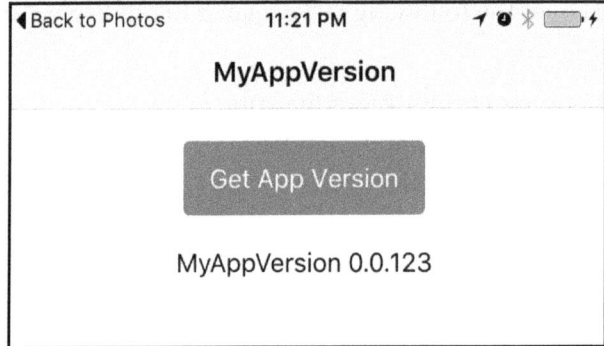

Getting ready

The following app example must run on a physical device or a simulator.

How to do it...

Take a look at the following instructions:

1. Create a new `MyAppVersion` app using the `blank` template, as follows, and navigate to the `MyAppVersion` folder:

```
$ ionic start MyAppVersion blank
$ cd MyAppVersion
```

2. Install the `app-version` plugin:

```
$ ionic cordova plugin add cordova-plugin-app-version
$ npm install --save @ionic-native/app-version
```

3. Edit `./config.xml` by changing the version number, as follows:

```
<widget id="com.ionicframework.myappversion637242" version="0.0.123"
xmlns="http://www.w3.org/ns/widgets"
xmlns:cdv="http://cordova.apache.org/ns/1.0">
```

Note that your `widget id` might be different from the one mentioned here. You only need to change the version number. In this case, it is the `0.0.123` version.

4. Create the `services` folder inside the `app` folder, as follows:

```
$ mkdir ./src/services
```

5. Create `myenv.ts` in the `services` folder with the following code:

```
import { Injectable } from "@angular/core";
import { AppVersion } from "@ionic-native/app-version";

@Injectable()
export class MyEnv {
  constructor(private appVersion: AppVersion) {}

  getAppVersion() {
    return this.appVersion.getVersionCode();
  }
}
```

This is your only service for this app. In a real-world project, you will need multiple services because some of them will have to communicate directly with your backend.

6. Open and edit your `/src/app/app.module.ts`, as follows:

```
import { BrowserModule } from "@angular/platform-browser";
import { ErrorHandler, NgModule } from "@angular/core";
import { IonicApp, IonicErrorHandler, IonicModule } from "ionic-angular";
import { SplashScreen } from "@ionic-native/splash-screen";
import { StatusBar } from "@ionic-native/status-bar";
import { AppVersion } from "@ionic-native/app-version";
import { MyEnv } from "../services/myenv";
```

```
import { MyApp } from "./app.component";
import { HomePage } from "../pages/home/home";

@NgModule({
  declarations: [MyApp, HomePage],
  imports: [BrowserModule, IonicModule.forRoot(MyApp)],
  bootstrap: [IonicApp],
  entryComponents: [MyApp, HomePage],
  providers: [
    StatusBar,
    SplashScreen,
    AppVersion,
    MyEnv,
    { provide: ErrorHandler, useClass: IonicErrorHandler }
  ]
})
export class AppModule {}
```

The main modification in this file is to inject the `AppVersion` and `MyEnv` providers for the entire app.

7. Open and replace `./src/pages/home/home.html` with the following code:

```
<ion-header>
  <ion-navbar>
    <ion-title>
      MyAppVersion
    </ion-title>
  </ion-navbar>
</ion-header>

<ion-content padding class="center home">
  <button ion-button (click)="getVersion()">Get App
Version</button>
  <p class="large" *ngIf="ver">
    MyAppVersion {{ ver }}
  </p>
</ion-content>
```

8. Open and replace `./src/pages/home/home.ts` with the following code:

```
import { Component } from "@angular/core";
import { NavController } from "ionic-angular";
import { MyEnv } from "../../services/myenv";

@Component({
  selector: "page-home",
  templateUrl: "home.html"
})
export class HomePage {
  public ver: string;

  constructor(private navCtrl: NavController, public myEnv: MyEnv)
{}

  getVersion() {
    console.log(this.myEnv.getAppVersion());
    this.myEnv.getAppVersion().then(data => (this.ver = data));
  }
}
```

9. Open and edit `home.scss` in the same folder:

```
page-home {
  .home {
    p.large {
      font-size: 16px;
    }
  }

  ion-content {
    &.center {
      text-align: center;
    }
  }
}
```

10. Go to your Terminal and run the app. If you want to run the app on your physical device, type the following command:

```
$ ionic cordova run ios
```

For Android, type the following command:

```
$ ionic cordova run android
```

How it works...

In a nutshell, the AppVersion plugin does all the *heavy lifting*. It's not possible for an Ionic app to find out the current version of its code using JavaScript. You may think that using local storage or cookie is an alternative, but the users could also delete that storage manually. In order to have a permanent solution, the AppVersion plugin should be used because it can read your config.xml file and get the version for you.

It's the best practice to create a separate service for all environment variables. That's why, you should have a service, called MyEnv. Also, you should inject MyEnv as a provider at the *app level* because you want to instantiate it only once, instead of doing it every time a new component is created. Take a look at the following code:

```
providers: [MyEnv]
```

Since all the AppVersion methods are based on promise, you should return the entire object as a promise. Let's take a look at the getAppVersion() method in your myenv.ts file:

```
getAppVersion() {
  return this.appVersion.getVersionCode();
}
```

Then, in your page files, such as `home.ts`, you should call the `getAppVersion` method, as shown, and use the `.then()` method to get the following result:

```
getVersion() {
  console.log(this.myEnv.getAppVersion());
  this.myEnv.getAppVersion().then((data) => this.ver = data);
}
```

If you open the console to inspect the `promise` object, you will see that it has your app version value and the `.then()` method. Take a look at the following screenshot:

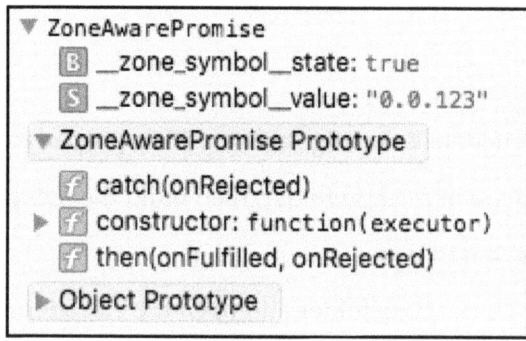

For more information about the `AppVersion` plugin, you may want to refer to the official AppVersion documentation at `https://github.com/whiteoctober/cordova-plugin-app-version`.

Building and publishing an app for iOS

Publishing on App Store could be a frustrating process if you are not well-prepared upfront. In this section, we will walk through the steps to properly configure everything in Apple Developer Center, iTunes Connect, and your local Xcode project.

Getting ready

You must register for Apple Developer Program in order to access `https://developer.apple.com/macos/touch-bar/` and `https://itunesconnect.apple.com` because those websites will require an approved account.

In addition, you should have the following:

- macOS
- Xcode

How to do it...

The following are the instructions to configure everything properly:

1. Ensure that you are in the app folder, then build the iOS platform:

   $ ionic cordova build ios

   Go to the `/platforms/ios` folder and open the `.xcodeproj` file in Xcode. Take a look at the following screenshot:

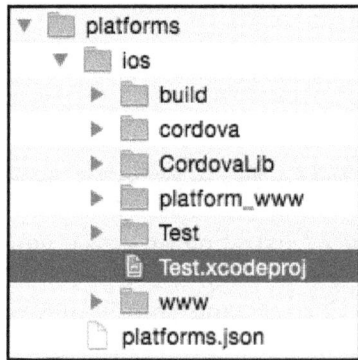

2. Navigate to the **General** tab, as illustrated in the following screenshot, to make sure that you have the correct information for everything, especially **Bundle Identifier** and **Version**. Change and save as needed:

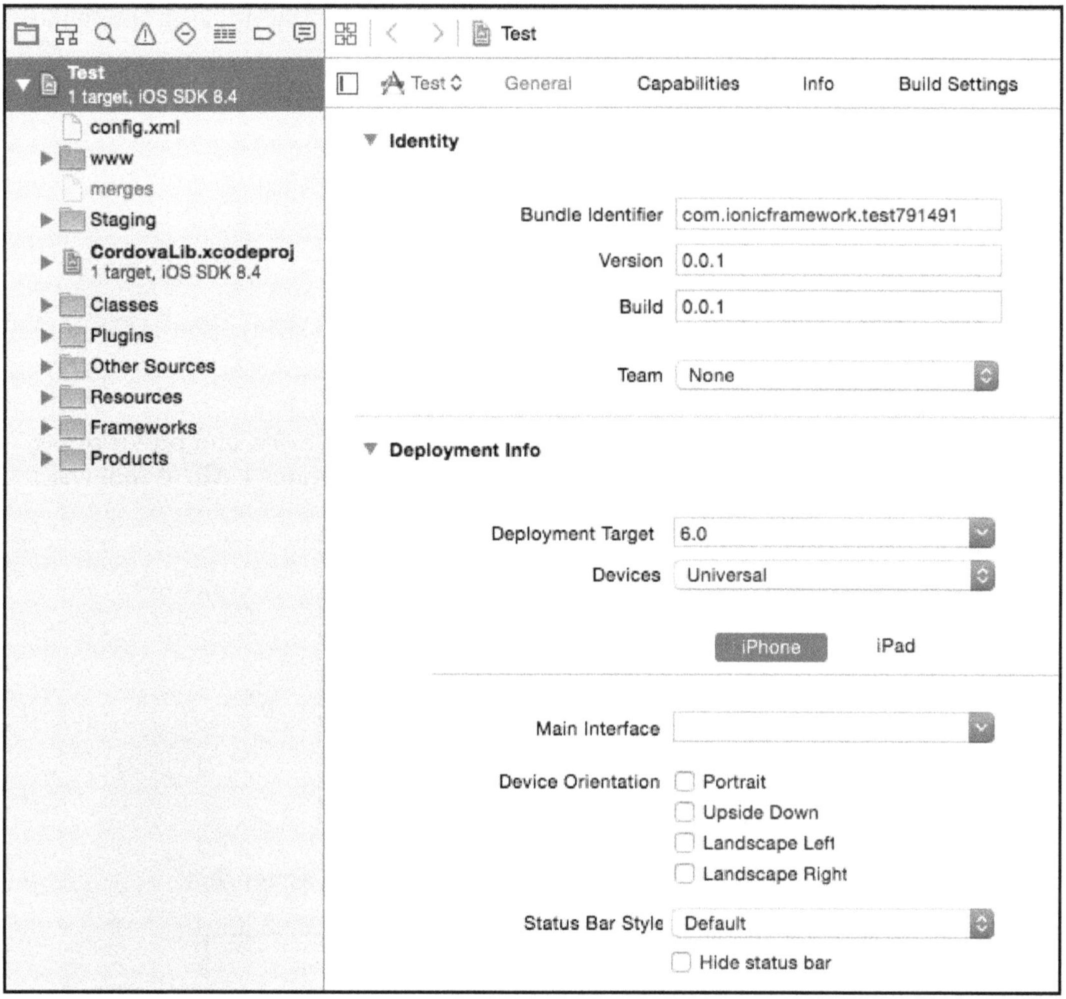

![Xcode project editor screenshot showing the General settings tab for the Test target. The left sidebar lists the project navigator with Test (1 target, iOS SDK 8.4), config.xml, www, merges, Staging, CordovaLib.xcodeproj (1 target, iOS SDK 8.4), Classes, Plugins, Other Sources, Resources, Frameworks, and Products. The main panel shows Identity section with Bundle Identifier com.ionicframework.test791491, Version 0.0.1, Build 0.0.1, Team None, and Deployment Info section with Deployment Target 6.0, Devices Universal, iPhone/iPad toggle, Main Interface, Device Orientation checkboxes (Portrait, Upside Down, Landscape Left, Landscape Right), Status Bar Style Default, and Hide status bar checkbox.](xcode_screenshot)

3. Visit the Apple developer website and click on **Certificates, Identifiers & Profiles**, as illustrated:

4. Select the correct device platform that you are targeting; in this case, it will be **iOS, tvOS, watchOS**:

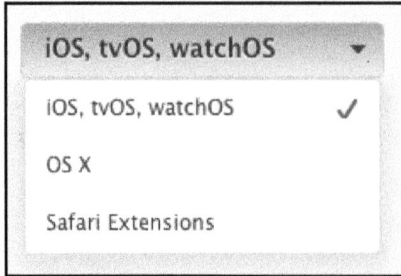

5. For the iOS app, you need the certificate, app ID, test device, and provisioning profile. To start with the certificate, navigate to **Certificates** | **All**, as follows:

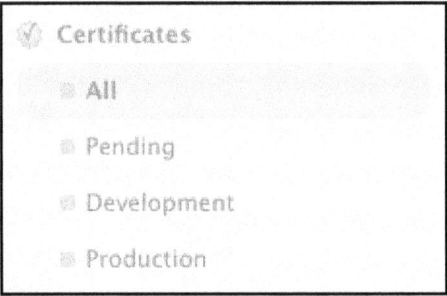

6. Click on the plus **(+)** button, as shown in the following screenshot:

7. You have to go through the steps on the website to fill out the necessary information, as depicted in the following screenshot:

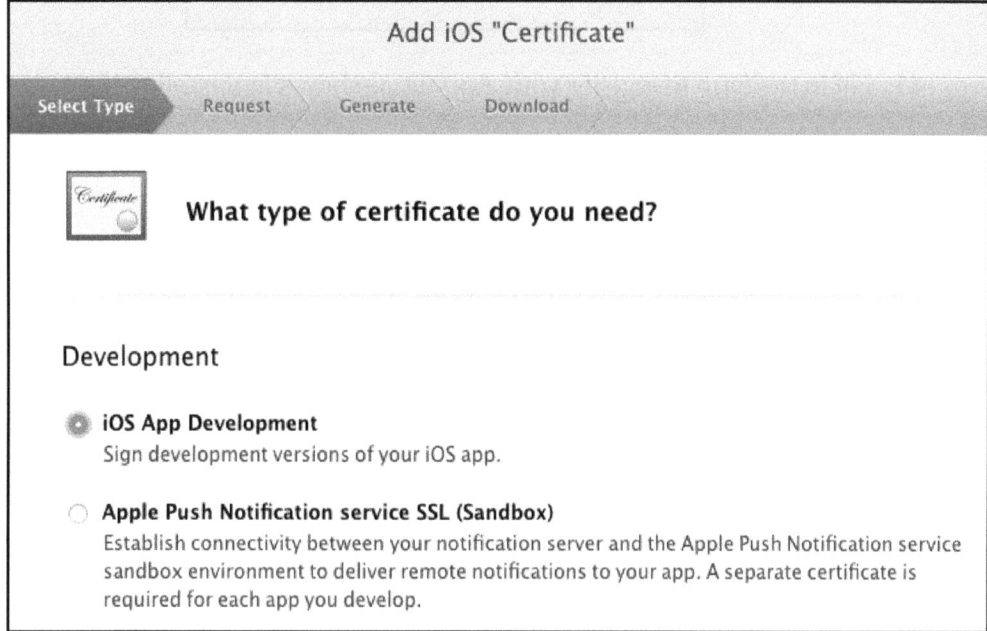

8. Once you've completed the form, you can save the CSR file and import it into your Mac's **Keychain Access**.

9. Navigate to **Identifiers** | **App IDs**, as follows, to create an app ID:

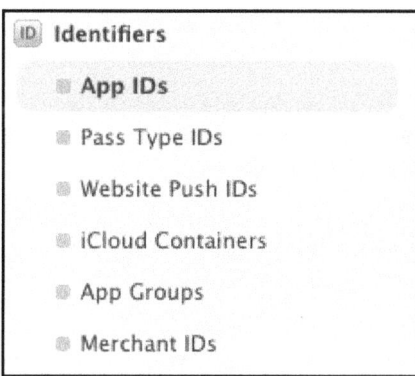

10. Click on the plus button at the top-right corner of the screen, as follows:

11. Fill in the form to register your App ID, as shown in the following screenshot:

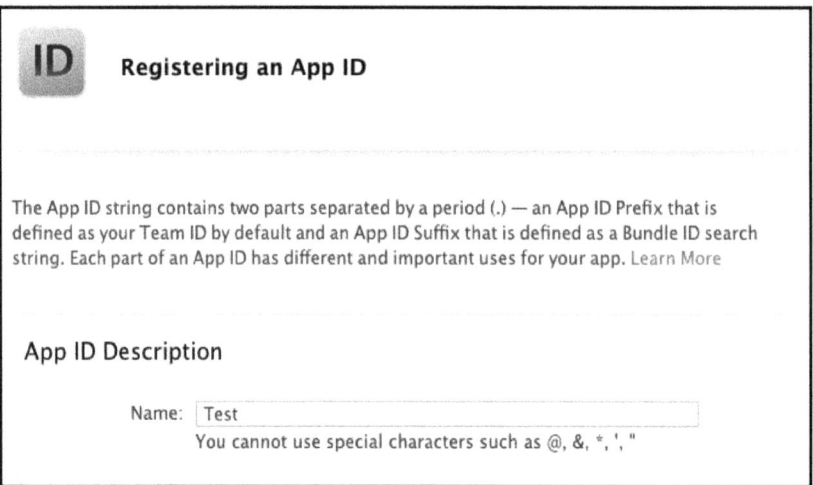

12. The important part here that you need to do correctly is the **Bundle ID**, as shown in the following screenshot because it must match your Bundle Identifier in Xcode:

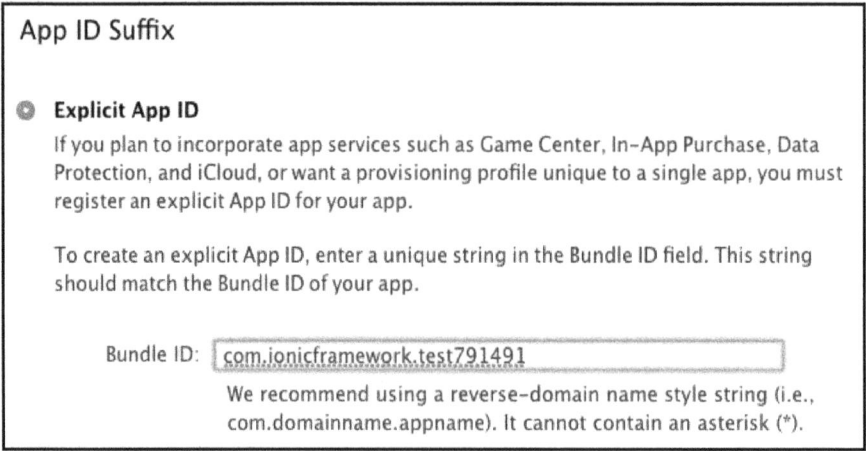

13. If your app needs **Push Notifications** or other **App Services**, you will need to check those services on the following page:

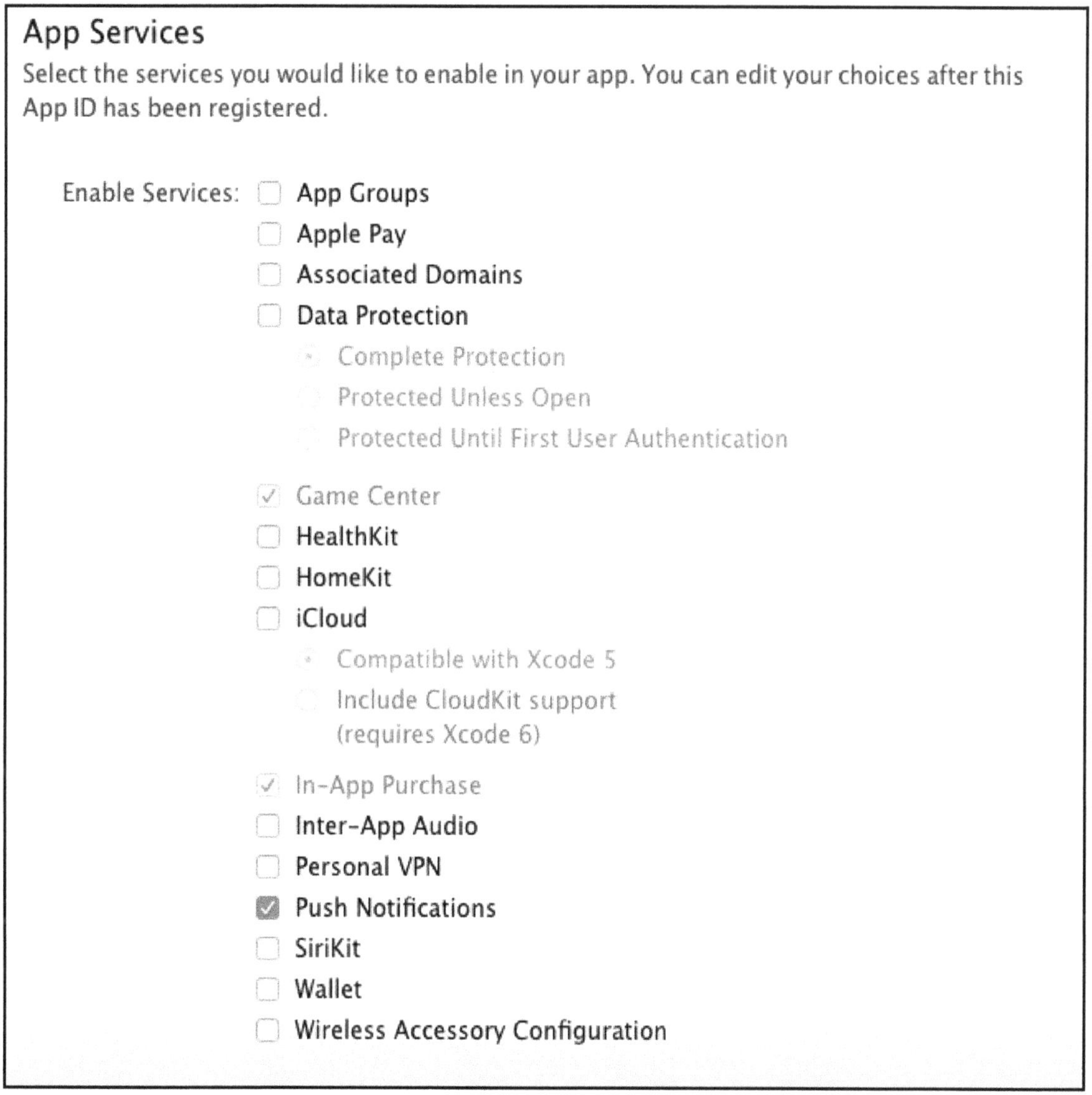

App Services

Select the services you would like to enable in your app. You can edit your choices after this App ID has been registered.

Enable Services: ☐ App Groups
☐ Apple Pay
☐ Associated Domains
☐ Data Protection
   ⊙ Complete Protection
   ○ Protected Unless Open
   ○ Protected Until First User Authentication

☑ Game Center
☐ HealthKit
☐ HomeKit
☐ iCloud
   ⊙ Compatible with Xcode 5
   ○ Include CloudKit support
     (requires Xcode 6)

☑ In-App Purchase
☐ Inter-App Audio
☐ Personal VPN
☑ Push Notifications
☐ SiriKit
☐ Wallet
☐ Wireless Accessory Configuration

14. If you need to push the app to a specific device, you must register the device. Navigate to **Devices** | **All**, as illustrated in the following:

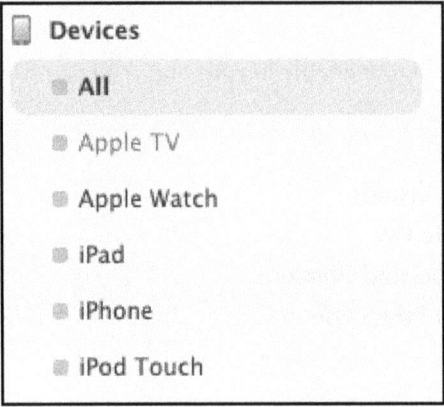

15. Click on the plus button, as shown:

16. Provide the device's **UDID**, as follows, and save it in order to register the device:

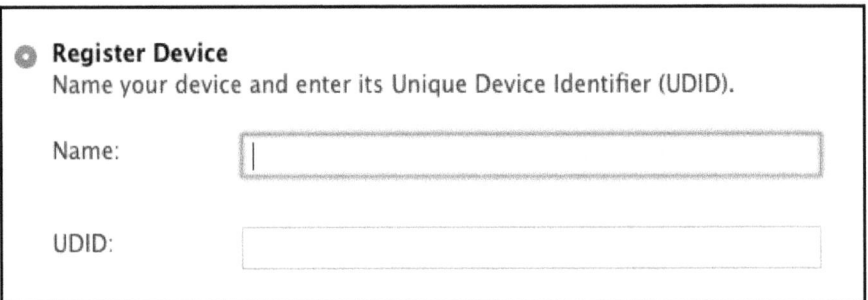

17. Finally, you will need a provisioning profile if one doesn't exist yet. Usually, Xcode will create one automatically. However, you could create your own by navigating to **Provisioning Profiles | All**, as shown:

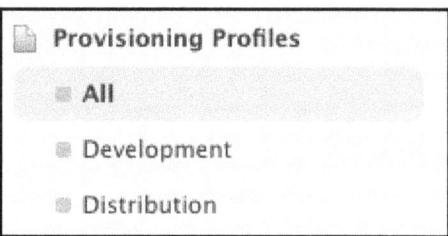

18. Click on the plus button, as follows:

19. Select **App Store** as your provisioning profile, as illustrated:

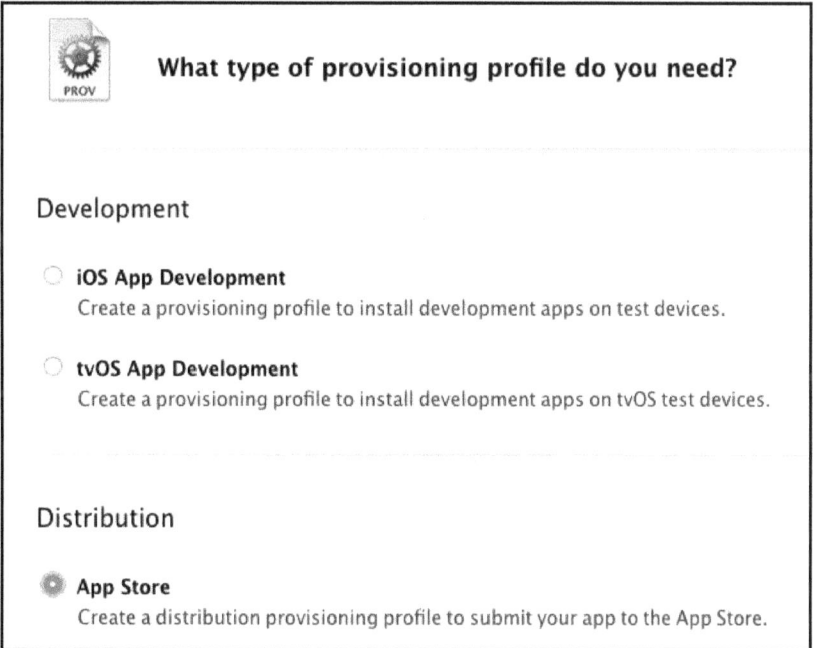

20. Select the correct **App ID** from the drop-down menu and save it to finalize your provisioning profile creation, as follows:

If you plan to use services such as Game Center, In–App Purchase, and Push Notifications, or want a Bundle ID unique to a single app, use an explicit App ID. If you want to create one provisioning profile for multiple apps or don't need a specific Bundle ID, select a wildcard App ID. Wildcard App IDs use an asterisk (*) as the last digit in the Bundle ID field. Please note that iOS App IDs and Mac App IDs cannot be used interchangeably.

App ID: test1 (Q9AH7H7W82.com.ionicframework.test1223125)

21. Visit iTunes Connect at `https://itunesconnect.apple.com` and click on the **My Apps** button, as follows:

22. Select the plus (+) icon and select **New App**, as follows:

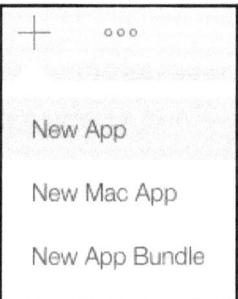

23. Fill out the form and ensure that you select the right **Bundle ID** for your app:

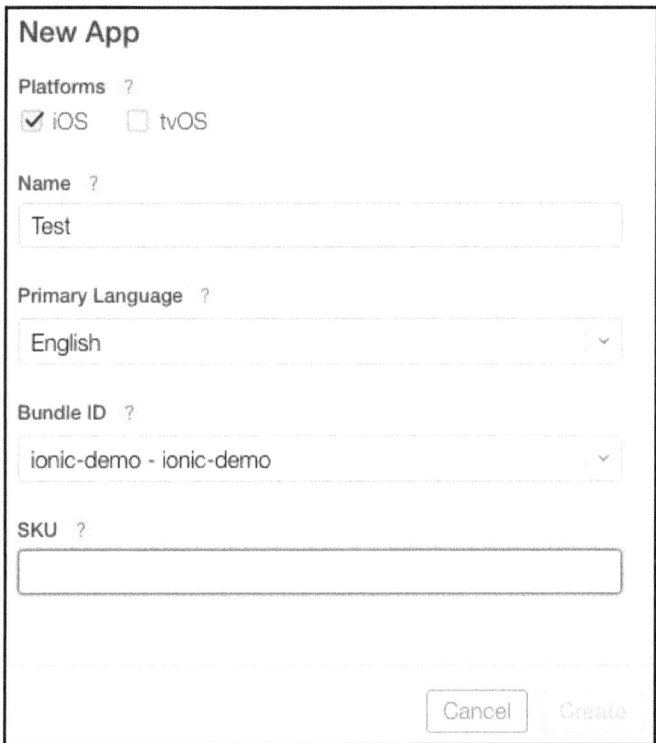

24. There are several additional steps to provide information on the app, such as screenshot, icon, and address. If you just want to test the app, you could provide some placeholder information initially and come back to edit it later.
    That's it to prepare your Developer and iTunes Connect account.
    Now, open **Xcode** and select **iOS Device** as the archive target, otherwise the **Archive** feature will not be turned on. You will need to archive your app before you can submit it to the App Store:

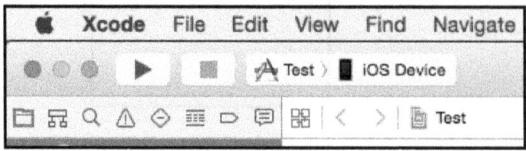

25. Navigate to **Product** | **Archive** in the top menu, as illustrated:

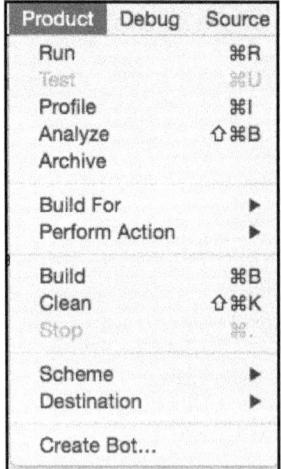

26. After the archive process is completed, select **Submit to App Store** to finish the publishing process.

27. To publish, select **Submit for Beta App Review**. You may want to go through other tabs, such as **Pricing** and **In-App Purchases**, to configure your own requirements.

How it works...

Obviously, this section does not cover every bit of detail in the publishing process. In general, you just need to ensure that your app is tested thoroughly, locally, on a physical device (either via USB or *TestFlight*) before submitting it to the App Store.

If for some reason, the Archive feature doesn't build, you could manually go to your local Xcode folder to delete that specific temporary archived app to clear cache, as follows:

```
~/Library/Developer/Xcode/Archives
```

There's more...

- *TestFlight* is a separate subject by itself. The benefit of *TestFlight* is that you don't need your app to be approved by Apple in order to install the app on a physical device for testing and development. You can find out more information on *TestFlight* at
  `https://developer.apple.com/library/content/documentation/LanguagesUtilities/Conceptual/iTunesConnect_Guide/Chapters/BetaTestingTheApp.html`.
- There is one more way to test Ionic Apps, that's with Ionic's DevApp. It allows you to test Ionic Application on iOS and Android without even compiling. You have installed the Ionic Devapp on your phone, and in your workstation run `ionic serve -c` in the Terminal. You can find more details at `https://ionicframework.com/docs/pro/devapp/`.

Building and publishing an app for Android

Building and publishing an Android app is a little more straightforward than iOS because you just interface with the command line to build the .apk file and upload it to Google Play's Developer Console.

The Ionic Framework documentation also has a great instruction page for this, which is `http://ionicframework.com/docs/guide/publishing.html`.

Getting ready

The requirement is to have your Google Developer account ready and then log in to `https://play.google.com/apps/publish`.

Your local environment should also have the right SDK and `keytool`, `jarsigner`, and `zipalign` command line for that specific version.

How to do it...

The following are the instructions:

1. Go to your app folder and build for Android using the following command:

   ```
   $ ionic cordova build --release android
   ```

2. You will note `android-release-unsigned.apk` in the `/platforms/android/build/outputs/apk` folder. Go to that folder in the Terminal:

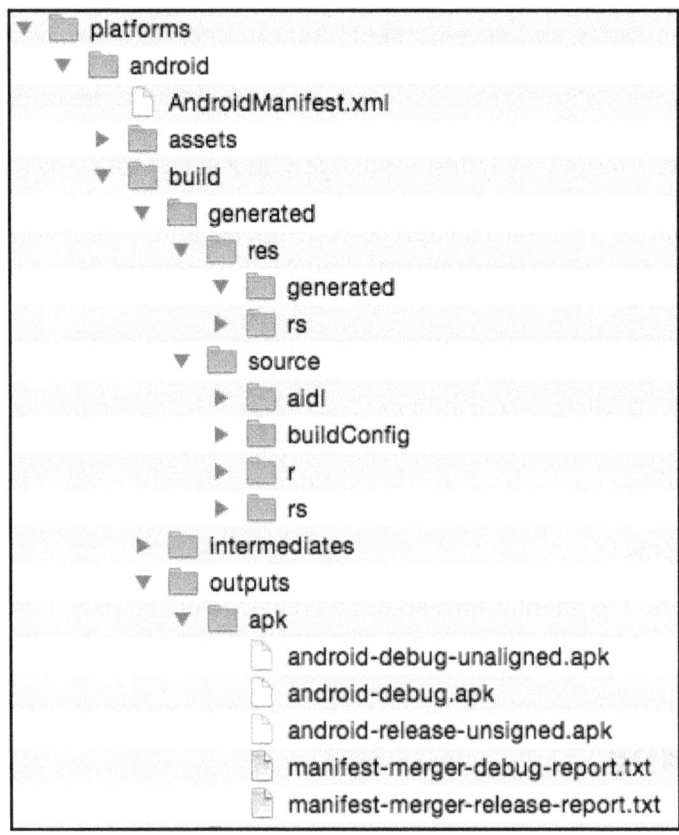

3. If this is the first time you created this app, you must have a `keystore` file. This file is used to identify your app for publishing. If you lose it, you cannot update your app later on. To create a `keystore` file, type the following command line and ensure that it's the same `keytool` version of the SDK:

```
$ keytool -genkey -v -keystore my-release-key.keystore -alias
alias_name -keyalg RSA -keysize 2048 -validity 10000
```

4. Once you fill out the information on the command line, make a copy of this file somewhere safe because you will need it later.

5. The next step is to use that file to *sign* your app so that it will create a new `.apk` that Google Play allows users to install:

```
$ jarsigner -verbose -sigalg SHA1withRSA -digestalg SHA1 -keystore my-
release-key.keystore HelloWorld-release-unsigned.apk alias_name
```

6. To prepare for the final `.apk` before upload, you must package it using `zipalign`, as follows:

```
$ zipalign -v 4 HelloWorld-release-unsigned.apk HelloWorld.ap
```

> You need to ensure that `zipalign` is in `PATH` or you have to specify the absolute path. The app name could be anything you like or you can use the same name as created in this chapter.

7. Log in to Google Developer Console and click on **CREATE APPLICATION** button, as follows:

8. Fill out the **Title** of the application in the opened popup and then click on **CREATE** button, as shown in the image below:

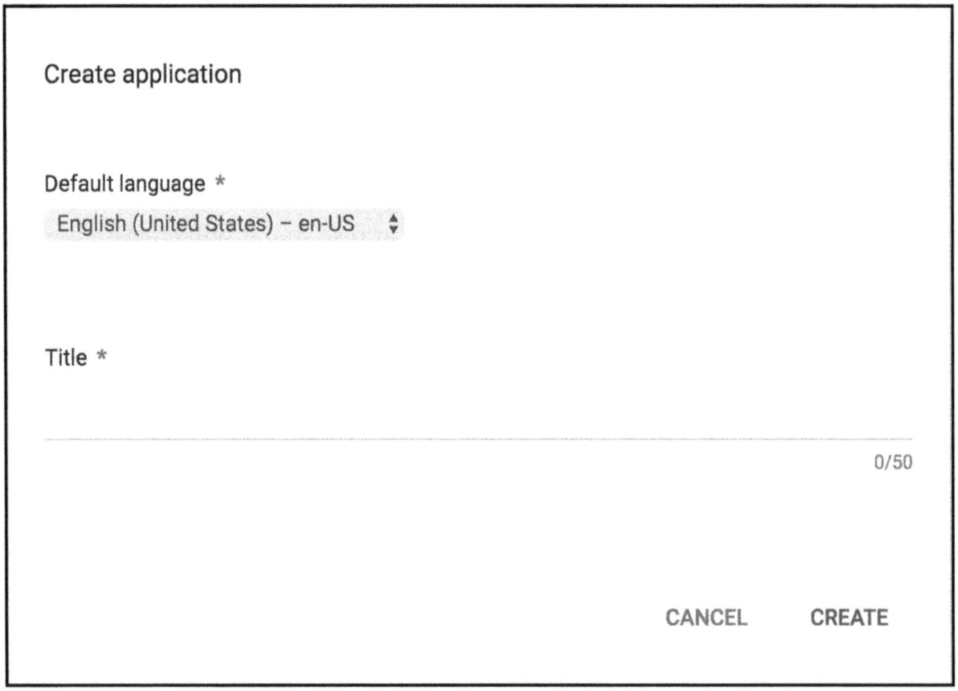

Create application

Default language *

English (United States) – en-US ⬍

Title *

0/50

CANCEL   CREATE

9. Fill out the store listing and other information as required for your app using the left menu:

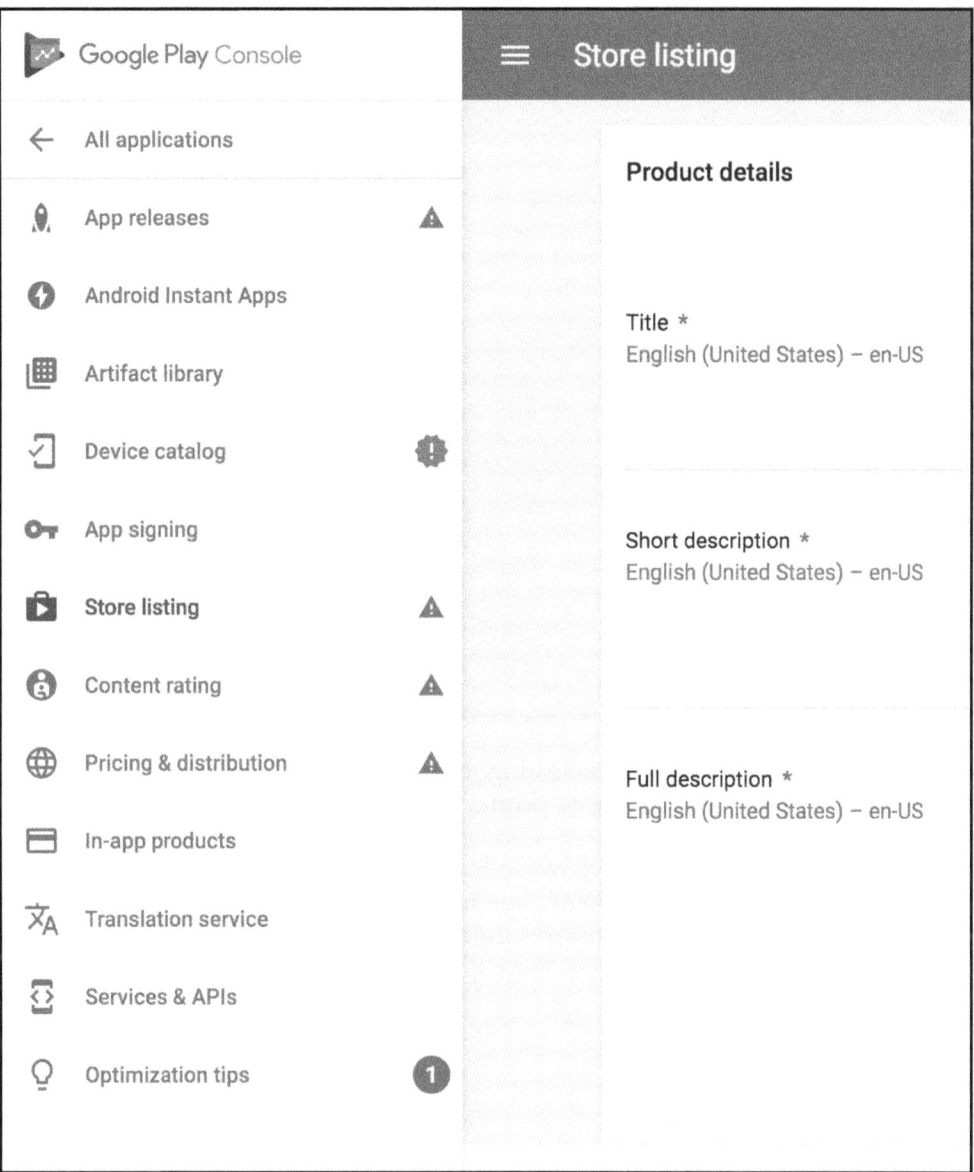

10. Now you are ready to upload your `.apk` file. The first thing you need to do is to do a Beta testing:

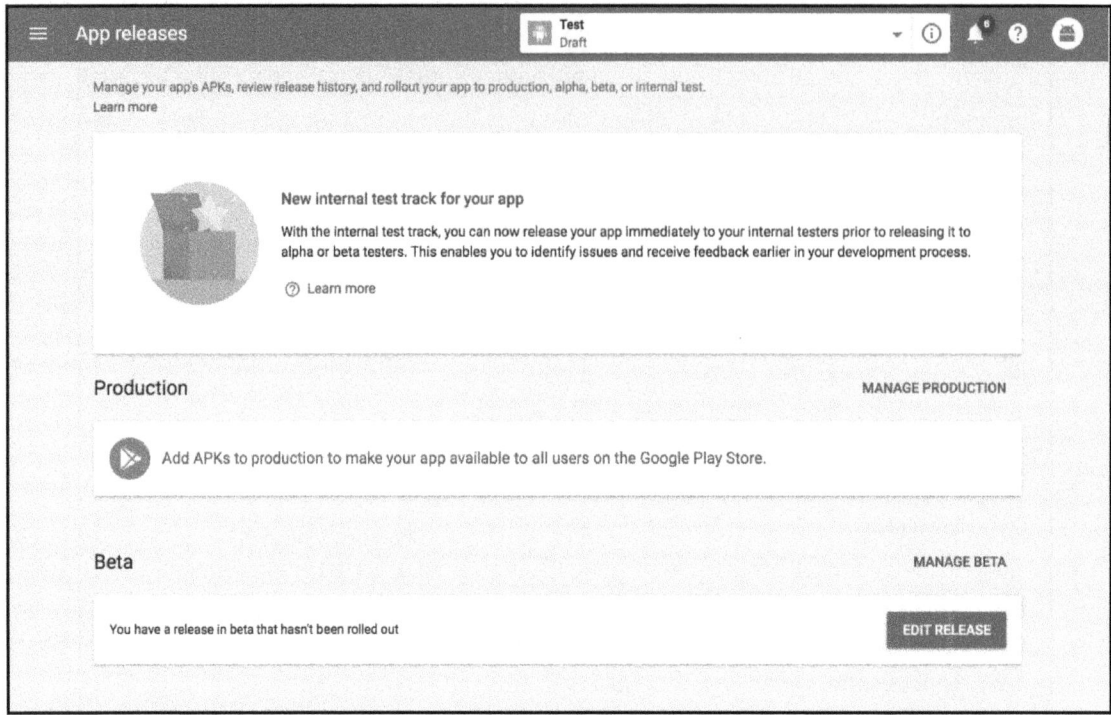

11. Once you are done with Beta testing, you can follow Developer Console instructions to push the app to production.

 If you run into any problem while publishing the app, it's helpful to look at the "Why can't I publish?" link in the dashboard's top-right corner. Google will guide you on specific steps that must be completed or fixed.

How it works...

This section does not cover other Android marketplaces, such as Amazon App Store, because each of them has different processes. However, the common idea is that you need to completely build the unsigned version of the .apk, sign it using an existing or new keystore file, and, finally, zipalign to prepare it for upload.

Read more about uploading the application for publishing at https://support.google.com/googleplay/android-developer/answer/113469?hl=en

Other Books You May Enjoy

If you enjoyed this book, you may be interested in these other books by Packt:

Learning Ionic - Second Edition
Arvind Ravulavaru

ISBN: 978-1-78646-605-1

- Understanding the world of the mobile hybrid architecture
- Scaffolding and working with Ionic templates
- Transforming a single page app to a multi-page app using Navigation Controller
- Integrating Ionic components, decorators, and services and rapidly developing complex applications
- Theming Ionic apps as well as customizing components using SCSS
- Working with Ionic Native to interface with device features, such as camera, notifications, and battery
- Building a production grade app using Ionic and Uber API to let users book a ride
- Migrating an Ionic 1 app to Ionic 2 or Ionic 3
- Performing unit testing, end-to-end testing, and device testing on your apps
- Deploying Ionic apps to store and manage their subsequent releases

Hybrid Mobile Development with Ionic
Gaurav Saini

ISBN: 978-1-78528-605-6

- Use every Ionic component and its customization according to the application along with some important third party components
- Recently released Lazy Loading and Grid System supporting desktop application with Electron
- Integration of the various Ionic backend services and features such as Ionic Push, DB, Auth, Deploy in your application
- Exploration of white-listing, CORS, and various other platform security aspects to secure your application
- Synchronization of your data with the cloud server and fetching it in real time using Ionic Cloud and Firebase services
- Integration of the Cordova iBeacon plugin which will fetch contextual data on the basis of location and Websockets for real time communication for IOT based applications
- Implementation of offline functionality in your PWA application using service-worker, cache storage and indexedDB

Leave a review - let other readers know what you think

Please share your thoughts on this book with others by leaving a review on the site that you bought it from. If you purchased the book from Amazon, please leave us an honest review on this book's Amazon page. This is vital so that other potential readers can see and use your unbiased opinion to make purchasing decisions, we can understand what our customers think about our products, and our authors can see your feedback on the title that they have worked with Packt to create. It will only take a few minutes of your time, but is valuable to other potential customers, our authors, and Packt. Thank you!

Index

Lightning Source UK Ltd.
Milton Keynes UK
UKHW02f0935150718
325678UK00004B/171/P

9 781788 623230